The Optina Elders Series

ELDER LEONID OF OPTINA

ELDER LEONID OF OPTINA
A portrait from the original Russian version of his Life, 1876.

ELDER LEONID
of Optina

by
FR. CLEMENT SEDERHOLM

ST. HERMAN OF ALASKA BROTHERHOOD
2002

Published with the blessing of His Grace
+ JOVAN
Bishop of the Western American Diocese
of the Serbian Orthodox Church

Copyright 1990 by the
St. Herman of Alaska Brotherhood

First Edition: 1990
Revised Second Edition: 2002

Address all correspondence to:
St. Herman of Alaska Brotherhood
P.O. Box 70
Platina, California 96076

Translated from the Russian. Original Russian Edition: *Biography of Optina Elder Hieromonk Leonid (in Schema Leo),* published by the Kozelsk Optina Monastery of the Entrance of the Mother of God, Moscow, 1876. This Russian edition was reprinted one hundred years later, in 1976, by the St. Herman of Alaska Brotherhood.

Front cover: A portrait of Elder Leonid, painted by Hieromonk Gabriel in the middle of the 19th century.
Back cover: A recent painting, from Russia, of the Optina Skete of St. John the Forerunner.

Library of Congress Cataloging in Publication Data:

Sederholm, Hieromonk Clement.
  Elder Leonid of Optina.
  Translated from the Russian.

Library of Congress Control Number: 90–64135
ISBN: 0–938635–66–2

Dedicated to the bright memory of
BISHOP NEKTARY (KONTZEVITCH),
a disciple of Optina and a carrier of
its spiritual transmission to
modern America.

The Optina Elders

Left, from bottom to top:
Elder Moses
Elder Leonid
Elder Ambrose
Elder Anthony
Elder Barsanuphius

Right, from bottom to top:
Archimandrite Isaac
Elder Macarius
Elder Joseph
Elder Hilarion
Elder Anatole

The Optina Elders Series

Original hagiographical monographs from the Library of Old Optina, illustrated with rare lithographs as well as views of the restored Optina today. The Lives of Elders Leonid, Anthony, Macarius and others, incorporating rare material that is now being discovered.

Preface to the Second English Edition

Over the course of one century—from Elder Leonid's arrival in 1829 until the Monastery's forced closure by the Communists in 1923—Optina, with its Skete of St. John the Forerunner, was at the center of a tremendous spiritual revival in Russia.

As a result of anti-clerical legislation during the reigns of Emperor Peter I and Empress Catherine II, a general decline in monastic life had taken place across Russia from the middle of the 17th century through the end of the 18th century. While several spiritually well-ordered monasteries still existed, such as Valaam and Sarov, the strict new regulations often forced those desiring to follow the Gospel commandments within the God-ordained monastic life to choose one of two alternatives: either to leave Russia in search of a monastery in one of the neighboring Orthodox countries, or to live this life in the depths of forests, hidden from view. The greatest example of those who chose the first path was St. Paisius Velichkovsky (†1794), who labored ascetically on Mount Athos and ended his days at the head of a vast monastic army centered in Moldavia, Romania. A number of his disciples later returned to Russia, bringing with them priceless patristic writings on the spiritual life which had been painstakingly translated by St. Paisius, and which became instrumental in bringing about a new blossoming of sanctity in Russia. An example of those who chose the second way was the community of ascetics who dwelt in the Roslavl Forest of the Bryansk Province in Russia. These ascetics were also nourished by St. Paisius by means of his patristic translations, which reached them through Elder Athanasius, one of St. Paisius' disciples.

When, at the beginning of the 19th century, a more propitious time for monasticism arrived, and the run-down Optina Monastery was being restored, it was by these ascetics that true monasticism was instituted in Optina. From the Roslavl Forest came the Putilov brothers, Elders Moses and Anthony, who took the reins of the Optina Monastery and established the Optina Skete nearby. They, in turn, brought in Elder Leonid, a disciple of Elders Theodore of Svir and Cleopas of Valaam, both of whom were direct disciples of St. Paisius.

With the arrival of Elder Leonid, the practice of eldership was introduced in Optina. This is the prophetic ministry of the Church, which has existed since apostolic times, and through which God's will is directly revealed to those seeking guidance. An elder is one who, through inward purification, has become a vessel and conduit of the action of the Holy Spirit. This ministry was passed on in Optina from one Elder to the next, in a remarkable chain of sanctity that lasted a full century.

The succession of Optina Elders had a profound effect on all levels of Russian society. Guidance by eldership—marked by a life of simplicity, unquestioning obedience to the Elder, and frequent revelation of one's thoughts—was a source of spiritual rebirth, not only for Optina's monks and monastics of other monasteries, but also for the thousands of lay folk who came to Optina in a steady stream day after day for spiritual direction. Famous Russian authors, such as Gogol, Dostoyevsky, and Tolstoy, were deeply affected by their contact with the Elders.

The Optina Elders also had a profound effect on the spirituality of Russia by fostering the publication of a significant body of patristic literature concerning the ascetic, spiritual life. The books that Optina Monastery published were sent out free to all monasteries in Russia, and were read by great numbers of laypeople, as well. This labor of love began under the leadership of Elder Macarius (Elder Leonid's disciple) and continued until the forced closure of Optina Monastery.

Through God's mercy, in spite of seventy years of Communist enslavement, "prima vitae" of the of many of the Elders have been preserved. Written by their immediate disciples, these rare biographies contain a multitude of priceless details and anecdotes that shed light into the secret corners of lives totally dedicated to Jesus Christ.

In the twelve years since the first English printing of Elder Leonid of Optina, interest in and veneration of the God-bearing Elders of Optina Monastery have grown tremendously, both in Russia and in the West. Since the 1988 re-opening of Optina, numerous men, inspired by the Lives of the Elders and thirsting for the kind of monastic life inspired by them during the 19th and early 20th centuries, have found shelter within the walls of this great monastic citadel. The Monastery and Skete, after years of neglect and destruction under the Communist regime, have gradually been restored by loving hands, and are already beginning to regain their former magnificence. At this time there are over forty monks settled in the Monastery and Skete, as well as many others in the Monastery's *metochia* in Moscow and St. Petersburg.

In 1990, when this book was first published in English, only Elder Ambrose had been glorified by the Orthodox Church in Russia (1988), while in April of 1990 all the Optina Elders were glorified by the Russian Orthodox Church Abroad. With the fall of Communism in Russia and the consequent freedom experienced by the Church there, preparations were undertaken for the glorification of all the Elders by the entire Russian Orthodox Church. During the restoration work on the Optina Church of the Kazan Icon of the Theotokos, which had been almost totally destroyed, the relics of Elders Moses and Anthony and those of Archimandrite Isaac (Antimonov) were uncovered and later placed in that church. At about the same time the relics of Elder Nectarius, which had been uncovered in 1989 in the village of Kholmishche and brought to Optina, were placed in the Optina Church of the Entrance of the Theotokos into the Temple. The local canonization of all fourteen Elders took place in Optina on June 13, 1996. Two years later, in June of 1998, the relics of the remaining Elders were uncovered (except those of Elder Nikon, who reposed in exile in the far north, and those of Archimandrite Isaac [Bobrikov], who was executed by the Communists and whose relics have not been found) and later that year placed in the newly rebuilt Optina Church of the Vladimir Icon of the Theotokos. Finally, on August 7, 2000, in connection with the glorification of the New Martyrs and Confessors of Russia, all the Optina Elders were universally canonized by the Russian Orthodox Church in the newly rebuilt Cathedral of Christ the Savior in Moscow.

The St. Herman of Alaska Brotherhood has had the privilege, over these past twelve years, of translating and printing six more volumes in its series of Lives of the Optina Elders: Elder Anthony, Elder Macarius, Elder Ambrose, Elder Nectarius, Elder Sebastian, and Elder Barsanuphius.

These Lives form a unified spiritual picture—the legacy of the great Elder and preceptor of the patristic revival of 19th-century Russia, St. Paisius Velichkovsky. Beginning with Elder Leonid, all these men of God hearkened to, preserved, and transmitted the ancient patristic wisdom of the Holy Orthodox Church. This wisdom is timeless, and is as fitting to our present age of apostasy as it has been throughout the two millennia of the life of the Church.

The Lives of the Optina Elders contain the flame of faith that can ignite in subsequent generations the impulse to die to this world and seek the unending Kingdom of God. In reading the Lives of these Elders, may we develop a hunger for true spiritual life, and may we strive, as they did, to fill it at the laden table of the Church.

St. Herman of Alaska Brotherhood, 2002

CONTENTS

BISHOP NEKTARY (KONTZEVITCH) OF SEATTLE
(†1983)
A disciple of Elder Nectarius of Optina.

Preface to the 1976 Centennial Russian Edition

WITH God's help we are publishing this volume of the *Prima Vitae,* original hagiographical monographs of the Optina Elders. This biography of Elder Leonid, in Schema Leo, was compiled by the learned ascetic Hieromonk Clement Sederholm. A former Lutheran, Fr. Clement converted to Orthodoxy and provided the impetus for these biographies of the Elders.

Father Leonid—the founding father of the line of the great Optina Elders—is the link between Optina Monastery and St. Paisius Velichkovsky, since his Elder, the Schemamonk Theodore, was himself a disciple of Paisius. In order to highlight this link with St. Paisius, we have appended to the end of this book the biography of Elder Theodore. There exist two versions of it: 1) a version compiled by Bishop Ignatius Brianchaninov,[1] published by Moscow University Press in 1839, while Fr. Leonid was still among the living, and later preserved in the Library of Valaam Monastery; and 2) the original Manuscript Life found in the Optina Library at the begin-

---

1. Leonid Sokolov, author of the definitive study of St. Ignatius Brianchaninov, states that among the papers of Bishop Ignatius remaining after his repose there were preserved several notebooks. The second of these was entitled *"The Life of Elder Theodore,* 1829, Ploshchansk Hermitage, Orel Province, compiled by D. A. Brianchaninov" [Bishop Ignatius was still a layman in 1929, known as Dimitry Alexandrovich Brianchaninov]. It was published anonymously. See Leonid Sokolov, *Bishop Ignatius Briancha-ninov,* Vol. III, 1915, pp. 6–7.

ning of the century by Sergei Nilus. In 1916 Nilus published the original Manuscript Life, the existence of which had been unknown to the world until then.

In the present edition, we have included only the more complete Manuscript Life of Elder Theodore. We have divided it into chapters, and at the end we have appended the testimony of a disciple of Elder Leonid concerning the incorruption of the remains of the holy Elder Theodore. The Life of Elder Theodore was undoubtedly compiled from the words of Elder Leonid.

With this new edition of Elder Leonid of Optina, we offer to the contemporary reader a rare, genuine spiritual treasure. We have reprinted without any alterations the first edition, which came out exactly one hundred years ago.

We dedicate this labor of publication to our dear preceptor, protector and inspirer, with whom we share oneness of soul, Bishop Nektary of Seattle, the brother by birth of I. M. Kontzevitch. In the person of our dear Vladika we have obtained a living link with Optina Monastery. From his childhood years (he eventually became a spiritual son of the last great Optina Elder, Hieromonk Nectarius), he was destined by the Elders to preserve himself to be a monk of Optina upbringing. At first in a wondrous manner Batiushka Nectarius gave him over to the spiritual guidance of his spiritual son Fr. Adrian (later Archbishop Andrew) Rymarenko; and thereafter he was confirmed in monasticism by another Optina disciple, Archbishop Tikhon of San Francisco, a spiritual son of the Spirit-bearing holy Elder Gabriel (†1915) of the Eleazar Monastery of the Savior, originally tonsured in Optina. We ask the reader to pray for the repose of the first Elder of Optina, Leonid, together with his Elder, Theodore, and likewise for the health of the ailing Bishop Nektary, the spiritual son of the Spirit-bearing Batiushka Nectarius of Optina.

Before the face of the emerging apostate "new humanity," we abroad, as also the young shoots of awakening Russia, are in dire need of our native Holy Russian roots for the purpose of strengthening ourselves. May God grant that the powerful image, the lion-like image, of the great Elder would reach even Rus, that her sons, hearing his "regal roar," might be strengthened and offer fruit to the Setter of the Contest, our Lord Jesus Christ. Amen.

Monk Herman
11th of October, 1976
The Day of the Repose of
Elder Leonid and the Day of
The Monastic Tonsure of Bishop Nektary

Since the publication of our Russian edition of 1976, Bishop Nektary reposed in the Lord (†1983). This book, along with the other Optina monographs, was preserved in the Kontzevitch family, and Bishop Nektary ardently desired to make it available to the new generations of Orthodox Christians.

ST. LEONID (LEO IN SCHEMA), ELDER OF OPTINA
(1768-1841)
Commemorated October 11/24

Forward to the 1876 Russian Edition

THE LATE BISHOP of Kaluga, Nicholas, during the lifetime of the Elder Leonid to all appearances was not kindly disposed toward him; but after the Elder's death it was he who first suggested the idea of compiling his Life. It was not possible to accomplish this soon after the death of the Elder because many of the materials had not yet been prepared. Moreover, the person who took upon himself this task, the devout disciple of Fr. Leonid, Hieromonk Anthony (Bochkov), later Abbot of the Chermenetsk Monastery, wanted to set down the life of the Elder in its entirety as he himself had witnessed it. He, however, was faced with the problem that the Elder had acted and expressed himself in his own peculiar way and had even acted somewhat as a fool-for-Christ. A person can see and understand this, but to express it in words and to relate it fully to another is not an easy task. For this reason Fr. Anthony twice undertook the compilation of the Life of the Elder but left only some notes. Realizing this difficulty, we have set for ourselves a more modest goal: to collect and describe what we can concerning Fr. Leonid.

In compiling this Life we have made use of the above-mentioned notes made by Fr. Anthony Bochkov,[1] and in addition we have also had in view:

1. The letter of Elder Leonid (unpublished), in which he recalls the events of his life in Valaam, in the Svir Monastery and in the Optina Monastery.

---

1. Part of these notes have been published in "A Description of the Skete of the Optina Hermitage."

2. The foreword to the *Life and Writings of the Elder Paisius Velichkovsky* (Moscow, 1847), where on pages vi-viii there is a brief listing of the most important events in the life of Fr. Leonid, as compiled by his closest disciple and successor, the Elder Macarius (Ivanov).

3. The collection of the letters of this same Optina Elder, Hiero-schemamonk Macarius (Moscow, 1862), in which he relates among other things the final illness and the repose of Fr. Leonid.

4. "The Historical Description of the Skete at the Optina Monastery" authored by Fr. Leonid (Kavelin), now the Archimandrite of the Resurrection Monastery called New Jerusalem (St. Petersburg, 1862), where on pp. 93-142 there is information concerning Elder Leonid which was possible to gather at that time.

5. By the same author, "The Historical Description of the Belev Convent" (St. Petersburg, 1863), where on pp. 67-89 there is an account of the persecution of the women disciples of Elder Leonid in 1839-1841.

6. A letter (unpublished) of the Abbot of the St. Tikhon Hermitage, Fr. Gerontius, concerning the final days of Fr. Leonid's life.

7. Accounts about the Elder by his spiritual children and persons closely associated with him. Some of these accounts have been related in writing, others orally.

We urgently beseech all those who knew Fr. Leonid to relate to us all the information they have which could serve to complete the Life of the Elder. We will use this information in the next edition of this Life.[2]

We plan to publish the letters of Elder Leonid to various persons in a separate volume.

October 20, 1875
Skete of the Forerunner at Optina

---

2. The Second Edition of the Life of Elder Leonid was published in 1917, considerably expanded by the monks of Optina.

The Life of
Elder Leonid

RUSSIA at the time
of Elder Leonid

0   100   250   500

Miles

I

The Youth of Father Leonid

HIS STAY AT THE OPTINA MONASTERY, WHITE BLUFF, VALAAM AND IN THE SVIR MONASTERY

Even so we speak, not as pleasing men,
but God, which trieth our hearts.
For neither at any time used we
flattering words as ye know.
(I Thess. 2:4, 5)

HIEROMONK LEONID was born in 1768 in the city Karachev, in the Orlov Province. In Holy Baptism he was named Leo. His parents were simple citizens of Karachev, Nagolkin by name. In his youth Leo Danilevich Nagolkin worked in business. As an agent of a merchant he made frequent and long trips, so that he knew all of Russia quite well. He had contacts with persons in all walks of life; and thus while he was yet in the world he acquired experience and an extensive knowledge of people, which he later employed for the benefit of his fellow man when they turned to him for spiritual counsel. In 1797 he left the world and first entered the Optina Monastery under the Abbot Abraham. He spent two years here and then went to the secluded monastery of White Bluff in the Orlov Diocese, where at the time the Abbot was Hieromonk Basil (Kishkin),[1] an Elder

---

1. See *Glinsk Patericon*, Monk Theodosius (Clare), St. Xenia Skete, Wildwood, California, 1984, pp. 78-82.

of spiritual life who had struggled for no short while on Mount Athos. In 1801, Leo was tonsured by him into monasticism with the name Leonid; in the same year, December 22, he was ordained hierodeacon and on December 24, hieromonk. This rapid advancement of Fr. Leonid to the rank of priestmonk, only two years after he had entered the White Bluff Monastery, shows that he surpassed the other brothers in his way of life and attracted the special attention of the Abbot. We do not know any further details about the beginning of Fr. Leonid's monastic life. We know only that while he was living in the Monastery he spent his days in uninterrupted labor, thus setting an example of sincere obedience for all the brethren. Once on the eve of the patronal feast, the brothers of the cliros were dissatisfied about something and refused to chant for the vigil, presuming that in this way they could force the Abbot to fulfill some of their demands. But the Abbot, not wanting to give in to their unreasonable insistence and in order to humble them, ordered that Fr. Leonid and a brother close to him be summoned and that the two of them chant the vigil. Fr. Leonid at that time was bringing in a load of hay for the barn. Tired and covered with dust, he had been intending to go for supper when he was informed of the wish of the Abbot that he come to the cliros. He obeyed without questioning and, without having had supper, hastened to the church where together with his companion he chanted the entire vigil to the delight of the Abbot. He had quite a strong voice (baritone), although it was somewhat sharp; he sang correctly and knew the order of the service quite well.

In 1804 Fr. Leonid, at the wish of His Grace Dorotheus, Bishop of Orlov and Svensk, was installed as Abbot of White Bluff Hermitage. His election to this position came about as follows. When the Abbot, Fr. Basil, left his post, the brotherhood gathered and debated for some time as to whom they should elect to take his place. Fr. Leonid avoided these discussions. "They can elect someone without me; I hear the supply of kvas has run out," he thought and went to make kvas. Meanwhile the brethren came to the decision, after long discussion, that apart from Fr. Leonid, there was no one else to elect as Abbot. The whole assembly came to the kvas kitchen, took the ladle he was holding out of his hand, removed his apron, and took him to the Bishop to be presented and confirmed in the position of Abbot.

Before he assumed these duties, Fr. Leonid spent some time at the Cholnsk Monastery, where at that time a new arrival from Moldavia had come to dwell, Schemamonk Theodore,[2] a disciple of the great Elder Paisius, the Archimandrite of the Moldo-Vlachian monasteries. Many of the brethren of the Cholnsk Monastery made use of the spiritual directions of Fr. Theodore, who was experienced in the ascetic life and wise with the grace of the Holy Spirit.

Under the direction of this guide Fr. Leonid also learned to war with the passions and attained spiritual enlightenment. The purest kind of love united the guide and his disciple with unbreakable bonds. When Fr. Leonid was appointed Abbot, it was difficult for him to interrupt his close relationship with his Elder. Yet Providence separated the co-strugglers only for a short while. The disruptions of visitors who interrupted the stillness of the desert life, and especially the fame of his virtues and struggles — fame which Fr. Theodore always fled because of his humility — forced him in 1805, for the sake of a more readily prayerful service to the Lord, to move to the secluded White Bluff community. The humble Elder was lovingly received by his disciple, the Abbot of this secluded Monastery, Fr. Leonid, who in turn rejoiced over the arrival of his wise guide as over the acquisition of a great treasure. His frequent conversations with his Elder and their life together strengthened Fr. Leonid even more for further

---

2. Schemamonk Theodore was born in the city of Karachev, the home town of his disciple and spiritual friend, Fr. Leonid. The Life of Fr. Theodore was published in a separate volume in Moscow, 1839, and a second edition in 1847. See p. 209 of this text.

advancement in spiritual endeavors and brought him to perfection. At this time Fr. Leonid had spiritual contact also with the Abbot of the Svensk Monastery in Bryansk and the inspector of the Orlov Theological Seminary, Abbot Philaret (who later became Metropolitan of Kiev), a person with extensive education, who through contact with monks like Fr. Leonid quickly learned to value the spiritual insight of experienced elders.

In White Bluff (in 1807), Fr. Theodore came down with a severe and prolonged illness. For nine days he took no food and for three days and nights was in a lethargic sleep. As the author of the life and struggles of Fr. Theodore relates, "During this illness, after his experience of the sweet sensations of the grace-filled gifts of the Spirit of God, the Elder thirsted all the more for the solitary and hesychastic life and expressed his desire for this to the Abbot and the brotherhood. Out of love and reverence for him, they immediately built a secluded cell for him in a thicket in the forest, more than a mile from the Monastery. Here he lived with another great ascetic, Hiero-schemamonk Cleopas. Humble Fr. Leonid soon came to join them, after voluntarily resigning from the position of Abbot in 1808." It is here, so they say, while living with Fr. Theodore in silence in the wilderness, that he received the tonsure to the great schema in their common cell and was named Leo.

Yet it is written: *Neither do men light a candle, and put it under a bushel, but on a candlestick; and it giveth light unto all that are in the house* (Matt. 5:15). Soon Providence revealed to men the great labors of the desert-loving Theodore. The fame of his lofty life and wisdom spread everywhere, and thousands of visitors began to flock to the doors of his cell. Then Fr. Theodore and his fellow-strugglers, exhausted by distraction — so pleasant for self-love and so weighty for humblemindedness — "were consumed with a strong desire to move to the very distant northern areas of the Russian Empire. For no brief time this longing continued and matured among them." Finally there came a directive that the humble Theodore leave White Bluff before his fellow strugglers. Entrusting himself to the will of the Almighty, Who *upholds all things by the word of His power* (Heb. 1:3), he directed his steps to the New Lake Monastery"[3] (in 1809), which lay in the eastern region of the Novgorod Province. However, he did not stay, but at the wish of the Metropolitan of St. Petersburg, Ambrose, he went to settle at the Palei Island Hermitage (on an island in Lake Onega), where he spent three years which were very grievous for him. From there, in 1812, he moved to the Skete of the Valaam Monastery.

Fr. Leonid and Fr. Cleopas did not remain long at White Bluff after the departure of Fr. Theodore. In 1811, already wishing to live somewhat nearer to their spiritual guide and friend, they moved their place of habitation to the Skete of Valaam Monastery, where in the following year they had the consolation of being reunited with ". . . the Elder Theodore, exhausted from his struggle with envy and hatred," according to the author of his Life.

"Glory to our compassionate God," wrote Fr. Theodore soon after arriving at Valaam to Fr. Athanasius, an ascetic of the Ploshchansk Monastery, "glory to our compassionate God, that He has granted me, the unworthy and defiled one, to live together with my fathers in the Skete at Valaam. Now we cannot offer any excuse or justification before our Maker and Redeemer; He has fulfilled our every wish. . . . In fact, we can even boast of the kindness of God toward us unworthy ones: He has brought us to a place that is silent, quiet, far from men and free of disturbance. Fr. Leonid has been appointed Superior in the Skete. Only pray to the compassionate God that He henceforth grant us now to make a

---

3. At that time Theophan Sokolov was Abbot there. He was himself a disciple of one of the fellow-conversers of Elder Paisius and was the childhood friend of St. Herman of Alaska.

beginning of loving Him and living according to His holy will and keeping His divine commandments."[4]

The three courageous co-strugglers spent about six years together in the Valaam Skete, as in a reliable haven for salvation. As Anthony Ivanovich,[5] a Fool-for-Christ of those regions, put it: "They traded well," referring on the one hand to their origin from the merchant class, and on the other to their spiritual trading — the acquisition of souls for Christ through their counsels and directions which are more precious than silver and gold. For here also the great Elders, by their spiritual wisdom and humility, attracted many brothers to themselves; these began to come to them, desiring to benefit from their spiritual direction.

At the same time as Fr. Theodore and Fr. Leonid, a hieromonk Barlaam (later the Abbot of Valaam) lived in the Valaam Skete. As a great lover of stillness, he was puzzled at how these Elders spent entire days in the midst of crowds of people, speaking with those who came to them for the sake of spiritual counsel, yet remained undisturbed. Once he turned to Elder Theodore with the words: "Father! I am scandalized by you, because you spend days at a time occupied and talking with outsiders; how can this be?" "Eh, what a funny fellow you are, little brother," the Elder replied. "Here I spend a couple of days in conversation out of love for my neighbor and I remain undisturbed." From this reply of an Elder known for his labors and gifts of grace, Fr. Barlaam became enlightened once and for all about how to discern the distinction between the paths of "the unique and the general."[6]

---

4. See the "Life of Elder Theodore of Svir," p. 226 of this text.

5. See Appendix II, pp. 255-257 for his life.

6. St. John of the Ladder says: "It is truly a great thing to struggle in stillness manfully and courageously; but it is incomparably greater to have no fear of turmoil and to remain steadfast under its assault with a fearless heart, while dwelling with men outwardly, but inwardly with

GENERAL VIEW OF VALAAM MONASTERY
1864 engraving showing the church built by Abbot Nazarius.

Among those making use of the spiritual direction of Fr. Theodore and Fr. Leonid was the cellarer of the Valaam Monastery, Fr. Eudocimus (later Schemamonk Euthymius, the spiritual father of the Valaam Monastery). He had formerly spent his monastic life without spiritual guidance, hoping to attain spiritual advancement by outward struggles alone and by absolute submission to the Abbot, who considered him to be a devout disciple. But neither obedience, expressed by a readiness to die in the fulfillment of a command of his Abbot, nor ascetic labors brought him the genuine fruits of the monastic life. Fr. Eudocimus did not notice any meekness, love, tears or humility within himself. Rather, dryness, hardness, disparagement of others and other yet-hidden passions consumed the Elder. He found no relief for himself, even though he fulfilled everything he should have fulfilled — according to books and according to his opinion and experience. The Elder fell into despair; his thoughts were already turning him towards suicide, telling him to hurl himself from a cliff into the bay. The Lord inspired Fr. Eudocimus, after he had abandoned hope in his own righteousness, to have recourse to Fr. Theodore and Fr. Leonid. The Elders quickly helped him, revealing, on the basis of the Holy Fathers, that external activity and physical struggles alone do not bring a monk to advancement, especially if they, being apparent to other men, drag him to vainglory and pride and to all the results of these passions, to insensitivity, judgment and despair; that without the internal, humble, secret labor of prayer and without complete

---

God." (Homily to the Shepherd, Chapter 9 in Russian; 43 in English.)

This measure, however, is attained by very few, and not easily; they receive it as a reward for many labors, and especially for humility. It is then, when they are summoned by Providence to the labor of ministering to their neighbors, that they are able to offer them great spiritual benefit, while they themselves are not harmed at all by contact with others. Such were these ever-memorable Elders, Fr. Theodore, Fr. Leonid and his successor, Fr. Macarius.

The cell of Schemamonk Nicholas, a contemporary
of Elder Leonid on Valaam.

self-abnegation[7] one cannot soften oneself, become humble and find happiness with childlike, evangelical joy. The Elders showed him the true key to opening the heart; and Fr. Eudocimus, a monk outwardly, yet sincere and prepared to suffer even death for the sake of salvation, understood the humble teaching of the Elders, began to be reborn, to humble himself and bit by bit to be at peace. Afterwards he was revered by everyone at Valaam. The Abbot at that time, Fr. Damascene, they say, made use of his counsels and told certain persons that the names of Fr. Theodore and Fr. Leonid were constantly on Fr. Eudocimus' lips and that he always remembered them with gratitude and the deepest reverence.

The fame of the Elders spread more and more. Together with Fr. Eudocimus, and following his example, more and more of the brotherhood began to come to them. Visitors to the Monastery from all walks of life also rushed to the cell of the Elders in order to profit from their divinely-wise counsels.

But at the same time that these wise guides were offering great spiritual benefit, among others there arose dissatisfaction with them, which partially derived from the weakness of the human heart and partially from the fact that they could not properly understand the way of life and teaching of the Elders. We already mentioned that formerly Fr. Eudocimus was considered to be the devoted disciple of the Abbot of Valaam, Abbot Innocent. But when he, and after him other brothers also, began to turn to the Elders, the Abbot with sorrow saw himself abandoned by one of the persons most devoted to him, and felt that he was being overlooked by the brethren, probably because he thought that the abbot should be the only spiritual guide in the monastery. In the simple times of old this was more often than not the case.

---

7. Self-abnegation, according to the teaching of St. Barsanuphius the Great, means to consider oneself to be nothing, to consider oneself dust and ashes, to compare oneself with no one, and not to speak of one's own good deeds, saying: "I did this too." (Answers 269 and 610).

But in our more formal times, the abbot alone, without the assistance of experienced spiritual fathers and elders, cannot easily guide the brotherhood. This was realized even in ancient times by one of the greatest monastic teachers, the saintly and Spirit-bearing Theodore of Studion, who, concerning the election and appointment of the abbot, in his last will and testament to the brethren, wrote thus: "First I leave you as your guide, my master and father and your father, our most venerable anchorite and father, and luminary and teacher. For 'he in the Lord is greater than both me' and you, and he is our head, even though he has submitted himself by living in stillness in Christ-like humility; by his instructions and prayers, I believe, you will find salvation, if only you show him the appropriate good submission and obedience." "And then," continues St. Theodore, "whomever by your common choice you appoint in a godly manner to be abbot, in keeping with his fatherly counsel, and whomever the entire brotherhood will desire, I am agreeable to his election."[8] It was not with such feelings and thoughts that Fr. Innocent regarded Fr. Theodore and Fr. Leonid. Their fatherly love for all, their ready accessibility and freedom of conduct seemed to him to be a lack of submission to the Abbot and interference with his governing; their teaching seemed to him to be a strange sort of novelty. His dissatisfaction with the Elders grew all the stronger when the Minister of Spiritual Affairs, Prince A. N. Golitsyn, during a visit to Valaam spent the entire time of his visit in the cell of the Elders, even asking that he be served tea there and inviting the Abbot to come from the Monastery to the Skete.

Finally, Fr. Innocent decided to file a complaint with the Metropolitan of Novgorod and St. Petersburg, Ambrose, against these newcomer Elders, who were, according to his opinion, disturbing the peace of the Monastery. The Metropolitan knew the good side of the Abbot of Valaam, as an

---

8. See *St. Theodore the Studite, Catechetical Instructions*, in Russian translation, Moscow, 1872, p. 334.

honorable and industrious ascetic; he was prejudiced against the Elders and was prepared to condemn them. Soon stories were circulating that Fr. Theodore, since he had been tonsured in Moldavia and not in Russia, and since in Russia he had simply been a merchant of the city of Karachev, was to be expelled from the Monastery and returned to his former state and that Fr. Leonid would not be able to avoid trouble either. However, the Metropolitan entrusted the investigation of the matter to Fr. Hilarion[9] (the late Archimandrite of the Tikhvin Monastery). Fr. Hilarion visited Valaam Monastery in February of 1817, questioned Fr. Theodore and his co-strugglers and put thirty written questions before them. Fr. Hilarion read their answers with amazement, and afterwards he always said that he had never read anything like what these simple Elders answered in their replies. Their sacred foolishness turned out to be loftier than the wisdom of men.

Fr. Hilarion did all he could to reconcile the Abbot with the Elders. He acted in this manner partially out of an awareness of the truth and a sense of justice and partially, perhaps, because together with him there had been sent to Valaam by the Minister of Spiritual Affairs, A. N. Golitsyn, one of his trusted men, a certain A. N. Nikolsky, to investigate the

---

9. Archimandrite Hilarion (1776-1850) began his monastic life in the Kargopol Monastery of the Savior in the Olonets Diocese and later with the help of Metropolitan Gabriel went to dwell in the secluded Konevits Monastery. He totally transformed this monastic citadel situated on Lake Ladoga during his term as Abbot between the years 1807 and 1823, doing for Konevits what Abbot Nazarius had done for Valaam. "Refraining from idleness, unprofitable conversations and all entertainment, through meekness and attentiveness he soon acquired not only the love but also the respect of the brothers." He spent his formative years enriching his soul with treasures from the Word of God and the writings of the Holy Fathers. The Konevits Monastery rule which he composed became a standard for other monasteries in the Empire. "He portrays in the rule the monastic life as it ought to be, according to its very nature, in a word, as a life equal to the angels." Appended to this rule was another for the recluses of the Konevits

matter that had arisen and to defend the Elders. At the same time, some of the persons devoted to them had informed two great Hierarchs, Philaret[10] and Innocent,[11] of the difficult situation of the Elders. These Christian philosophers, who had some knowledge of Fr. Leonid, took up the side of the Elders and came to their defense. Their words had an effect on the Metropolitan. At this time the report of Fr. Hilarion was received.

With bitterness the Metropolitan saw that he had almost committed a great injustice. Abbot Innocent was summoned and met with the foreboding and unceremonious question: "What are you trying to do to me, you old . . . ? Thanks to you I almost condemned persons who are better than the both of us." The Abbot was ordered to put the Elders at ease in every possible way in his Monastery with the warning that, if they made any complaint, he would be removed. The Elders were told that they could be certain of the defense of the highest church administration. But the experienced and humble ascetics, knowing the hearts of men, did not harbor any hope that the Abbot would be totally reconciled with them. Aware that it is easier to bear the hatred of the entire brotherhood than ill intentions on the part of the Abbot,

---

Desert for which the recent exemplary lives of the Elders Zosima and Basilisk served as models. "He was strict towards himself, sober, unacquisitive, zealous for the Church, exemplary and a model Abbot-ascetic." In addition to his many writings on the monastic life he also composed the Church Services to Sts. Sergius and Herman of Valaam and likewise to St. Arsenius, the Wonderworker of Konevits. Hence, his testimony on behalf of the persecuted Elders was very weighty indeed. In 1823 he was elevated to the rank of Archimandrite and appointed Superior of the Tikhvin Monastery and remained in this capacity until his repose in 1850. (See *Biographies of National Ascetics of Piety of the 18th and 19th Centuries,* October, Moscow, 1909, pp. 526-537.)

10. Later the famous Metropolitan of Moscow. —trans.

11. Bishop of Penza, a very influential church figure at that time. —trans.

and in order to avoid a prolonged sin, they decided to leave Valaam. Soon after this, in June 1817, they moved to the St. Alexander of Svir Monastery, considering themselves to be rejects from the world and unworthy of an abode on earth.

Concerning Abbot Innocent we have noted that he made a mistake due primarily to misunderstanding. This grievous experience for him, one should assume, served as a profitable lesson for him because afterwards he was remembered as an outstanding figure.

During the time that the Elders were living at the St. Alexander of Svir Monastery, it is related that Emperor Alexander I visited this Monastery; from this account of his visit one can see how human fame everywhere pursued the humble-minded ascetics, while they did all they could do to deflect it, thus giving everyone a great lesson in sincere humility.

In 1820 the Emperor traveled throughout the northern parts of his realm. His route lay near the Svir Monastery. The Elders, Fr. Theodore and Fr. Leonid, who were living there respectfully suggested to the Archimandrite that he prepare to meet the Tsar, even though the Svir Monastery was not listed on his itinerary. The Archimandrite heeded this advice and at the time appointed for the journey was standing at the gates. Meanwhile the Emperor, as was his custom, inquired along the way about the area and its inhabitants, questioning his drivers — sometimes personally, sometimes through his attendant, Elias, who was his inseparable coachman. As they were approaching the road junction where a cross had been erected, indicating that a monastery was nearby and showing the way to it, the Tsar asked, "What is that cross for?" When he learned that the Svir Monastery was nearby, he directed that he be driven there and began to ask what the Monastery and its brotherhood were like. The driver, who had been there many times, said that now it was doing much better.

"Why?" asked the Tsar.

"Not long ago the Elders Fr. Theodore and Fr. Leonid settled there; now the chanting on the cliros is much better[12] and it looks like everything is in much better order." The Tsar, who had heard these names from Prince Golitsyn, wanted to make the acquaintance of the Elders.

Meanwhile, as they awaited their royal guest, the Elders, experienced in afflictions, consulted briefly with one another about what to do if the Tsar deigned to direct his attention to them. "If we had temptation because of Prince Golitsyn," said Fr. Theodore, "what will happen because of the Tsar? So, Fr. Leonid, don't be talkative; for the most part keep your mouth shut and don't expose yourself."

The Tsar, when he approached the gates, was surprised to be met by the Abbot and immediately asked whether they had been expecting him. The Archimandrite had not considered in advance what to say and replied that he had come out to meet their beloved Monarch at the advice of the Elders. When they had entered the church and had venerated the relics of St. Alexander (one of the Elders was present at the reliquary), the Tsar in his humility expressed his desire to receive the blessing of the hieromonks, with the request that they not pull their hands away when he kissed them. Then he asked, "And where are Fr. Theodore and Fr. Leonid?" The Elders came forward a bit; but they replied to all of the questions of the Tsar with the greatest possible brevity and succinctness, so that the Tsar himself noticed this and put an end to the questions, perhaps thinking that it was improper to ask them in church. Finally, coming up to Fr. Theodore, he asked his blessing. "I'm a monk who is not ordained, an un-ordained monk," said Fr. Theodore. "I am just a peasant." The Tsar bowed respectfully and went on his way.

In 1822, on the 7th of April, which was Bright Friday, Fr. Theodore came to the end of his earthly course which

---

12. Fr. Theodore was an excellent chanter and an expert on the order of church singing.

had been so filled with toil. He gave up his spirit in the arms of his beloved disciple and at the same time spiritual father, Fr. Leonid. Here is the beautiful description of his end penned by the eloquent writer of his Life: "Half a year before his death, Fr. Theodore fell gravely ill. 'Glory to God, Glory to God!' he kept repeating during his intense suffering — 'At last I see the shore of the sea of life, where up till now my soul has been cast about by the gales and tempests like a tiny boat.' The evening of Bright Friday arrived. The face of the Elder began to shine, and a joyful smile animated his face. His sorrowful disciples stood silently around his death bed; they forgot about their tears and mourning while with reverent trembling and awe they watched the blessed end of the servant of the Lord. Archimandrite Macarius administered the Sacrament of Holy Unction and the Communion of the Holy Mysteries; and his pure, radiant soul flew off to the lofty mansions of eternal bliss."

After the repose of his Elder Fr. Theodore, Fr. Leonid did not want to remain in the St. Alexander of Svir Monastery, not only for the sake of his disciples who could not yet withstand the disruptions due to the great flow of pilgrims to the Svir Monastery, but also for certain other reasons; he had the intention to go with his disciples and brothers of like mind to a more secluded place. Here is what he wrote about this to Hieromonk P.: "You were pleased to write that in our most difficult times it seems needful for us all to gather into one and to petition some monastic-loving archpastor for a quiet refuge. We also approve of this opinion. . . . And our father Theodore more than once emphasized the point that we should all be united so as not to be separated, and should preserve the common life together. Especially after he received the gift of clairvoyance before his death, he would say in a fatherly manner, 'My fathers! For the sake of the Lord do not separate one from another, because in the present time, so filled with afflictions, one can find very few to whom he can speak a word according to his conscience.' And now you behold this in your own experience as in a mirror. But, regrettably, because of the great multitude of my sins, we do not have a courageous and worthy superior in our midst, one who could maintain a monastery and care for us according to the Holy Fathers, and who could give direction with the proper discretion. . . . But it seems beneficial for us to join together in order to strengthen one another."

When the desire of Fr. Leonid to leave the Svir Monastery became known, his disciples were soon invited to various places. The famous Archbishop of Kazan, Ambrose (Podobedev), having heard about Elder Leonid from his spiritual father, Hieromonk Job (who later lived at the Optina Skete), expressed his willingness to receive him in his diocese. In addition, he was invited to move to the Ploshchansk Hermitage in the Orlov Diocese. The Elder completely refused to move to the Kazan Diocese. He was more inclined to move to the Optina Skete, where he had been invited by the Archpastor of Kaluga, Philaret; by the Abbot of Optina, Daniel; and by the founder of the Skete, Fr. Moses, together with the Elders of the Skete. "Our hearts," he wrote, "are inclined in that direction, in so far as it was there that I laid the foundation of the monastic life and lost my health; and our former friend and benefactor, Bishop Philaret, being a monk-loving soul, is desirous of this." His closest disciples were in agreement with this desire of the Elder. One of them, Hieromonk Gabriel, who had remained at Valaam Monastery, was the first to move to the Optina Skete in 1823.

In this same year on August 17, Bishop Philaret visited the Optina Monastery and stated positively to the Optina Elders that he felt that Fr. Leonid would certainly be in Optina, or at least somewhere in his diocese.

The prophecy of the Bishop did in fact come to fulfillment, but not right away. For five years, Fr. Leonid, in spite of his intensified petitions, was retained in the Svir Monastery; he was not even allowed to make a pilgrimage to Kiev. In this refusal of his authorities, Fr. Leonid saw that it was not yet God's will for him to move to another place. Many of the visitors to the Svir Monastery were very glad that the Elder remained there, because they were thirsty to hear a word of instruction from him. But this devotion of the people to him could not keep him there. "Yes, there is nothing else that we are so sorry to leave behind," he wrote, "as the remains of our most beloved benefactor, Fr. Theodore, so worthy of blessedness. But, in this matter, may the will of our Creator and Redeemer be done. We think and judge as men who are still carnal. But the all-merciful Lord knows all things, even what we have not yet done." "Whenever the will of God indicates," he wrote in another letter, "then even the most powerful interference cannot prevail." This faith of his in the Providence of God was justified in actual fact. For five years, as we said, he was forcibly detained at the St. Alexander of Svir Monastery; but at the beginning of the sixth year, the Lord arranged that he be released without any difficulty. And even after leaving the Svir Monastery, Fr. Leonid did not immediately decide to take up his abode at the Optina Monastery, but, as it were, still wanted to make certain that it was the will of God for him to settle in this Monastery. First he went to live in the Ploshchansk Hermitage, where he was drawn by the desire to live together with the Hieromonk Macarius (Ivanov) with whom he had spiritually become closely acquainted. On October 6th, 1828, Fr. Leonid arrived in the Ploshchansk Hermitage; but due to certain circumstances he lived there only half a year, and in April of 1829, together with his disciples, he finally moved to the Optina Monastery.

Concerning the inner, spiritual life of Fr. Leonid, we have no detailed and reliable information of the period he spent at the Svir Monastery. But judging by the fact that he was the disciple of one of the devout disciples of the great instructor of mental activity, Paisius Velichkovsky, and likewise judging by the questions of the disciple and replies of the Elder which are appended to this Life, we can say that Fr. Leonid was not a stranger to the activity of prayer according to the teachings of the Holy Fathers. To the question: Is mental prayer granted to all, he replied to his close disciple, "Whomever the Lord visits with a grievous trial, sorrow, or the deprivation of a beloved person or ones close to him, such a person will involuntarily pray with his whole heart and all his thoughts and with all his mind. Consequently the wellspring of prayer is in everyone; but it is tapped either by gradually delving deeper and deeper into one's self in accordance with the teachings of the Holy Fathers, or instantaneously, by God's drill."[13] We cannot positively confirm that when he spoke these words, Fr. Leonid had in mind the experience of his own life, but it is known that during the final year of the life of his Elder Fr. Theodore, Fr. Leonid, according to the Elder's own testimony, made more progress in the monastic life than in all the previous years. This, beyond any doubt, served as preparation for him to receive the grace-filled gifts of God. Likewise it is certain that after the repose of Fr. Theodore and his seven-year stay in the Svir Monastery, Fr. Leonid emerged in the complete armament of spiritual power for his new ministry to mankind, to which he was called by the Providence of God in the new and final place of his earthly sojourn — the Optina Monastery.

---

13. See the Spiritual Counsels of Elder Leonid, question 8, p. 201 of this text.

Beehives (apiary) near where Elder Leonid originally settled at the Optina Skete.

II

Father Leonid Settles
at the Optina Monastery

THE INSTALLATION OF ELDERSHIP

FATHER LEONID arrived at the Optina Monastery in April of 1829, as we have already noted, with six disciples. He was given a cell which had been especially prepared for him at the apiary near the Skete, and all his disciples were situated with him in cells in the Skete also.

The settling of Fr. Leonid at the Optina Monastery is very significant because he is the one who introduced and established in this Monastery what is called "eldership." This form of monastic life, founded on the Gospels and the teachings of the Holy Fathers, in our time has been almost forgotten; therefore we consider it appropriate to say a few words about it.

Eldership consists of the sincere spiritual relationship of spiritual children to their spiritual father or elder.

Saints Callistus and Ignatius, in the *Philokalia*, set down five indications of such a sincere, spiritual relationship: 1. complete faith in one's guide and superior; 2. truthfulness — to be truthful before him in both word and deed;

3. not to do one's own will in any way, but in every way
to strive to cut off one's own will — that is, not to do anything
in keeping with one's own wish and understanding, but
always to ask about everything, and to act according to the
advice and will of one's guide and superior; 4. in no way to
contradict or be contentious as contradiction and conten-
tiousness issue from thoughts mixed with unbelief and conceit; 5. complete confession of sins and the secrets of one's
heart (Volume II of the *Philokalia*, Chapter 15).[1]

"They deceive themselves," says St. John Climacus,
"who, placing their hope in themselves, suppose that they
have no need of a director" (Chapter 1, Step 7).[2]

"As a ship which has a good helmsman comes safely
into harbor with God's help, so the soul which has a good
shepherd, even though it has done much evil, easily ascends
to Heaven. Without a guide it is easy to wander from the road,
however prudent you may be; and so he who walks the monastic way under his own direction soon perishes, even though
he may have all the wisdom of the world" (Step 26, Chapters 236 and 237).[3]

"For the man who goes (by way of the monastic path)
his own way, traveling without understanding of the Gospels
and without any guidance," says St. Mark the Ascetic, "often
stumbles and falls into many pits and snares of the devil;
he frequently goes astray and exposes himself to many
dangers, not knowing where he is going. For many have
endured great ascetic labors, much hardship and toil for
God's sake; but because they relied on their own judgment,
lacked discrimination, and failed to accept help from their

---

1. *Writings from the Philokalia on Prayer of the Heart,* "Directions
to Hesychasts," Chapter 15, pp. 176-7. Faber and Faber Ltd., Fifth
Impression, 1967.

2. St. John Climacus, *The Ladder of Divine Ascent,* Revised Edition,
Holy Transfiguration Monastery, Brookline, Massachusetts, 1978, p. 5.

3. *Ibid.,* Summary of Step 26, Chapters 52-53, p. 195.

neighbor, their many efforts proved useless and vain" (Letter to Nicholas the Solitary).[4]

"It is impossible," says St. Gregory the Sinaite, "for anyone to learn by himself the art of virtue, although some have used their own experience as a teacher. For acting by one's own inclination, instead of following the advice of those who have succeeded, leads to a high opinion of oneself. For if *the Son can do nothing of himself, but what he seeth the Father do: for what things soever he doeth, these also doeth the Son likewise* (John 5:19), and the *Spirit shall not speak of himself* (John 16:13), who can think that he has reached such heights of virtue that he has no need of someone's guidance amid mysteries? In his delusion such a man seems to be more mad than virtuous" (in Volume I of the *Philokalia,* Chapter 15 on hesychasm).[5]

"One should not question everyone, but only him who has been entrusted with the guidance of others, whose life shines, and who is himself *poor, yet making many rich,* according to the Scriptures (II Cor. 6:10). Many inexperienced men have done harm to many unwise people, for which they will be judged after death. For not everyone has the right to guide others, but only those who have been endowed with *discernment of spirits,* according to the Apostle (I Cor. 12:10), namely that discerning of spirits which separates good from evil by the sword of the word. Each man has his own reason and his natural discernment, either practical or scientific, but not all have *spiritual* discernment. Therefore the wise Sirach says: *Be in peace with many: nevertheless have but one counsellor of a thousand* (Eccles. 6:6). It is hard to find a guide unerring either in

---

4. St. Mark the Ascetic, "Letter to Nicholas the Solitary," *The Philokalia,* Faber and Faber Ltd., 1979, Volume I, pp. 151-2.

5. St. Gregory of Sinai, "Instructions to Hesychasts," *Writings from the Philokalia on Prayer of the Heart,* Faber and Faber Ltd., Fifth Impression, 1967, Chapter 15, p. 93.

deeds, words or understanding. That a man is unerring can be recognized if he has testimony from the Scriptures both for practice and for understanding, and is humbly wise in the realms of wisdom" (Volume I of the *Philokalia*, Chapter 7 on prelest).[6]

A spiritual relationship requires on the part of those being guided, not just the usual confession before Communion of the Holy Mysteries, but also frequent confession, whenever needed, to the elder and spiritual father, not only of one's actions and deeds, but of all one's passionate thoughts and movements, even the secrets of one's heart; as Basil the Great (in the "Long Rules," question 26),[7] Symeon the New Theologian (in Volume I of the *Philokalia*, Chapter 122),[8] and other Holy Fathers have spoken about this.

"It is impossible," says St. Cassian the Roman, "for anyone who orders his life on the basis of the judgment and knowledge of the spiritually mature to fall because of the wiles of the demons. In fact, even before someone is granted the gift of discrimination, the act of revealing his base thoughts openly to the fathers weakens and withers them " (2nd Conference on Discrimination, Chapter 10[9]).[10]

---

6. *Ibid.*, Chapter 7, "Of Prelest and Other Subjects," pp. 81-2.

7. St. Basil the Great, "The Long Rules," *Ascetical Works,* Catholic University of America Press, Inc., 1962, question 26, pp. 288-9.

8. St. Symeon the New Theologian, "Active and Theological Chapters," *Philokalia* (Slavonic) Volume I, Synodal Press, Moscow, 1840. Chapter 122, folio 72, reverse.

9. St. John Cassian, "On the Holy Fathers of Scetis and on Discrimination," *The Philokalia, op. cit.,* pp. 288-9, 327-30.

10. Note: Those who wish to have a more detailed understanding of the way of eldership should read: St. Basil the Great, "An Ascetical Discourse and Exhortation on the Renunciation of the World and Spiritual Perfection," *op. cit.,* pp. 19-22, and "The Long Rules," *op. cit.,* pp. 288-9, 327-30; St. John Climacus, *op. cit.,* "On Blessed and Ever-memorable Obedience," Step 4, pp. 20-54 and "To the

The great importance and great significance of the spiritual relationship to one's elder is demonstrated by the following two examples.

St. Theodore the Studite writes, "A certain elder on several occasions told his disciple to perform a certain task, but the latter kept putting it off. The elder, disturbed over this, in his indignation laid a penance on the disciple, forbidding him to eat bread until he had finished the appointed task. While the disciple went to perform his assignment, the elder died. After his death, the disciple wanted to be released from the *epitimia* laid on him. But there was no one he could find in that desert place who would take it on himself to resolve this problem. Finally the disciple went with his petition to the Patriarch of Constantinople, Germanos, who gathered other bishops in order to examine the matter. But neither the Patriarch, nor the synod which gathered, found it possible to lift the epitimia of the elder, concerning whom it is not known whether or not he had the rank of priest. For this reason the disciple was forced to eat only vegetables."[11]

In *The Prologue* for October 15 there is the following account: In Scetis there was a monk who for many

---

Shepherd," pp. 231-50; St. Dorotheos of Gaza, Discourse 5, "On the Need for Consultation," *Dorotheos of Gaza — Discourses and Sayings,* Cistercian Publications, 1977, Chapter 5, pp. 122-30; St. Theodore the Studite, *Catechetical Homilies,* especially 2, 4, 8, 9, 10, 12, 17, 26, 29, 46, 47, and 95; St. Symeon the New Theologian, "Practical and Theological Precepts," *Writings from the Philokalia on Prayer of the Heart,* Chapters 15-19, pp. 100-1, Chapters 38-44, pp. 104-6. [Also Chapter 37, p. 104, and 45, p. 106 on the same subject. —Trans.]; Sts. Callistus and Ignatius, *op. cit.,* pp. 94-108; St. Theodore (of Edessa) the Great Ascetic, "A Century of Spiritual Texts," *The Philokalia, op. cit.,* Volume II, 1981, Chapters 40-46, pp. 21-2. Also read the collected letters of Hiero-schemamonk Macarius (of Optina), especially part 4, to nuns.

11. St. Theodore the Studite, *Catechetical Homilies* (in Russian), Moscow, 1872, p. 133.

years was obedient to his father; in the end, however, due to the envy of the demons he fell from obedience, and without any good reason left his elder, disregarding his epitimia, for he had an epitimia from his elder for his disobedience. He came to Alexandria, was arrested and forced by the governor there to deny Christ; but he remained unshaken in a firm confession of the faith, and for this he was tortured and put to death. The Christians of the city took the body of the new martyr, put it in a casket and placed it in the holy church. But during each Liturgy when the deacon proclaimed: "All that are catechumens, depart," the casket with the body of the martyr, to the amazement of all, was removed by an invisible force to the narthex; and after the completion of the Liturgy, on its own returned again to the church. One of the noblemen of Alexandria prayed for an answer concerning this problem; and it was revealed to him in a vision that the martyred monk was the disciple of a certain elder, and that for his disobedience he had been bound by him. As a martyr he had received the crown of martyrdom; but being bound by the epitimia of his elder, he could not remain present for the celebration of the Divine Service until the one who had bound him absolved him. Then the elder was sought out; he came to Alexandria and absolved the monk bound by his epitimia. After that time the casket no longer moved from its place.

At the present time, many, especially those who reject the path of spiritual guidance, in order to justify themselves point to the dearth and waning of spiritual guides. But St. Basil the Great says that if a person diligently seeks a good teacher, he will surely find him (Ascetic Homily).[12] And St. Symeon the New Theologian teaches: "With prayers and tears implore God to give you a man who could keep you free from passions."[13] He further says, "It is better to

12. St. Basil the Great, "An Ascetical Discourse and Exhortation on the Renunciation of the World and Spiritual Perfection," *op. cit.*, p. 20.
13. St. Symeon the New Theologian, *op. cit.*, Chapter 33, p. 103.

be called the disciple of a disciple than to live by one's own devices and pluck the worthless fruits of self-will" (Volume I of the *Philokalia*, Chapter 33; and Homily 12, p. 109).[14]

However, if after diligent and fervent searching one cannot find a spiritual guide and instructor, in that case the Elder Paisius Velichkovsky, in his letter to the Priest Demetrius, offers the following advice:

"But in the present cruel times, which are worthy of much weeping and lamentation, so few have such instructors; therefore if any zealots among the monks should desire to please God by means of such a coenobitic life, their teacher and instructor must be God Himself and the divine writings of those Holy Fathers, the instructors of the common life, which have been preserved by God's Providence even up to now. And if these zealots pay careful heed to these writings as if it were to those Fathers themselves, by reading them with the fear of God and understanding, and with God's help, they may be in part imitators of their God-pleasing life, being guided and helped to understand by their own father who has gathered them in the Name of Christ or who has been unanimously chosen by them — as long as he instructs his spiritual children not from himself, but from the Holy Scripture and from this same teaching of the Holy Fathers" (*The Life and Writings of Paisius Velichkovsky*, Moscow, 1847, p. 248).[15]

The path of guidance by an elder has been recognized throughout all the ages of Christianity by all the great desert dwellers, fathers and teachers of the Church as being the

---

14. Homily 12 of St. Symeon refers to the numbering in the Russian edition of Optina Monastery from the work of St. Paisius — *Twelve Homilies of St. Symeon*, Moscow, 1869; *St. Symeon the New Theologian: The Discourses*, Paulist Press, New York, 1980, Discourse XX, "The Ideal Spiritual Guide," p. 232.

15. St. Paisius Velichkovsky, letter "To the Priest Demetrius," *Blessed Paisius Velichkovsky*, St. Herman of Alaska Brotherhood, 1976, pp. 147-8.

most reliable and surest of all that are known to the Church of Christ. Eldership blossomed in the ancient Egyptian and Palestinian communities; it was afterwards planted on Athos, and from the East it was brought to Russia. But in the last centuries, in view of the general decline of faith and asceticism, it has gradually fallen into neglect, so that many have even begun to reject it. In the times of St. Nilus of Sora, the way of eldership was already scorned by many; and by the end of the past century [that is, the 18th] it had become almost entirely unknown. For the restoration of this form of monastic life, which is founded upon the teaching of the Holy Fathers, much was done by the famous and great Elder, the Archimandrite of the Moldavian monasteries, Paisius Velichkovsky. With great labor he gathered together on Athos and translated from Greek into Slavonic the works of the ascetic writers, which set forth the patristic teaching on monastic life in general and the spiritual relationship to an elder in particular. At the same time in Niamets and in the other Moldavian monasteries under his rule, he exhibited in practice the application of this teaching. One of the disciples of Archimandrite Paisius, Schemamonk Theodore, who lived in Moldavia almost 20 years, transmitted this teaching to Hiero-schemamonk Father Leonid; and through him and his disciple, the Elder Hiero-schemamonk Macarius, it was planted in the Optina Monastery.

The Abbot of Optina at that time, Fr. Moses, and his brother, the Skete Superior Fr. Anthony, who laid the beginning of their monastic life in the Bryansk forest in the spirit of the ancient great desert dwellers, wished for a long time to introduce eldership into the Optina Monastery. By themselves, however, they could not fulfill this task; they were burdened by many difficult and complicated occupations in conjunction with the development and governance of the Monastery. Furthermore, although in general the combining of the duties of the abbacy and eldership in one person was possible in the ancient times of simplicity of character, as

ST. MOSES, ABBOT OF OPTINA
(1782-1862)
Commemorated June 16/29

we have already mentioned, in our times it is very hard and even impossible. However, when Fr. Leonid settled in Optina, Fr. Moses, knowing and taking advantage of his experience in the spiritual life, entrusted all the brothers who lived in the Optina Monastery to his guidance, as well as all others who would come to live in the Monastery.

From that time the entire inner order of the monastic life at the Optina Monastery changed. Without the counsel and blessing of the Elder nothing of importance was undertaken in the Monastery. Every day, especially in the evening, the brotherhood came to his cell with their spiritual needs. Each one hastened to reveal before the Elder how he had transgressed during the course of the day in deed, word or thought, in order to ask his counsel for the resolution of problems that had arisen, consolation in some sorrow that he had met, help and strength in the internal battle with the passions and with the invisible enemies of our salvation. The Elder received all with fatherly love and offered all a word of experienced instruction and consolation. Here is a description of the cell of Fr. Leonid by an eyewitness, his disciple, Hieromonk Anthony.

"The cell of the Elder, from early morning until late at night, was filled with those who came to him for spiritual assistance; it was a picture worthy of an artist's brush. The Elder, clothed in white with a short mantia, could be seen amid the circle of his disciples who stood around him on their knees,[16] their faces animated with the expression of various feelings. One came with repentance for some sin that he had committed, something which a person not under obedience would not even think about confessing; another,

---

16. The confession of thoughts while kneeling, as a sign of humility, is an ancient Christian practice. (See the *Ladder of Divine Ascent,* Step 4, Chapters 66 and 34, which refer to kneeling. [The Russian notes Chapter 62, which is similar but vague.])

with tears and fear, admitted to an unintentional offense against a brother. On one face was burning shame that he could not overcome his thoughts, thoughts from which he wished he could flee to the ends of the earth; on another's face there showed the indifferent smirk of distrust of all that he saw — he had come together with the others just to make an appearance before the Elder and to go away un-healed. But even he, fearing the piercing gaze of the Elder and his word of rebuke, kept his eyes lowered and spoke in a soft voice, as if desiring to placate his judge with false hu-mility. Here in Fr. Leonid's cell one could see genuine obedi-ence, readiness to kiss the feet of the Elder; another person, stricken and rejected by the entire world, a sickly youth, re-fused to leave the knees of Fr. Leonid, like a suckling from its mother.[17] Along with the others could be seen the gray head of a soldier,[18] who at one time had served in the War of 1812 and now was waging war under the command of [an equally] skilled general against invisible foes. Here, too, shone the hoary head of an Elder[19] who, recognizing his own lack of skill in monasticism, had undertaken the spiritual alphabet at a time when the world considered him to be a teacher. It was this kind of varied society which surrounded the great Elder and spiritual commander. In this marvelous cell one would see sights which were just as instructive as any incidents which the best ages of Christianity can bring to mind. 'The assembly of the humble is beloved of God like the assembly of the Seraphim,' said St. Isaac the Syrian."[20]

---

17. Novice Dimitry Sh. [Hiero-schemamonk Anthony, of the Kiev Caves, while describing the cell of the Elder mentions "the Novice Dimitry Alexandrovitch Brianchaninov, later Bishop Ignatius." *National Ascetics of Piety* . . ., Moscow, 1909, October, p. 298. —Ed.]

18. Alexius Ivanovich Zhelyabuzhsky

19. Hieromonk Macarius (Ivanov)

20. St. Isaac the Syrian, *The Ascetical Homilies of Saint Isaac the Syrian*, Holy Transfiguration Monastery, 1984, Homily Fifty-one, p. 245.

The divinely-wise instructions of the Elder began to have a good effect on the Optina brotherhood, which gradually began to come to perfection in a spiritual sense.

The skillful healing of ailing souls and the wisdom of the Elder, to which the love and reverence shown him by the Abbot and brotherhood bore witness, soon made Fr. Leonid well-known outside the Monastery as well. Like gold that had been tried and purified in the crucible of 30 years of ascetic life, the Elder, by God's Providence, was finally called to the great labor of ministering to mankind. For spiritual counsel, persons of various ranks from the cities and villages began to come to the doors of his cell: noblemen, merchants, craftsmen, and simple folk of both sexes. All were received by the Elder with a heartfelt, fatherly disposition and love, and not one of those who came departed from his cell without being consoled spiritually by him. After they had revealed to him their ailments and wounds of soul, they departed consoled and healed. Those suffering physical illnesses, and even those possessed by demons, received relief when he read the prayers (from the Book of Needs) over them and anointed them with oil from the ever-burning lamp before the Vladimir Icon of the Mother of God, which he always kept in his cell. It was with this icon that the great Elder Paisius had blessed the journey of Schemamonk Theodore when he departed from Moldavia for Russia; and he, in turn, before he departed to the Lord, had blessed Fr. Leonid with it, for he had shared his afflictions with him and was the inheritor of his spiritual gifts.

With each year the flow of people to the Optina Monastery began to grow significantly, and thus the Monastery flourished. Persons who had a good understanding of spiritual life but who were living in seclusion or stillness[21] began to send from all parts of Russia persons of every rank

---

21. George the Recluse of Zadonsk, Hilarion of Troekurovo, and others.

who were seeking a more trustworthy haven to the guidance of Fr. Leonid in the Optina Monastery, in order to be instructed in the monastic life. Like bees to a hive, brothers began to come from all directions in order to nourish their hearts with the flow of Divine sweetness which flowed from the mellifluous lips of the Elder.

In 1834, Hieromonk Macarius (Ivanov) moved to Optina from the Ploshchansk Hermitage; he was later the Superior of the Skete and Elder. Having lived in the monastic life since 1810, he had always been aware that without experienced guidance one cannot attain either to spiritual vision or to the fruit of monastic life; and for several years he had been under the spiritual guidance of one of the disciples of Elder Paisius Velichkovsky, the Schemamonk Athanasius. After this Elder's death, Fr. Macarius grieved over being a spiritual orphan and begged the Lord to send him an experienced guide. When Fr. Leonid arrived in the Ploshchansk Hermitage in 1828, this was like the fulfillment of his prayerful petition. In Fr. Leonid he found that for which his soul had hungered for so long — a man with the gift of spiritual discernment, something given very rarely, and moreover, given not just for labors and asceticism, but more so because of humility. After growing close to Fr. Leonid during his brief stay at the Ploshchansk Hermitage, Fr. Macarius continued his spiritual contact with him by correspondence after the Elder had departed to the Optina Monastery. In 1834, as was mentioned, he moved to the Optina Monastery in order to live together with him. From the moment he entered the Monastery, he assisted the Elder with his extensive correspondence with persons asking him for spiritual counsel and instruction. He was also an assistant for the Elder in the spiritual care of the brothers and visitors, especially after 1836, when he was appointed spiritual father of the Monastery.

The relationship between Elder Leonid and Fr. Macarius was very instructive and edifying. Fr. Macarius for more than seven years had been the spiritual father of the Sevsk

Convent, and many referred to him as their director and turned to him for spiritual counsel. But in spite of this he humbled himself, considered himself to be nothing, fled from human glory and sought, as if for a special honor and privilege, to be at the feet of another elder. Filled with faith and love for his Father, Fr. Macarius was also the primary spiritual father for the Monastery and the Superior of the Skete. Still he did nothing without first asking Fr. Leonid, and out of humility attributed all his successful enterprises to the secret and public prayers, counsels and blessing of his Father. Up to the blessed repose of Fr. Leonid, he remained one of his most fervent disciples.

On the other hand, the same kind of humility was shown by Fr. Leonid to Fr. Macarius; his Elder, Schema-monk Theodore, had once jokingly called him a humble lion. From the beginning of his monastic life he had always walked the path of obedience, and had spent almost twenty years under the spiritual guidance of Elder Theodore; he so loved to submit himself in every way to the counsel of his guide that he never did anything on his own. During the life of his Elder, Fr. Leonid in his letters to various persons always signed together with Fr. Theodore; after the Elder's death, out of his deep humility Fr. Leonid joined his signature with that of his spiritual son, Fr. Antiochus, even though this latter took no part in the correspondence. And when Fr. Antiochus was not with him, then he usually signed: Hiero-schemamonk Leonid with his devoted brothers. (Then, later, he signed together with Fr. Macarius: Hiero-schema-monk Leonid and Hieromonk Macarius.) In this way the Elder wished to show all that only with the help and prayers of the fathers and brothers living with him was he able to offer spiritual advice. When he met Fr. Macarius, Fr. Leonid was glad to unite with a monk who was so gifted and skillful, and he regarded him not as a disciple but as his co-laborer and spiritual friend. In this regard he imitated his own humble-minded Elder, Fr. Theodore, who, while he had

ST. MACARIUS, ELDER OF OPTINA
(1788-1860)
Commemorated September 7/20

been his instructor and guide, at the same time had regarded him as his spiritual father and frequently asked his advice as of his friend and brother. However, giving place to the unfeigned petitions, humility and importunity of Fr. Macarius, Fr. Leonid decided to treat him as his beloved son and disciple in the Lord, and, following the instruction of St. John of the Ladder,[22] did not miss an opportunity to provide his skillful struggler with crowns by testing his patience. With this purpose he subjected him to rebukes and reprimands, frequently in the presence of others, so that they could benefit from his humility.

Here is one of many examples of this. The Abbot, Fr. Moses, summoned Fr. Macarius (after he had been appointed spiritual father of the Monastery) and asked him to be the sponsor for the tonsure of certain brothers. Fr. Macarius, regarding the request of the Abbot as a command, replied with a humble bow. When he came to the Elder, he found his spiritual instructor, as usual, surrounded by a multitude who were asking about their spiritual needs and problems. Fr. Macarius briefly informed him about why the Abbot had summoned him.

Fr. Leonid, with a stern look, asked Fr. Macarius, "And what did you do; did you consent?"

"Well, I almost consented, or it would be better to say, I did not dare refuse," Fr. Macarius replied.

"Yes, that is typical of your pride," said the Elder, raising his voice and making it seem as if he were angry. He then began to reprimand Fr. Macarius. The latter stood with his head bowed, humbly bowing and from time to time repeating: "I'm guilty. Forgive me, for God's sake, Father." Everyone present was accustomed to treating Fr. Macarius on an equal level as the Elder and watched this either with bewilderment or with reverent awe.

---

22. St. John of the Ladder, *op. cit.*, Step 4:27, p. 30.

When the Elder fell silent, Fr. Macarius bowed at his feet and meekly asked, "Forgive me, Father; do you bless me to refuse?"

"Refuse? How can you refuse? You asked for it yourself, and now you want to refuse? No, you can't refuse now; the matter is settled . . ." said Fr. Leonid, who in no way intended to deprive of spiritual benefit those who had been entrusted to the spiritual guidance of this experienced instructor. There was a different reason for his reprimand: to test the humility of the Elder-disciple, in which he was advancing, and thus to provide profit for others. This was accomplished in its entirety.

By acting in this way, the Elder at the same time not only nourished a fatherly love but also a heartfelt reverence for Fr. Macarius as his spiritual friend and confidant; and when he considered it beneficial he expressed these feelings to such a degree that his listeners were astonished. Some persons once asked the Elder about the spiritual level of Fr. Moses, Fr. Anthony and Fr. Macarius. The Elder replied briefly, "Fr. Moses and Fr. Anthony are great men, but Macarius is a saint." Those who heard this later explained the words of the Elder by the saying of St. John Climacus, "People of high spirit bear offence nobly and gladly, but only the holy and righteous can pass through praise without harm" (Step 22:12).[23]

Above all, Fr. Leonid showed his humility of wisdom and his respect and love for Fr. Macarius in the fact that he especially confided in him and made him his helper, sharing with him the labor of the spiritual nourishment of the brotherhood and visitors. In the last five years of his life, Fr. Leonid, for the most part, blessed those who sought his spiritual guidance to turn also to Fr. Macarius and to reveal to him all that they had revealed to Fr. Leonid himself. On his part, Fr. Macarius, too, when he learned of anything of

---

23. St. John Climacus, *op. cit.*, Step 22, Chapter 12, p. 133.

importance from his spiritual children or of some predicament, always asked whether they had explained this to the
Elder; and if they had not, sent them to him to make an
explanation. In this way the soul of each person who turned
to them was equally open before both Elders, and both of
them equally knew all the circumstances of their spiritual
children. If anyone, when he confessed to Fr. Macarius,
came to ask the blessing of Fr. Leonid, the Elder, who had
the gift (as will be shown below) of revealing and calling
to mind forgotten sins, would ask whether he had said this or
that to Fr. Macarius; and if he had not said it out of forget-
fulness or for some other reason, he sent him back to explain.
When Fr. Macarius was asked about anything, he gave no
reply without the Elder. And likewise the Elder without
Fr. Macarius did not decide anything; in such instances he
would say, "Let's wait. Fr. Macarius is coming; we will
talk it over together." It was touching to see such a oneness
of soul and mutual love between the two Elders. "It was
often the case," related a spiritual daughter of Fr. Leonid
and Fr. Macarius, "that as one would be talking with Fr. Leonid, Fr. Macarius would come in; and Fr. Leonid would say
to him, 'Father! Talk with her; she needs to explain something
to you.' Or they would sit, like the angels of God, side by
side; and we would stand before them on our knees and
reveal our souls to the two of them, as if to one person,
and never separated them or made any distinction between
them. In truth, they had one heart and one soul. Therefore
when Fr. Leonid died, although we grieved over him, still our
sorrow was tempered because we were deprived of only
one half, while the other remained with us."

Being Elders, inspired with humble-mindedness and
joined by mutual love and oneness of mind, they instructed
their spiritual children in these primary Christian virtues
not only in word but above all by their own example. They
did not allow any kind of contention to arise between them,
since disciples, out of human weakness, are often inclined

to words. It is for this that the Apostle Paul rebuked the Corinthians, saying: *For it hath been declared unto me of you, my brethren . . . that there are contentions among you. Now this I say, that every one of you saith, I am of Paul; and I of Apollos; and I of Cephas; and I of Christ. Is Christ divided?* (I Cor. 1:11-13). Among the spiritual children of Fr. Leonid and Fr. Macarius there were no such divisions or parties; the openness of mind and soul of the Elders was reflected in their children. In this way there were two Elders in one Monastery; but there was no division, nor was the unity of the Elders' care lost.

The spiritual activity of Fr. Leonid was not limited to the Optina Monastery alone with its many visitors. In 1837, one of the disciples of Fr. Leonid (who had come with him to the Optina Monastery from the St. Alexander of Svir Monastery), Hieromonk Gerontius, was appointed Abbot of the St. Tikhon of Kaluga Monastery. Five of the like-minded brethren were sent with him; and, in time, some others also went to live with him, with the blessing of the Elder. From that time the Elder himself annually visited St. Tikhon's Monastery and would spend about a month there, caring for the spiritual confirmation of the brotherhood and the good order of the Monastery. In addition, through persons devoted to him, he was a benefactor to the Monastery materially as well; and it began to flourish from that time.

In 1839, the Superior of the Skete, Fr. Anthony, was appointed Abbot of the Maloyaroslavets Monastery, to where some of the disciples of Fr. Leonid went with him. While living in Maloyaroslavets, they continued to make use of the instructions of the Elder.

Thus the spiritual influence of Fr. Leonid extended beyond the Optina Monastery to two other monasteries in the Kaluga Diocese as well, where he introduced eldership; and for future times it strengthened the internal well-being of these monasteries, granting both the brotherhood and visitors the opportunity to reap great benefits for their souls.

Consequently, all those who make use, even at the present time, of the instructions and consolations of the spiritual Elders in these three monasteries should always remember with gratitude that it was Fr. Leonid who laid the foundation for the way of eldership in these locations. Finally, from other dioceses, also, there were nuns who made use of the spiritual direction of Fr. Leonid, especially those from the Trinity Convent in Sevsk, the Borisov Tikhvin Convent and the Belev Convent of the Exaltation of the Cross. In each of these Convents Fr. Leonid had several devoted disciples who advanced more than others in the spiritual life; and they became guides and eldresses for many sisters, both during the lifetime and after the death of the Elder. Thus Fr. Leonid's spiritual seed grew and expanded far beyond the borders of the Kaluga Diocese.

Apart from his usual care for monastics and lay visitors, the Elder received a multitude of letters from various persons seeking a resolution of their problems from him, and out of his love for his neighbor he did not leave them without his attention. Either he himself wrote or he dictated replies, appropriate to each person, to strengthen and console them in their sorrows.

III

The Opponents of Eldership

THE PERSECUTION OF ELDER FR. LEONID
IN 1835 - 1836

IT IS NOT in vain that the Holy Fathers say that whoever is performing a task pleasing to God is sure to meet with temptation, and that every good deed is preceded or followed by temptation. The words of the Chronicler of the Kiev Caves that monastic institutions are built by the sweat and tears of prayer can be applied also to the introduction of eldership — the foundation of monasticism — at the Optina Monastery. It was introduced and established here with many labors and sorrows. This is in keeping with the assurance of the Holy Fathers that the enemy of mankind harbors no love for the revelation of thoughts, not even the very sound of the words of such revelation, because he knows that by means of this all his snares and cunning are laid to waste. So it is not surprising that he does not hesitate raising opposition to this monastic path which is so hateful for him, employing various snares. Because of the introduction of eldership, he raised up a strong persecution against Fr. Leonid. The tools of this persecution were simple persons who did not know and did not understand the path of eldership.

Among the former brotherhood of Optina there were pious, kind monks; but each of them had lived according to his own understanding and had struggled as he was able. Their primary attention was focused on external labors and *active* virtues. But when Fr. Leonid settled in the Monastery with his disciples, then they began to hear of eldership and spiritual nourishment, of purifying the conscience and revealing thoughts, of cutting off one's own desires and understanding, of *inward activity;* and all of this seemed to many of them to be some kind of new, unintelligible teaching, which some of them called outright heresy. The former brethren (especially those among them who because of their age had difficulty in changing the concepts with which they had passed the greater part of their lives) openly rose up against these novel innovations and began to regard the disciples of Fr. Leonid with distrust and dislike. In keeping with the directions of the Elder, his disciples humbled themselves in every possible way before these venerable old men, and for their part observed everything so as not to disturb the peace of the Monastery. But the dissatisfied monks were not happy with the new order of things. They began to turn to the diocesan authorities with various kinds of complaints, and finally managed to get the chancery to issue an ukase that four hieromonks of the older brotherhood, together with the abbot and treasurer, were to participate in the discussion of all the most important matters of the Monastery, and that without their common consent nothing concerning the general welfare of the Monastery was to be undertaken or put into effect. This was in 1830, one year after the Elder, Fr. Leonid, had settled at the Optina Monastery. However, the expectation of the opponents did not meet with success. When the Archpastor of Kaluga, at that time Bishop Gabriel, visited the Optina Monastery he showed very sympathetic attention

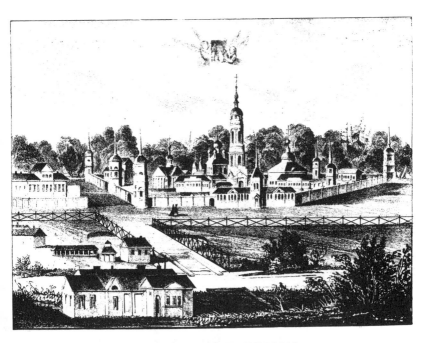

OPTINA MONASTERY IN 1840

to the Abbot, Fr. Moses, in the presence of the entire brotherhood and reprimanded the disgruntled brothers, ordering them to correct themselves. Though the unrest in the Monastery did not completely quiet down after this, nevertheless, by their long-suffering over the course of many years Fr. Moses and Fr. Leonid overcame these difficult circumstances, strengthening themselves with the good hope that through the help of the grace of God the affairs of the Monastery, in time, would come into better order.

"The most merciful God of peace," Fr. Leonid wrote to Fr. Macarius in Ploshchansk Hermitage, "is powerful and almighty to turn the storm, unrest and temptation which He has permitted into quiet, fair weather and to usher in peace. Blessed be His name henceforth and for evermore. As is pleasing to His all-holy will, so may He govern us, His creation." In fact, after some time the unrest in the Monastery did quiet down somewhat. Some of the dissatisfied brethren left the Monastery; more and more new disciples of the Elder arrived and his influence in the Optina Monastery grew stronger and stronger.

But there still remained a group of the monks who retained a hidden dissatisfaction for the Elder and were unable to watch the course of Fr. Leonid's action peacefully. And so a new temptation began for the Elder.

Fr. V., a monk of the Skete, was moved with false zeal against Fr. Leonid because so many people came to him. He wrote reports to the Bishop on several occasions, presenting this traffic of crowds of people as something disgraceful and a disruption of the stillness of the Skete, even though the visitors did not come directly to the Skete but went to the apiary where Fr. Leonid's cell stood. This place had its own separate entrance, and no one was bothered. Also, we should note that this monk who rebelled against Fr. Leonid acted in this manner at the prompting of the brothers who were discontent with the Abbot and the Elder. They took advantage of his simplicity and made use of it as

THE OPTINA SKETE IN 1840

an instrument for their own secret intentions.[1] Almost all of these brothers later could find no peace in the Optina Monastery and wandered off to various monasteries. Some of them also suffered very grievous deaths.

Dissatisfied with the written reports of Fr. V., the new Bishop of Kaluga, Nicholas, first left them unnoticed. Then the opponents of the Elder finally put together a false complaint against the Elder and Fr. Moses, and they sent it to the Bishop as from some unknown person. Unseemly rumors were circulated about Fr. Moses among the people at that time, primarily by persons who did not know him at all, who had never seen him, or by persons who had heard exalted reports about the Elder (from those who had received spiritual benefit from him) but who did not believe such things and then came with their own preconceived notions and curiosity, saying scornfully: "Let's go see what kind of saint this is they have over there." It is quite natural that such persons, instead of being edified, were scandalized and spread degrading stories that others manipulated. Finally, there were also persons who confused the Sacrament of Confession with a life according to spiritual guidance, and therefore beheld with great indignation how the people flocked to the Elder-monk for spiritual counsel. This took place in the Kaluga Diocese at a time when, perhaps for all of Russia, this was something *new*. For many did not know what the ancient practice of the Church of Christ had been: that throughout Christian times the monastic elders who had advanced in spiritual life never refused to be spiritual guides for those who turned to them in faith.[2]

---

1. Among those who initiated complaints against the Elder and provoked this simple monk to such actions were certain persons sent by the chancery under penance to the Monastery for correction.

2. Of the great desert dwellers and monastic fathers, only a few, following the example of Arsenius the Great and Theodore of Pherme, fled as much as they were able from the duty of instructing others and

Persons who had forgotten this — or it is better to say, people who did not know — and in general a great many who did not understand the spiritual activity of the Elder, spread unfavorable opinions about him. The Bishop, wanting to put an end to the rumors and perhaps concerned lest the spreading of unseemly rumors result in something unpleasant for himself, directed that Fr. Leonid be transferred from the apiary of the Skete to the Monastery and forbade lay persons of both sexes to see him. Fulfilling the wish of the Archpastor, the Elder instead was moved in November of 1835 to one of the cells inside the Skete because there was no cell in the Monastery that was free or convenient for him. But soon there came an insistent directive that, no matter what, Fr. Leonid was to be moved into the Monastery. This was on February 2, 1836. It was not without tears and lamentation that

---

turned away (only in part, not entirely) from those who came to them for spiritual counsel. The greater part of the Holy Fathers followed the example of the founder of monasticism, Anthony the Great, who, after spending 35 years in ascetic labors and stillness, afterwards became, as Athanasius the Great expressed it, the good physician of all Egypt — that is, a spiritual guide and instructor for all monks and laymen who turned to him. Even the holy stylites after prolonged withdrawal from the world and extended asceticism in solitude, devoted the end of their lives to ministering to suffering mankind, not turning away anyone who turned to them for spiritual healing.

In the monasteries of Egypt not only the monks and clergy who came were received, but also laymen and women; and there were special hostels built for them. According to the rule of Pachomius the Great, the founder of coenobitic monasticism, special care should be taken for women as they are weaker and have a greater need of spiritual nourishment. Also, Pachomius the Great, not far from the monastery in Tabennesi, built a convent for women which was governed by his sister and was under his own personal guidance. Basil the Great did the same.

St. Isidore of Pelusium, zealous for the welfare of the Orthodox Church and the spiritual benefit of all Christians, wrote instructive letters (according to Nicephorus Callistus, almost 10,000 of them) to persons of every rank and occupation, from the emperor to simple soldiers, from patriarchs and bishops to readers and simple monks.

the brothers with him accompanied him from the Skete to the Monastery, like a family with one mind which was being deprived of their own father and guide. Nor was it any less grievous for the Abbot of the Monastery, Fr. Moses, and the Superior of the Skete, Fr. Anthony, to see that these measures were enforced. They were, as the saying goes, caught in a cross-fire. They had to submit to the will of the Bishop, while at the same time they understood what a spiritual loss would result. They knew that the Elder was innocent and that his life was equal to that of the angels. What can be said about those multitudes of devotees and spiritual children of the Elder, of those who possessed in him a ready resolution of their problems and doubts, a support in their needs, an experienced guide in spiritual warfare and predicaments, a ready consolation in their sorrows? Their grief defies description. But the Elder himself endured this persecution magnanimously and did not even consider himself persecuted. "Out of your unbounded devotion," he wrote to one of his spiritual sons, "you are discouraged about my situation and by mistake consider me to be under persecution. . . . But I am certain that nothing can happen to me without God's permission; and when it is pleasing to Him to send me something because of my sins, I have to accept it with submissiveness, for we can never flee from His hand." "If all were to speak of me with praise," the Elder wrote to another person, "then woe to me, according to the words of the Savior Himself: *Woe to you, when all men shall speak well of you* . . . (Luke 6:26). Truly the Lord does everything for our benefit, and without Him not even a hair of our head can perish. As for those who are so fervent for my wretchedness and who find profit according to their faith, the Lord is not in need; and even now He can grant consolation to each person who is worthy and who seeks — both through the pastors appointed by the Holy Spirit and also, especially, through His hidden servants. But those who seek benefit and consolation in their sorrows and bewilderment have to be prepared with faith and with the intention of fulfilling all the commandments of the Lord and the regulations of the Church, and must seek with humility and accept advice with simplicity of heart. For my part I thank the Lord; I sense a calm in my conscience and am in no way burdened by my move."

The Bishop of Kaluga received from the secret police in Moscow an anonymous report in which various accusations were repeated at the same time against the Elder Fr. Leonid and also against the Abbot of Optina. Among other things it was reported that the Abbot showed a preference for those Elders living in the Skete over those living in the Monastery, that the Skete was bringing great harm to the Monastery in every way, and that if the Skete were not closed, then this ancient Monastery would fall into decline and destruction, and so forth. As a result of this report the Abbot of Optina had to submit his defense. Since Fr. Leonid had been tonsured to the great schema in a monastic cell environment without a directive from the chancery, the Bishop of Kaluga forbade him to wear the schema and also strictly repeated his order that the Elder receive no visitors.

This prohibition was repeated more than once, and each time, submitting to the will of the Bishop, Fr. Leonid stopped receiving visitors. In fact, he himself was happy to have some rest from his labors as he was then 68 years old. "Concerning myself and my circumstances, I have the honor to inform you," the Elder wrote to an acquaintance of his in 1836, "that I, glory be to the all-merciful Lord God, Who yet endures my sins, am still among the living and in the same cell, but my visits with those who come to the guest house to see me have been terminated. And if I may speak frankly to you, even if this were permitted, it seems that my weakness and frailty no longer possess the strength to satisfy those who are hungry, because my physical strength has been exhausted. In keeping with this situation of ours, I most respectfully request you: do not cut off relations with the

Monastery and explain, concerning my own position, that people should not expect to receive any kind of profit from my wretchedness through some pseudo-devotion. Here is what happened just yesterday: A certain person with good intentions, acquainted with the Abbot and my unworthiness, asked the Abbot that she be allowed to have a visit with me in his quarters, so that she could speak about what she needed. But I was too weak. Even though I fought to gather the strength to carry out this obedience and satisfy this person, I was unable to go; she left without being satisfied." Sometimes the Elder, wishing to fulfill the will of the Bishop to refuse visitors, would depart for a time from the Optina Monastery to St. Tikhon's. "Circumstances and the remarkable flocking of devoted people," he wrote on another occasion to the same person, "scarcely allow me to remain, but I have to leave at least for a time. If the Lord wills and I remain alive, I have this intention. It is only now, glory be to the all-merciful Lord God, that the authorities have taken strict measures; the gates are locked and the doors are bolted shut. But is my rest going to last long? . . ."

In fact, in spite of the desire of the Elder to fulfill the will of the authorities, he was not able to refuse guests for long. Individuals soon appeared coming to the Monastery to consult Fr. Leonid. After they were not permitted to see him they turned to the Abbot, explained their spiritual needs on account of which they had hoped to see the Elder and persuasively begged the Abbot not to deprive them of spiritual assistance. The Abbot, being a spiritual man himself, could not refuse such visitors having extreme needs, and sometimes personally brought them to the Elder. But when he did not make up his mind to do this, it sometimes happened that these visitors would appeal to the Bishop himself, and after being convinced by their tearful petitions the Bishop would finally give permission for Fr. Leonid to receive them. After he had received the persons sent by the Bishop or those whom the Abbot had brought, Fr. Leonid would open his door for everyone on every occasion, saying that if he was not to receive anyone then he would receive no one at all, but if he was to receive one then he would receive all.

Since he acted in this manner Fr. Leonid was the victim of much criticism, and because of rumors even certain spiritual persons considered him to be self-willed and anxious to teach others. The persecution which was brought at that time against Fr. Leonid because of his ministering to suffering mankind is reminiscent of the ancient life of St. Abramius of Smolensk, about whom St. Demetrius of Rostov gives the following account: "Many persons, not only monks but also layfolk, came from various places especially to him in order to hear from his lips a word of instruction profitable for their souls. But the devil who hates what is good, unable to endure the sight of such profit from the Saint of God, initiated persecution against him by arousing envy and hatred for him among certain of the monks. But the guileless servant of the Lord endured all this with meekness and humility. He did not stop his own work and continued to teach and console those who came to him, through the grace of Christ. Finally, the abbot, provoked partially by the monks, partially by the invisible enemy, forbade the blessed one to teach, saying: 'Here you are attracting everyone to yourself and have grown proud and vainglorious that you are educated and learned and better than we are; so stop teaching — I will answer for you before God.' Then the abbot, after reprimanding Abramius, in anger drove away all those who had come to him for soul-profiting counsel and greatly insulted the servant of the Lord by stopping the wellspring of grace which flowed from his lips. In the end, with dishonor he expelled him from the monastery. Then the servant of Christ Abramius went to Smolensk and lived in another monastery; but he did not abandon his work here either, because even more people began to come to him for spiritual instruction."

Likewise in the account of the life of Seraphim of Sarov,[3] we read that on one occasion the Abbot Niphon, while revering the Elder for his ascetic labors, made it a point to inform him that the brotherhood, because of the strictness of its asceticism, did not approve of Fr. Seraphim since he was receiving persons of both sexes and from every walk of life, albeit for edification unto salvation. The Abbot Niphon said this only because some of these brothers were scandalized, while he himself deeply loved and respected the Elder Seraphim. After listening to the words of the Abbot, the Elder fell at his feet and gave him a wise and salutary reply: that he not give himself over to false accusations in the future and that he not accept any word of the brothers against anyone without discretion. "You are a pastor," he said, "do not permit everyone to speak in vain, to distress you and those who are journeying into eternity. For your word is powerful and your staff, like a whip, is fearsome to all." Abbot Niphon was moved by these words of the Elder and stated that he agreed that Fr. Seraphim not change his way of life and that he continue to receive everyone who came to him for profit of soul, as before.

In keeping with the example of St. Abramius and the blessed Elder Seraphim, and as a genuine performer of the commandments of Christ, Fr. Leonid did not pay attention to human interference. We think that had his opponents looked more closely at his activity, they would have thought differently about him. Let us recall what lay at the beginning of the persecution of Fr. Leonid and Fr. Theodore at Valaam. It began when Fr. Eudocimus (Euthymius), formerly the disciple of the abbot of Valaam, worn down by depression and despair and even contemplating suicide, turned to these Elders for help. Could they have refused him help because of some human reservations when he was in such a

---

3. At the time this book was written St. Seraphim had not yet officially been glorified by the Church. —Trans.

terrible plight? Now there were many such predicaments and they continued to occur. Apparently the opponents of Fr. Leonid never gave a single thought to what spiritual needs brought people to him for his advice.

On one occasion, Abbot Moses, walking about the monastery, saw an enormous crowd of people before the cell of the Elder; and at that time a strict order from Kaluga had recently been received that no one be permitted to see him. The Abbot entered the cell. "Fr. Leonid!" he said, "How can you receive people? You know the Bishop forbade you to receive anyone." Instead of replying, the Elder, after letting the persons with whom he had been occupied depart, told his cell-attendants to bring in the cripple who at that time was lying at the door of his cell. They brought the man in and placed him before Fr. Leonid. The Abbot watched this with bewilderment. "Now," Fr. Leonid began his reply, "look at this man. You see how all the members of his body are afflicted. The Lord punished him for sins of which he did not repent. He did this and this, and for all of that he is now suffering — he is alive in hell. He needs help. The Lord brought him to me for sincere repentance, so that I might rebuke and instruct him. Can I refuse to receive him? What do you say about that?"

Listening to Fr. Leonid and looking at the suffering man before him, the Abbot shuddered. "But the Bishop," he mumbled, "is threatening to send you away under arrest."

"So what? You can exile me to Siberia, you can build a bonfire, you can burn me at the stake, but I will still be the same Leonid. I don't beckon anyone, but when a person comes of his own accord I cannot chase him away. Especially among the simple folk, there are many who are perishing out of ignorance and they need spiritual assistance. How can I disregard their clamor about their spiritual needs?"

Abbot Moses could not say anything in reply and he left in silence, leaving the Elder to live and act as God Himself directed him.

In 1837, that is, in the year after Fr. Leonid was moved from the Skete to the Monastery, a member of the Holy Synod, His Eminence Metropolitan Philaret of Kiev, visited the Optina Monastery on his way to St. Petersburg accompanied by the Bishop of Kaluga, Nicholas. The Metropolitan demonstrated his extremely sympathetic archpastoral approval both to the Optina Abbot, Fr. Moses, and to the Elder, Fr. Leonid, whom, as was previously mentioned, he had known while in the White Bluff Hermitage. Moreover, he noted that Fr. Leonid was not wearing any of the apparel of the great schema, and in the presence of Bishop Nicholas the Metropolitan asked him, "Why aren't you wearing the schema?" The Elder was silent. "You are a monk of the great schema," the Metropolitan continued, "and you are supposed to wear the schema." From that time to the end of his life Fr. Leonid wore without any prohibition as previously, in the manner of the Moldavian monasteries, the great *paraman* of the schema (which some persons mistakenly call *analavos*). The Kiev Archpastor also expressed his fatherly regard for the fathers of the Skete, which had been built in keeping with his concepts and blessing. "His Eminence made us happy with his visit to our hermitage," Fr. Leonid wrote to one of his spiritual sons, "and strengthened our souls with his special blessing. 'Our benefactors' seeing this were completely disarmed, and now it seems they have begun to learn a little humility. As to how delighted His Eminence was over seeing the Optina Monastery, I think that it is difficult to give a description."

The visit to the Optina Monastery by the Metropolitan of Kiev and the attention which he showed the Abbot of Optina and the Elder brought very beneficial results to the Monastery, for Bishop Nicholas began to attach less significance to the rumors of their detractors. The suppressed position of the Elder began to improve.

Still in the summer of 1836, in order to give Fr. Leonid some respite, a devout landowner who lived in the Monastery,

Alexei Ivanovich Zhelyabuzhsky, had built a special wooden building in which there were two cells: one for himself and one for the Elder. This unforgettable benefactor of the Optina Monastery was spiritually attached to Fr. Leonid and was also loved by him. They always read the Divine Scriptures together and performed the prayer rule, with the assistance of the cell-attendants of the Elder and the brothers who came to him to ask about their thoughts.

After Fr. Leonid left the Skete for the Monastery, his spiritual bond with the fathers in the Skete was not broken. Fr. Macarius visited him daily. He would come for advice pertaining to his duties as spiritual father and would bring letters prepared for the Elder to sign, which had been written at the direction of the Elder and which they always signed together. Likewise the Superior of the Skete (until 1839), Fr. Anthony, also visited him frequently. He always had the most sincere and friendly relations with him and often profited from the frank conversations of the Elder. All the other brothers of the Skete, too, remained devoted to him with filial love as their spiritual instructor and ceased not from coming to him in the Monastery for the healing of their diseases of soul and the resolution of their problems. On his part, the Elder never ceased to show his love for the Skete and its brothers. On Saturdays and Sundays he always walked — and in the later years when he was too ill to walk he was driven — to the church services in the Skete. After the Liturgy he would usually stop by the cell of the Superior of the Skete, Fr. Anthony; and later Fr. Macarius and the rest of the brotherhood would gather there for spiritual converse with their spiritual instructor. Sometimes laymen from the nobility and merchants who had been at the Liturgy would also come by "for a cup of tea" with the Superior of the Skete; and when they found this spiritual discussion in progress, they joined in as listeners and participants, to their own spiritual benefit.

Fr. Leonid lived five years longer after moving from the Skete to the Monastery; and he continued to offer spiritual instruction to the brotherhood and visitors, recalling the words of the Savior: . . . *Him that cometh to me I will in no wise cast out* (John 6:37), and . . . *Freely ye have received, freely give* (Matt 10:8). Disregarding his deteriorating health the Elder never refused to receive anyone, and up to his blessed repose he showed an unflagging zeal to serve God in the person of suffering mankind. He was especially well-disposed to receive simple people, for the needs of the poor required immediate assistance and their mortal sorrows quick consolation. Many of them lived in the guest house for weeks at a time, waiting to see the Elder face to face. Some of them when they came to him could hardly utter a word from their pain of heart and could only express themselves with groans. Others possessed by demons would be dragged into the cell of the Elder by their sympathetic relatives or neighbors. Still others brought their children to receive his blessing.

The Elder at those times was like a great tree covered with abundant fruit to which everyone stretched forth his gaze and hands, so that it was difficult to make one's way through the crowd in order to see him. In such instances he would say, "God Himself helps those coming to me who receive benefit."

Seeing Fr. Leonid in such a crowd of people, some of his visitors expressed a kind of dissatisfaction with the Elder, probably considering that spending his time with the simple folk was not all that important, and perhaps useless or even inappropriate. But the Elder had a way of making such persons understand.

Once the Optina Monastery was visited by the Dean of the city of Belev, the venerable Archpriest John Glagolev, who loved and revered Fr. Leonid and who was likewise respected by the Elder. When he came to the Elder, Fr. John found him surrounded by peasants. "Are you really that eager to spend time with peasant women?" he said with his characteristic simplicity. "What can I do, Fr. John. You're right — this isn't our business," the Elder replied, "but tell me, how do you confess them? You ask them two or three words, and that's the end of the confession. But if you were to put yourself in their position, if you would delve into their plight, would sort out whatever is on their soul, would give them worthwhile advice, would console them in their grief. . . . Do you do all that? Of course not, you don't have time to spend a while with them. Well then, if we do not receive them, where would they go with their grief?" Put to shame, the Archpriest admitted that his words to the Elder had been inconsiderate.

"Once," wrote Hieromonk A., "I passed through Kozelsk on my way to the Smolensk Province. Along the way, in the isolated villages when the villagers learned that I was coming from Kozelsk, they kept rushing to interrupt me and find out something about Fr. Leonid. To my question as to how they knew about him, they would reply: 'O come now, Father, how can we not know Fr. Leonid? He is more than a father for us poor ignorant folk. Without him we would all be complete orphans!' Such is a monument that is far more enduring than one of marble and granite!"

IV

The Distinctive Qualities and Spiritual Gifts of Elder Leonid

IN OFFERING the reader an account of the most important events of the life of Fr. Leonid, we would like to depict along with his outward activity at least some of the primary characteristics of his inward life as well. But the inner life of spiritual persons always remains a mystery known only to God, Who knows the hearts of men; and not a single one of them could, or, better to say, would even want to express himself in full and disclose the treasury of his soul. The inner life of Fr. Leonid was especially difficult to capture; and although he spent his days in public amid a crowd of people, it remained a mystery even for the closest observers and his most devout disciples. Therefore, we can now speak only about a very few of the distinct characteristics of the inner qualities and spiritual gifts of Fr. Leonid, as far as they found expression in his external activity.

Here is what Bishop Ignatius (Brianchaninov) has to say about Fr. Leonid and his co-laborer and successor, Fr. Macarius.

"Both of the Elders were saturated with the reading of the patristic writings on the monastic life; they themselves were guided by these writings and it was through these that they also guided others who turned to them for instructive advice. Their memory was richly adorned with holy thoughts. They never gave counsel from their opinion, and they always set forth as their advice the sayings of the Holy Scriptures or the Holy Fathers. This imparted power to their counsels. Those who wanted to oppose the counsel of man, reverently hearkened to the word of God and found it proper to submit their own way of thinking to this.''[1]

But what imparted even greater power to the counsels both of Fr. Leonid and Fr. Macarius was the fact that they learned not only "from books," but "in practice," and that they properly ordered their own spiritual life: that is, they themselves first, over the course of many years, lived under sincere obedience and submission to experienced instructors. After first becoming good doers of obedience, by their obedience they acquired the gift of spiritual discretion; so that in their own time they became experienced elders and instructors, and with firmness and skill could guide others along the path that they themselves had travelled.[2]

Thus, Fr. Leonid was a living book for all that came to him for spiritual counsel and instruction. He instructed by deed, which is the most effective of all in moving our heart. He also instructed by word: how to understand the teaching of the Gospel, how to put it into practice and how to use it to heal our infirmities.

After attaining spiritual understanding through divine enlightenment, Fr. Leonid clearly discerned between . . . *the spirit of truth and the spirit of error* (I John 4:6), between the action of the grace of God and the delusion of the

---

1. *Ascetic Experience*, Vol. I, pp. 535-542. See Bishop Ignatius (Brianchaninov), "On Monasticism" in *Ascetic Experience*, Vol. I of *Collected Works,* 2nd Ed., St. Petersburg, 1886, pp. 482-489.

2. "For what reason are there so few experienced elders at the present time?" an Athonite spiritual father was asked. He answered, "For the reason that now there are few [obedient] novices. The former proceed from the latter."

enemy, even though the latter be subtle and concealed. In every instance and every matter he clearly perceived and showed others what is pleasing and what is not pleasing to God; and he would judge accurately concerning the state of soul of others, even of such persons whom many revered as spiritual persons. This is not granted to everyone. In 1836, when various rumors and blasphemous slanders were being circulated against him, Fr. Leonid wrote to his spiritual children, "Not everyone can pass proper judgment on the lofty monastic life or the life of the monks of the great schema, especially they who have not purified their spiritual eye. Read in St. Symeon the New Theologian about this, Chapters 79, 80, 81, and in these you can catch a glimpse of the validity of human judgment. . . .[3] As for V., let people think as each one pleases, and let them glorify his lofty way of life; but we do not have any confidence in it and do not wish that anyone pursue his kind of loftiness, which bears no fruit. *By their fruits*, it is said, *ye shall know them* (Matt. 7:20). Spiritual fruit is love, joy, peace, long-suffering, faith, meekness, temperance and the like. We

---

3. Here are the chapters which the Elder indicated:

Chapter 79: Many people, the eyes of whose souls are not cleansed (to enable them to see clearly) and who are unable to recognize men by their fruits, regard some as passionless and saintly who pretend outwardly to be virtuous but are inwardly otherwise, and who are often filled with all kinds of unrighteousness, envy, and the tumult and stench of sensory lusts. Such people are unable to distinguish true saints — living in devotion to God, virtue and simplicity of heart — from the rest of mankind; they pass them by with disdain and regard them as nothing.

Chapter 80: Such people take a showy babbler for a spiritual man and teacher, while they regard as a dumb and illiterate savage a man who is silent and refrains from idle talk.

Chapter 81: Presumptuous men, sick with pride born of the devil, turn their backs on a man who speaks from the Holy Spirit, accusing him of presumption and pride since his words wound them, rather than produce contrition or move their hearts. Conversely, they accept and praise a man who talks like a windmill, either from his belly or

feel sorry for him and wish that he would come to the knowledge of truth.''

In agreement with St. Symeon the New Theologian, the other Holy Fathers also teach that ordinary people who do not possess spiritual discretion are unable to judge correctly about the state of soul of others; and that, on the other hand, those who have attained spiritual enlightenment not only are able to rightly judge others, but they are also obligated to make the word of truth known to their neighbors. So St. Callistus Telecudes writes, ''While you are still unenlightened, do not take on what is fitting only for the enlightened. Such an undertaking is extremely sinful; such striving is most catastrophic. *So let them say* [the enlightened] and let them openly speak judgment, therefore, they *that have been redeemed by the Lord*, as the Blessed David counsels (Ps. 106:2), *whom the Lord hath redeemed from the hand of the enemy*, that is, the intelligible enemies; and *from the lands*, that is, lands not of the same tribe, which do not share their common practice, *hath He gathered them*, after uniting them to Himself and to His glory. These persons, who truly have been gathered and united and enlightened *as ones redeemed and saved, let them speak* and let them judge'' (Chapter 93).[4]

Fr. Leonid followed the teaching of these Holy Fathers. By the grace of God he had been delivered from the torment

according to mere learning, although he misleads them in everything concerning the work of salvation. Thus there is no one among such people who can rightly see and discriminate, either between men or as regards the work for salvation. [St. Symeon the New Theologian, ''Practical and Theological Precepts,'' *Writings from the Philokalia on Prayer of the Heart*, Faber and Faber Ltd., Fifth Impression, 1967, Chapters 79-81, p. 115.]

4. The Russian text has St. Callistus Antilicudes or Angelicudes. Seventeen chapters are found in the Greek and Russian *Philokalia*, none in the Slavonic. Optina possessed a Paisian manuscript in Slavonic by this St. Callistus, which Fr. Clement Sederholm translated into Russian.

of the soul's enemies, and with all his power he took care to deliver others from destruction of soul. Possessing the word of profit, he abundantly granted it to others and did not limit himself because of any human consideration. In any case, wherever it was necessary, he openly proclaimed the word of truth.

At the end of the 1820's or beginning of the '30's, Fr. Leonid visited the Sophroniev Hermitage. At that time Hiero-schemamonk Theodosius was living there in seclusion (in the orchard). Many people considered him to be a spiritual man and clairvoyant because he had foretold the War of 1812 and several other occurrences. Fr. Leonid found his state dubious. After speaking with the recluse, the Elder asked him how he was able to foretell the future. The recluse replied that the Holy Spirit made the future known to him; and to the Elder's question about the manner in which He makes this known, he explained that the Holy Spirit appeared to him in the form of some type of dove and spoke to him in a human voice. Fr. Leonid, seeing clearly in this the delusion of the enemy, began to warn the recluse that one should not believe this sort of thing. But the recluse was offended and indignantly retorted to the Elder, "I thought that you, like the others, wanted to derive profit from me, but you came to teach me!" Fr. Leonid withdrew and when he was leaving the monastery said to the abbot: "Watch out for your holy recluse; don't let anything happen to him." Fr. Leonid had hardly journeyed as far as Orel when he learned that Fr. Theodosius had hanged himself. From this one can conclude that although this recluse was deluded by the enemy, the mercy of God did not at first abandon him entirely. But when he rejected the well-intended warning of a wise and experienced Elder, the Lord abandoned him and he perished by a wretched death.

Without being distracted by zeal for some supposedly lofty way of life and without seeking the great gifts of God before their time, Fr. Leonid himself first traveled, and afterwards conducted his spiritual children, along the path that is free of danger. This path is described in the writings of the divinely wise guides of monasticism, who teach that the Christian who is beginning the ascetic life must first of all devote his efforts to knowing himself and humbling his passions. For this reason Fr. Leonid turned his especially keen attention to the passions of soul of those who came to him. He instructed all of them to keep track of these things, not to act under their suggestion, and by calling on the help of God to fight against them, above all not to justify them; and to learn one's own infirmities of soul, not to mix vainglory or any other impure inspiration with good undertakings, but to serve the Lord alone in sincerity and "with a pure intention, unfeigned simplicity and guilelessness."[5] Regarding fasting and the other bodily ascetic labors, Fr. Leonid instructed his disciples to fulfill everything conscientiously. If a person through self-will broke one of the established rules, the Elder rebuked him severely, saying that heedlessness even in something small is harmful for the soul and leads to destructive results. On the other hand, he did not approve of concluding that all spiritual perfection consists in observing the external rules of the monastic life; or in laying down one single rule for everyone, both weak and strong without distinction; or in disregarding reasonable measure and giving oneself over to excessive physical labors, as if hoping to find salvation in them alone. Some of those who came to Fr. Leonid revealed to him that they wore chains and at the same time complained that they could find no peace of soul. As it turned out, by undertaking severe labors on their own, they were not able to humbly endure the other afflictions sent by God or the deriding words of other people. While exhausting their body with chains, at the same time they nourished within their soul enmity and remembrance of wrongs against those who

_____

5. As he himself wrote in a letter.

derided them; and being carried away with self-opinion, they would even end in a state of delusion. It was from such ascetics who lacked discretion that Fr. Leonid would remove the chains,[6] teaching them that excessive physical labors without humble-mindedness and spiritual discretion cannot bring profit and sometimes can even harm those who are fervent for their salvation. He taught that Christians above all must turn their attention to the Gospel commandments of the Lord which are indispensable and obligatory for all, and that without observing the Gospel commandments one cannot find salvation.

The Elder especially urged his disciples to preserve mutual love for one another, peace and oneness of mind. Fr. Leonid would often repeat the touching words of Christ, *By this shall all men know that ye are My disciples, if ye have love one for another* (John 13:35). This was his most beloved admonition to his closest disciples.

All of the counsels of Fr. Leonid were saturated with seasoned spiritual wisdom. But he veiled his wisdom with the extreme simplicity of his speech and conduct; and he frequently mixed humor with his instructions, which at first sight at times seemed inappropriate but which were always justified by the course of events. In this way even in the midst of a crowd he frequently was able to apply spiritual healing to secret wounds of soul for persons suffering in various ways; and what is more important, in this way he made himself accessible to everyone. Some of the disciples of Fr. Leonid admitted that in the presence of other elders who were stern of countenance and serious in their conduct, their souls somehow grew tense and they were not able to confess all their hidden ailments of soul freely. On the other hand, the free conduct of Fr. Leonid relaxed their

---

6. After Fr. Leonid's death, the novice who was appointed to keep these chains found that he had almost 25 sets of them, weighing from 25 to 40 pounds each.

souls, and before him they easily spoke out such things as are difficult for a person to admit even to himself.

In the Elder's manner of speech and conversation there was a mark of very distinct uniqueness, characteristic of him alone. Uniting the spiritual power of the words of the Scriptures and the writings of the Fathers with his own succinct, but expressive, Russian folk dialect, he would mix the one with the other interchangeably, wherever he found this profitable. Sometimes, by lowering and raising his tone of voice (when necessary), even by changing his voice, he imparted a special power to his sayings, so that they fell directly into the heart and brought about the proper effect in each person.

The unequalled simplicity of Fr. Leonid at times became a sort of foolishness-for-Christ's sake, which it is impossible to describe and depict in full.

Some persons surmised that the circumstances of our times, the worldly concerns of men, hidden envy and, finally, open persecution and suppression forced him to adopt this manner of conduct. But one can say with greater surety that the Lord Himself wisened him, under the appearance of folly-for-Christ's sake, in order to offer profit to the souls of his fellow men. By acting in this way he hid himself from the glory of men, so dangerous even for great ascetics; and in this way he readily tested those who came to him, turning away empty curiosity and granting unhindered spiritual assistance to all who were in genuine need, or, more precisely, who were seeking it.

Fr. Leonid showed no concern for what people would say about him or how his conduct might appear to them. For this reason it is not surprising that some of them who had no concept of spiritual life were frequently scandalized by the Elder. Some of them were scandalized that a schemamonk, who according to the understanding of the world should spend his time exclusively in the labors of prayer and seclusion, was constantly surrounded by a crowd of people. The persons distressed by this did not realize that Fr. Leonid had left his life of stillness because he was moved by spiritual love for his suffering and ailing brethren, according to the Savior's words, *No man hath greater love than this, that a man lay down his life for his friends* (John 15:13). These people did not realize that, in the words of the holy John Climacus, even though "it is truly a great thing to endure courageously and manfully the burning heat, the tranquility, and the deprivation suffered in stillness . . . yet it is incomparably greater to have no fear of turmoil, and to remain steadfast under its assault with a fearless heart, while living with men outwardly, but with God inwardly."[7]

Others were scandalized by the simplicity and humorous sayings and conduct of the Elder, still others by his appearance of being physically overweight, when in fact his heaviness was the result of illness. During the final years of his life, because of his poor health the Elder could scarcely find any food that would agree with his stomach; and he always ate very modest portions. The Optina Hieromonk P. related that when he traveled for the first time to the Optina Monastery and came to Fr. Leonid and saw how heavy he was, he was scandalized and stopped at the door of the cell thinking, "What kind of schemamonk is this?" The clairvoyant Elder noticed this. He stood up and, slapping his stomach, called out loudly over all the crowd that surrounded him, "Hey, Koptsev! The tambourines sound great across the mountains, but when you get there, they're just bark baskets.[8] Take a look, brother, see what a belly I have!" The newcomer was seized with fear. He had known Fr. Leonid only through correspondence and had never seen him in person up to that moment. When he arrived in Optina he had not gone to anyone else, but had come directly to the Elder; how could

---

7. *op. cit.*, "To the Shepherd," chapter 43, p. 237.
8. A Russian folk proverb.

the Elder, without ever having seen him before, call him by name? How could he know his secret thought? With involuntary trembling he fell at Fr. Leonid's feet. Right then and there, in front of everyone, the Elder scolded him for arguing with his driver on the road.

There were encounters and incidents which were yet stronger. Archimandrite A. relates that when he first came to Fr. Leonid, he found him surrounded by peasant women. The Elder was dressed in a greasy, plain linen peasant's coat. In one hand he was holding a bottle full of some kind of liquid and in the other a shot-glass; he poured out a shot and gave it to one of the peasant women around him. At this sight, the Archimandrite froze. "What surprises you?" the Elder asked him. "Don't you remember how you used to brew this herb by the barrel-full?" These words served as a very simple explanation of this unexpected sight for the Archimandrite. The Elder was giving a sick peasant woman "bitter water" which the visiting Archimandrite while still a layman had used to treat many sick folk, and for this reason he had prepared it in large quantities. The Archimandrite's shock turned into astonishment: How could the Elder, who was seeing him for the first time, remind him of a circumstance in his life about which he himself had forgotten?

Once an old-timer at Optina, Hieromonk P., told how when he was still a beginner he, together with the other novices, came to Fr. Leonid with trembling. "And we," he said, "were standing on our knees before him explaining what each of us needed. Some visitor from afar came in, a gentleman with full epaulets on his shoulders. The Elder asked him, 'How may I help you?' The gentleman replied, 'I have heard a great deal about you and have come to the Optina Monastery to have a look at you.' 'Have a good look,' said Fr. Leonid, and with that he stood up, brushed both his hands over his chest and stomach and turned his side to the visitor, next his back and the other side; then he turned

his face to him again, repeating, 'There, have a good look
at me.' The gentleman, puzzled and offended by this, immediately went to the Abbot to complain that he had come
to the Monastery for the benefit of his soul and that the
Elder had received him in a very strange manner — by standing up and turning around in front of him. Fr. Moses asked
the gentleman, 'How did you come to the Elder and what
did you say to him?' He replied, 'I told him that I have
heard a great deal about him and wanted to have a look
at him.' 'His response was in keeping with your request,'
said the Abbot. 'Fr. Leonid sometimes does things which
appear half-way foolish, but I assure you that he is a wise
and holy Elder.' We were just leaving," continued Hieromonk
P., "when this gentleman with the full epaulets returned from
the Abbot to Fr. Leonid; he bowed at his feet, even though
the Elder held him back to keep him from doing this. 'Forgive me, Father,' he said, 'I didn't explain myself very well
and did not understand you.' Then the Elder waved his hand
at us and we left. The Elder spent two hours with this visiting
gentleman. I don't know what they talked about, but afterwards this gentleman lived for a whole month in the Monastery guest house, came very frequently to Fr. Leonid and
afterwards wrote him many times, explaining in his letters
that he had been in a desperate plight and that the Elder
had brought him to life and resurrected him."

In the midst of these and other similar outward actions
of Fr. Leonid, it was hard for the worldly, pharisaic viewer
to appreciate their inner meaning and spiritual significance.
A person had to live with the Elder, see the benefit of his
wise counsels, recognize how great was his heart, brimming
with faith and hope in the Lord and love for God and his
neighbor, in order not to be shocked at him and at his actions
which were incomprehensible for many. Only an ascetic
who had completely separated himself from the world
could live and act as he did, as one who had cast off all
worldly ties and who was inspired by the spirit of Christian

love. And this is what Fr. Leonid was like. Bold and magnanimous, he always acted openly. By his way of life he virtually asked for persecution; by his foolishness he seemed to be provoking it. "So what? Take me; condemn me if you have been given the authority for that. I live and walk before my God; I live for my neighbors. I have cast off all hypocrisy and fear of worldly judgment; I fear no one but God. When my conscience is at peace, my heart merrily rejoices like an infant's. And since my whole life has been a single day of serving my Elder and my children in Christ, what do I have to worry about?"

This is how the great Elder felt and thought. And the persecutions, the inescapable lot of virtually all true servants of God, pursued him right up to his very end.

The uninterrupted labors of Fr. Leonid in ministering to his fellow man and the great sorrows he endured because of this ministry exceeded human strength, but his faith in the help of God was also supernatural. In all his life's difficult circumstances, Fr. Leonid looked with hope . . . *unto Jesus the author and finisher of our faith* (Heb. 12:2). "Our Archpastor," he wrote in 1831, "is unhappy with us because of rumors. But the High Priest of future blessings, the Lord our God, knows more than he does; and therefore He can govern us the better. And so once again I speak concerning this: May the Lord's will be done." "Recall, my dearly beloved, our mutual Elder Fr. Theodore"; he wrote on another occasion to a close disciple, "recall our Elder Fr. Theodore, how he always entrusted himself to the will of the almighty Provider and Providence. He did not go wrong in his ways, but attained to the haven of good hope; and he entrusted us, together with you, to almighty Providence. He always counselled and urged us to rely on the Providence of our Redeemer and guileless Provider. The merciful Lord fulfills and turns all to His will and our profit, even though it be through means and results which might seem objectionable to us. With the help of the all-

merciful Lord God, we will be patient, and we will see. . . ."
All minor precautions were disregarded by Fr. Leonid,
who relied on his Lord Jesus Christ and His holy Angels,
the Guardians of men. To their invisible guidance he entrusted the coming and going of his visitors; like a cliff
amid stormy waves, he remained unshaken by the assaults
of enemies both visible and invisible. He had no favorites.
He had no special attachments or love for any particular person; therefore sorrow over one who went astray was tempered in him by faith in the Providence of God.

When the Elder was restricted in the reception of
guests, he was happy to have some rest from his labors, as we
have already seen. But at the same time, he never took care
either for rest or for fame; he was only sorry and suffered
pain of soul over the people that came, that the needs of
their souls remained unattended. Yet even in this matter,
with hope he entrusted himself to the will of God. "I ask
you," he wrote to his spiritual son, "not to advise others
to come to me. If they come on their own, then so be it,
but without encouragement. God is powerful to give help
even without my unworthiness." In general, by dedicating
himself to ministering to his fellow men, Fr. Leonid out of
humility did not attribute any special worth to himself.
"I am amazed at your unbounded faith in my nothingness,"
he wrote to this same spiritual son. "There can be no argu-
ment that, apart from my own unworthiness, this is very
praiseworthy. Among other things, however, you are pleased
to ask that I accept under my so-called protection Brother P., who desires to be saved on the true path. O, my most
beloved! I ask you to reconsider: This, it seems, is not
proper for me. You yourself know that I am from a low
social class and that I deserve no attention in the Lord;
yet, because of the commandment of God, for my part
I am obliged to counsel according to their faith those who
require it in the difficulties that they encounter, in keeping
with the testimony of the Holy Fathers."

Always keeping in view the glory of God alone and the benefit of his fellow man, and entrusting the salvation of all to the Heavenly Father, Fr. Leonid was a stranger to all human precautions. On occasion, some of the visitors to the Monastery would become acquainted with those brothers who were ill-disposed to the Elder. When his disciples noticed this, they, out of human weakness, grieved and were afraid that these brothers would distract the visitors and not allow them to see the Elder. But Fr. Leonid himself regarded the matter indifferently. "Eh! Don't worry," he would say in such instances to his disciples, "each kind always finds its own." The Elder wished to express thereby that if someone sincerely and with his entire soul is seeking salvation, God will bring him to a true instructor; but the person who, while desiring salvation at the same time gives consideration to or is distracted by double-mindedness, disbelief or self-opinion and self-justification, will end up with the same kind of guide and counsellor.

In casting aside all efforts to please men, the humble-minded and forthright Elder never assured anyone that came to him that he favored him, nor did he ever take care to show flattery or adulation. Keeping a holy simplicity, free of hypocrisy, he spoke with virtually everyone in a familiar way.[9] Where necessary, he was not particularly delicate in touching on the self-love of his spiritual children; rather, all the attention of the Elder was focused on uprooting this hidden, but pernicious vice. Concealing his spiritual wisdom and humbling himself, the Elder at the same time knew how to humble others also. He knew very well how and by what means to put someone to shame and to teach him a lesson which he would never forget. But at the same time he had a very subtle knowledge of what

---

9. In Russian, the "familiar" second person, singular; rather than the "polite" second person plural; this "familiar" form of address was in common use by Russian peasants and simple folk. —Trans.

each person could bear and how and by what means to console and put each person at ease. With his manifest simplicity, and even, it seemed, rudeness at times, his conduct was never offensive; and in this regard it was the complete opposite of what we sometimes see in persons of high society, in whom the words of the Psalm are frequently fulfilled: *Their words were smoother than oil, and yet they are darts* (Ps. 54:24). Fr. Leonid, on the other hand, albeit in forms that were sometimes apparently harsh, always spoke the holy truth; his guileless and loving soul was open, as was his fatherly care for the salvation of his spiritual children.

Here, for example, is how Abbot I. speaks of his first visit with Elder Leonid: "While I was still a layman, I came for the first time to the Optina Monastery and waited to receive the blessing of Fr. Leonid. I came to the Elder early in the morning. There was no crowd as yet; there was only a woman standing before him on her knees. His cell-attendant told him about me, 'John I. A. has come.' 'He can wait,' said the Elder loudly. I sat down in the reception room on a bench. After dismissing the woman, the Elder called out loudly, 'Johnny!' I had no idea that this meant me and sat there quietly. The cell-attendant, with a smile, whispered, 'Father is calling you.' This 'patriarchal' form of address was quite a surprise for me, a young dandy from the city, but I was not at all offended; on the contrary, the great Elder's manner of address was to my liking, and for some reason consoled me very much. Down to this very moment I remember it with a joy in my soul. 'Johnny, come here,' the Elder continued. I approached Fr. Leonid, received his blessing and, standing on my knees, set before him the circumstances that were disturbing me. The Elder listened to everything with fatherly love, greatly consoled me with his words and, when he dismissed me, prophesied to me that with time I also would be a monastic. Several years later this came to pass."

"It would sometimes happen," relates another disciple of Fr. Leonid, "that the Elder would give me such a strict and stern reprimand that I could hardly stay on my feet. But right then and there the Elder would humble himself like a little child and would impart such peace and consolation that my soul would be full of lightness and joy; and I would leave peaceful and happy, as if the Elder had praised rather than scolded me."

Sometimes Fr. Leonid, acting half-foolishly while speaking with persons of the upper class, would use harsh folk expressions. But the spiritual power of his words was so great that these people not only could not be offended by the simplicity of the Elder, but they even received instruction of great benefit for their souls. Not far from the Optina Monastery there lived a certain gentleman who boasted that as soon as he laid eyes on Fr. Leonid he would see straight through him. This gentleman did come to the Elder; and at the time there were many visitors. The man came in; he was tall and heavily built. Fr. Leonid had the custom that when he wanted to make a special impression on someone, he would shade his eyes by putting his left hand to his forehead as if he were examining some object in the sun. When this gentleman came in he lifted his left hand and said, "Eh, the blockhead is coming! He's come to look straight through sinful Leonid. But he, the rascal, hasn't been to confession and Holy Communion for 17 years." The gentleman was shaken like a leaf and began to weep and repent that he, a sinner and unbeliever, in fact had not been to confession and had not recieved the Holy Mysteries for 17 years.

No matter whom Fr. Leonid was speaking with or about, he always expressed his thoughts frankly and openly, taking no care to soften his expressions. His speech always breathed of sincerity and truthfulness. He had no use for what he labelled, in one of his letters, "the learned style of the diplomat and the artful conversation of the natural man."[10] "Boys! Sell for the same price you buy," he would tell his disciples, teaching them to retain a simple, straight-forward, unpretentious behavior. "If you were simple-hearted like an apostle," the Elder once told a close disciple, "if you wouldn't hide your human failings, if you wouldn't think so highly of yourself, if you would act without hypoc-risy . . . — such a path is the closest to salvation and attracts the grace of God. Unaffectedness, the absence of cunning, openness of soul — this is what is pleasing to the Lord, Who is humble of heart. *Unless ye become as children, ye shall not enter the Kingdom of Heaven* (Matt. 18:3).

Cunning people and politicians were incapable of be-coming disciples of Fr. Leonid. They could not endure his gaze; and even though they might become attached to him, it would not be for long. With a stricken heart they would quickly flee from this disciple of Christ when they saw that in practice their pretentious, worldly etiquette, gentility and false adulation had no place in the Elder's cell, where spiritual simplicity and Christian childlikeness reigned. Every-one believed that it was impossible to deceive Fr. Leonid either by cleverly woven lies or by an assumed humility in words. The Elder knew the value of all outward expressions; and he did not like it when someone attributed value to something which had no particular importance, even when persons would give strong expression by their words or out-ward actions to their humility, zeal and reverence without any flattery or hypocrisy. Fr. Leonid called this a "Chimera." Once someone asked him what he meant by this word. The Elder replied, "Have you noticed how cucumbers blos-som? There is a genuine blossom, and there are blossoms without pollen on which no cucumbers grow, that is, in-fertile flowers. That is what a 'Chimera' is." The Elder wanted his disciples to prove their devotion to him not with

---

10. *The natural man receiveth not the things of the Spirit of God* (I Cor. 2:14).

outward expressions, but more through observing his instructions. "You want to catch my words on the fly," he said to one of his spiritual sons. "You want to find salvation in passing, to learn in a hurry. That's why you have all this exaltation — kissing the elder's shoulders or hands. But I was under Fr. Theodore without any fanaticism [Fr. Leonid frequently used this word], yet mentally I was prepared to fall at his feet in filial devotion."

Fr. Leonid, while he was of simple background and had not received a formal education, still knew how to size up and distinguish persons of every rank. He attached the proper value to external giftedness if it was directed properly and if there was humility in the person's spiritual life.

Fr. Leonid always regarded the complaints and accusations of his spiritual children with extreme discretion and caution, no matter against whom they were directed. He frequently cited the example of Fr. Philaret of the Glinsk Hermitage, who was a wise and spiritual man but suffered much from his excessive trust in his spiritual children. Fr. Philaret compiled the rule for the Borisov Convent at the appointment of the Bishop of Kursk, and he established good monastery order there. He was a great support for the proper ordering of the Convent, and therefore he had many spiritual daughters in the Convent. Fr. Leonid had spiritual daughters in the Borisov Convent, too. Although the disciples of Fr. Leonid were fewer in number, for some reason they had greater importance and privileges in the Convent than the disciples of Fr. Philaret; and they occupied various posts of responsibility there. The disciples of Fr. Philaret were jealous over this and began to bring complaints against Fr. Leonid's disciples, as if they were holding to some kind of strange and incorrect teaching at the direction of their Elder. Trusting in his spiritual daughters, Fr. Philaret did not verify their complaints. Without investigating the matter he referred it to the bishop, who in the end entrusted an experienced archpriest, together with the rector of the neighboring (Chotmyzh) monastery, to make a strict investigation. This investigation ended in favor of the disciples of Fr. Leonid, as the complaints of Fr. Philaret's disciples turned out to be unjust and without any foundation. Then Fr. Philaret, who had established the good order in the Borisov Convent, was told by the indignant Bishop of Kursk, "After this, make sure that you never step foot in this Convent again." Recalling this instance, Fr. Leonid frequently said, "Trust in your zealous children, and they will chastise you."

The rules that Fr. Leonid observed in his conduct with his spiritual children can be observed in the following directions he gave to his disciple, the Abbot of St. Tikhon's Hermitage, Fr. Gerontius. "You, our most beloved Father," wrote the Elder, "are asking my lowliness that I, the most unprofitable of the unprofitable, offer your love some profitable counsel as to how you should govern and instruct the rational sheep entrusted to you by God and administer the affairs of the monastery. While your question is profitable, being set forth with faith and reverence in every way, it surpasses my thought and strength; but according to the measure of your faith alone, I will offer you my unworthy feelings. First, I advise you to entrust yourself and all those around you to the almighty Lord and to His all-merciful will, for the Savior Himself has said in the Holy Gospel, *Without Me, ye can do nothing* [John 15:5]. For this reason we must heed these words of Christ in every undertaking. If we call on His all-compassionate help, then everything will turn out well and will invisibly, through the grace of God, be put at peace. Likewise I ask and beg you, as I advised you previously, not to be pedantic and demanding, but in everything to observe moderation. Where correction is required, employ the necessary means tempered with discretion and long-suffering."

While advising others to observe such a measure [of moderation] and leniency in their treatment of those under their authority, the Elder himself always showed a fatherly condescension towards the weaknesses of his spiritual children. However, he knew how to show fatherly strictness where necessary, as well. Frequently he would say, "If you ask me, then take heed; but if you are not going to listen, then don't come to me." Here is how the Elder wrote to a monk who had been entrusted to him in front of the Gospel at [this monk's] tonsure, when this monk strayed off into some self-willfulness. "Beware! Although I cannot tell you directly that you will be cast out of our assembly — for the bond of the Holy Gospel is an unbreakable bond — nevertheless, from the examples of the Holy Fathers and especially that of St. Isaiah of Scetis, this [self-rule] is a fearsome matter. Yet for the alleviation of my own conscience it is necessary to tell you, 'Watch out!' If you are not going to listen to your very sinful, opinionated Elder Leo in what is lawful and for the edification of your soul, your going astray will punish you."

Fr. Leonid never took care in advance about what to say to anyone; he spoke and acted without preparation, according to his spiritual sense or at the inspiration of God. Sometimes a person guilty of something would come to him. The Elder, not fearing to hurt him or to tempt others, would reprimand him (depending, of course, on the situation) right there in front of everyone, as the Apostle commands, *Rebuke the sinner before all, that others may fear; preach the word, be instant in season and out of season . . .* (I Tim. 5:20; II Tim. 4:2). While the Elder acted in this way without any preconceived plan, still his word unfailingly corresponded with the needs of the soul of the person whom he was reprimanding and with other circumstances. Each person was administered the appropriate remedy. For this reason Fr. Leonid's word, while apparently so simple and artless, was filled with grace and spiritual insight; and it made a powerful impact on everyone. One person would be consoled in his sorrow, another aroused from sinful insensitivity; a hopeless person would be inspired — the very bonds of despair would be loosed; the unbeliever would be made to submit and have faith. In short, his word was able to convert a carnal person to the path of spiritual life.

By the grace of Fr. Leonid's instructions, many families were reconciled. Persons who had spent their lives in vice were instructed in the way of truth, and many schismatics were converted to the Orthodox Church.

All those who consulted Fr. Leonid with faith bear witness with one voice that in his presence they sensed an inner peace, quietness of heart and joy. Frequently they came to him with great sorrow; but as soon as they entered his cell, they forgot for what they had come and what sorrow had distressed them. It had all been left at the threshold. Thoughts which had seemed terrible and insurmountable would vanish in the presence of the Elder as if they had never existed, but they would appear once again if the person who sought counsel with the Elder became lazy about coming to him.

From the accounts of Fr. Leonid's disciples one can see that he read, as it were, the souls of each of them — that even their hidden thoughts could not be kept from his piercing gaze. These he frequently openly exposed, to the profit of soul of those who came to him. The Elder had the special gift from God of revealing and calling to remembrance forgotten sins. Hieromonk Hilarion (in the world John Ivanovich Gurianov) of the Skete was from the merchants of Kozelsk; he died in 1872. He told many of the brothers the following story about himself: "Before I had yet entered the brotherhood, I came once from Kozelsk to the Optina Monastery. I wanted to partake of the Holy Mysteries. But after I had made my confession to the spiritual father of the Monastery I felt some kind of unaccountable unrest in my soul, and just before the Liturgy I went to reveal this to Elder Leonid. The Elder told me, 'Your unrest clearly proceeds from the fact that you did not reveal to the spiritual father in confession all that you committed.' Then in the course of a few minutes he himself very skillfully reminded me of sins which I had not confessed, saying, 'Maybe you might have committed this and that?' When I admitted that I was in fact guilty of that at which the Elder had hinted, the uneasiness vanished; I was totally at peace, and with peace of soul I partook of the Holy Mysteries of Christ." Another disciple of Fr. Leonid, Fr. P., related that when he confessed his thoughts to the Elder sometimes he involuntarily concealed something, or sometimes he even did so willingly out of fear or shame. Fr. Leonid listened to this confession, then he himself related everything that his disciple had concealed, adding, "And why didn't you mention this?" In this way the Elder encouraged his disciple to make a pure-hearted confession of thoughts.

Fr. Leonid took a fatherly interest in all the needs of those who came to him. In addition to caring for their souls, he did not refuse to offer them assistance in their physical ailments by pointing out certain proven folk remedies. Primarily he made use of his so-called "bitter water" for treatment; sometimes he would dispense up to a bucket and a half in a single day. The preparation of "bitter water" did not stop after the passing of the Elder; but after his death this water lost its power of healing every illness, although it did help in certain cases.

The Elder sent some of those who came to him to the shrine of St. Metrophanes of Voronezh; and there were instances when sick persons after traveling hundreds of kilometers were healed on the road, and, like the Samaritan, they returned to thank their benefactor.

For many of those who suffered from the physical ailments frequently associated with emotional sicknesses, which are not always understood by common people, Fr. Leonid gave grace-filled help by anointing them with oil from the vigil lamp that always burned in his cell before the Vladimir Icon of the Mother of God. The icon, as we already mentioned, was the blessing of his Elder, Schema-monk Theodore. By employing this means the Elder visibly put all his hope in the mercy and help of God, in the intercession of the Queen of Heaven and in the prayers of his spiritual father. Corresponding to the faith of the Elder and of those who came to him, this anointing imparted grace-giving power; through this means many received healing of their physical ailments,[11] consolation in their sorrows and relief in their emotional warfare. But since the Elder anointed ailing women with the sign of the cross not only on the forehead, lips and cheeks, but sometimes also made the cross on their throat and breast, he suffered much criticism from those who were thereby scandalized. Some of his disciples even asked him to abandon this means of healing, but they were unable to persuade him. In the end, it was Fr. Leonid who knew better than they the power and meaning of this anointing, as he made use of it until his final illness — and always with good results.

Many possessed persons were also brought to Fr. Leonid. There were also not a few who did not know themselves that they were possessed by a demon; it was only in the presence of the Elder, when he exposed the delusion concealed within them, that they began to act demonized. This was not a rare occurrence with those lay ascetics who, lacking in understanding, believed their salvation of soul depended upon the wearing of heavy chains without giving thought to purifying their heart from the passions. We have already mentioned that Fr. Leonid ordered chains to be removed from such persons. If his will was not fulfilled, they were stricken with demonic possession. The Elder would place his epitrachelion over such persons and read the short prayer of exorcism over them from *The Book of Needs.*

---

11. Abbot P. related that when the cell-attendants of Fr. Leonid would complain of some illness, he would anoint them with oil from the lamp and the illnesses would disappear.

In addition, he would anoint them with oil or give it to them to drink, and there were a great many striking instances of miraculous healings. There were those who said then, and perhaps there are those who will say even now, "Anyone can anoint with oil and read the exorcism prayers." In reply to this objection we can recall the example of the sons of the Jew, Sceva, who were attempting to cast out spirits like the holy Apostle Paul with the Name of Jesus Christ. *Jesus I know*, the demon replied, *and Paul I know, but who are ye?* (Acts 19:15).

Victory over the demons, of course, was attained by Fr. Leonid after the victory over his own passions. No one ever saw him disturbed by passionate anger or irritation. During the hardest days of his life, no one heard a sound of impatience or grumbling from him; no one saw him downcast. One could not help but marvel at his joyfulness. Calmness, the childlike state of the Gospel and Christian joy never abandoned the child-loving Elder.

Such was Fr. Leonid! One of his closest disciples, finding him once in an especially happy and open mood, asked him: "Father! how did you latch on to such spiritual gifts as we see in you?" The Elder replied, "Live as simply as possible; God will not abandon you." Then he added, "Leonid was always the least person in the monasteries; he never refused any assignment from the abbot. On the eve of the great feasts, the others would hurry to church, but Leonid would be sent to the barn to fetch hay for the horses of the guests that had come. Then, worn out and without supper, he would be sent to the cliros to chant; and he would submit without complaining. Try, also, to live that way, and the Lord will show His mercy to you."

Also, Fr. Leonid would say, "In our times, God does not send ascetics trials like the ancients because we would not be able to bear them, and He does not give the gifts of the ancients, so that we be not puffed up beyond measure." This is how he spoke, in general, concerning our present weak times. But he himself was like one of the ancients by his Christian simplicity and humility, by the sorrows he endured and by his spiritual gifts.

Contrary to all the accusations against Fr. Leonid's supposedly strange way of life, it was quite genuine; and if it differed from the usual monastic life, it was only because of the immeasurable labors of his ministry to his neighbors. In his last years, the Elder scarcely ever left his cell. He slept with the light sleep of an infant, not more than three hours a day. He would wake up at two o'clock, when he could have rested without disturbance; but the night hours were dedicated to receiving the brotherhood. At two o'clock the morning cell rule began with the canon to the saint of the day and the first hour. He read the third and sixth hours separately, during the [time of the] early Liturgy. Vespers, with the three canons and akathist, was at the same time as in the Monastery. After the evening meal in the Monastery, the disciples of Fr. Leonid would gather in his cell to hear the evening prayers, two chapters from the Epistles and one of the Gospel. This rule was kept in St. Tikhon's Hermitage, also, with great reverence. The brothers who gathered for this rule made up a united family, as it were. Coming in from their work in the summertime, they sat on the floor and rested, taking spiritual food after scarcely strengthening themselves with physical food. One could recommend to any church the good order in the services and the readers that Fr. Leonid had. The reader had to read without dragging and without false expressiveness, without vanity in his voice; moreover, the Elder would interrupt him with his comments. Those eager to read had to admit to this in front of everyone, and in this way they learned to be aware of their weakness. The Elder himself read the Gospel in his high voice, in the Moldavian way, as his Elder Theodore brought this tradition from the lavra of holy Paisius. The canon of the day was usually read by the Elder's cell-attendant, Fr. Macarius (Gruzinov).

Among those who read primarily in the morning there was, for a time, a certain Alexius Polycarpovich Bochkov [later Fr. Anthony]. Here is how he related what fervor and attention to oneself the Elder demanded of his disciples:

"We had to arise a quarter of an hour before two o'clock. Once the Elder, who arose five minutes before two, did not find me in the reception room; and when I arrived just one minute before the time to begin the rule, he gave me a reprimand, "You boast of being so devoted to me; why, then, can't you devote a quarter of an hour to the Lord God before the midnight service? During that time you could prepare yourself through mental prayer for oral prayer, that is, for reading."

The time of the prayer rules was the only free time Fr. Leonid had. During all the remaining time, except for a brief rest (and this not at the established time of day, but whenever it might come), he was always at the service of his fellow man. But while he was dealing outwardly with men, inwardly he remained with God. The great spectacle of human passions and woes, to which he listened at every hour and in which he took a genuine, Christian part, would evoke deep sighs and tears from him, shaking his whole being. And then, a sigh directed to the Lord or a glance toward the icon of the Mother of God, before which there was always a vigil lamp burning: these simple signs of heartfelt feeling took the place of oral prayer. When he had only a few visitors, the Elder would frequently so immerse himself in internal prayer that he would not notice what was happening around him. Thus one of Fr. Leonid's close cell-attendants relates that when he was with the Elder without any visitors, the Elder would frequently forget about him and immerse himself in prayer, not hearing any comments he made and asking him to repeat the same thing several times.

The Elder usually partook of the Holy Mysteries of Christ every two weeks in the church of the Skete, where he first walked to the Liturgy from the Monastery, but later was driven. "Once," tells Fr. Anthony Bochkov, "when the Elder was walking along the path to the Skete to receive communion, I noticed a teardrop of spiritual compunction sparkle in his eye. But because he did not want to be noticed, Fr. Leonid restrained himself and immediately these drops of heartfelt feeling vanished from his eyes."

The Elder took food twice a day, whatever God would send; he would sometimes drink a small glass of wine or a glass of beer. During the meal there was usually a lively conversation — modest and harmless jokes and stories were permitted which, through the Elder, imparted a spiritual lesson. The Elder would sometimes tell anecdotes from Roman history, which he knew very well from old translations of Tacitus and other writers. He used to jokingly call one of his disciples[12] the last Roman, perhaps because this disciple sometimes expressed the opinion that we were living in the last times of monasticism, which was falling, according to his words, from the same causes which brought about the fall of the Roman republic: from luxury, delicacy and man-pleasing. Yet the Elder was simply an inaccessible island for the worldly spirit; the rivers of this world flowed around him without shaking him in the least. On the contrary, those battered by the waves of the world found salvation in the cell of the Elder as in a calm harbor.

The small Vladimir Icon of the Mother of God was the sacred treasure of his unforgettable cell. In this holy countenance there was no trace of contrived compunction or female beauty; her features were stern and the face was more Russian than Greek. The Queen of Heaven by her appearance inspired calm, and unbearable emotional and physical ailments were healed here by oil from her lamp.[13]

---

12. Fr. Anthony (Bochkov).

13. This icon was later in St. Tikhon's Hermitage, where it was taken after the death of Fr. Leonid by his disciple, the monk Ioannicius,

During his very laborious occupation with the crowds that came to him, the Elder did not leave off his handiwork. While he was receiving visitors he constantly braided little belts, which he would give away as blessings. When he was living in the Skete, after the noon meal he would chop wood for exercise, and at the same time receive the brotherhood and other visitors, who would come up to him, one at a time, and explain their needs to him.

Caring for St. Tikhon's Hermitage, where many of his disciples moved, did not hinder his care for those at Optina. No one could note any preference for one monastery over the other, even though the abbot at the St. Tikhon's Hermitage was his disciple and cell-attendant. When the Elder would go there to visit for about six weeks at a time, he had more freedom from the crowds; but at the same time his illnesses would increase. His life at Optina, while being cramped and deprived of regular sleep and food, did not exhaust the Elder as much as his rest at St. Tikhon's. In every respect it was clear that the Lord had appointed him to toil.

During his journey from Optina to St. Tikhon's, the Elder would be silent the entire way and pray inwardly. A wagon — without springs, not very spacious and with a disciple for the driver — carried the unparticular Elder over the bumpy road. The Elder found consolation and relief in the simplicity and poverty of the monastic life. It would have been very strange to have seen Fr. Leonid in a carriage — open or closed — wearing a soft overcoat or an expensive ryassa. His poor, monastic appearance did not disturb anyone; rather, on the contrary, his simple clothing, food and transportation served as an example for everyone. If one were to ask him about his way of life, he could confidently reply, *Come and see* (John 1:46).

---

named Leonid in the great schema. [It was dearly venerated by Archimandrite Gerasim (Schmaltz) when a young novice in the St. Tikhon of Kaluga Hermitage, 1906-1910. —ed.]

When he traveled back from St. Tikhon's to Optina, the Elder would stop his wagon in view of the Monastery on a small hilltop, and Fr. Gerontius would give everyone accompanying him a glass of beer. This simple beverage was literally mixed with the tears of his disciples. They loved Fr. Leonid not for his kindness and friendliness, which the Elder never made special efforts to show: the souls of his disciples loved the holy soul of their compassionate Elder, and their salvation was contained, as it were, in his fatherly bosom. As for the accompanying portrait of Fr. Leonid, while it bears a resemblance, still the artist was unable to capture and express that fearlessness, that calm, which shone on the face of Fr. Leonid. He did not want, did not seek and did not expect any reward from the world; and therefore he was not afraid to lose anything. Those traces which are to be seen on the faces of worldly persons: traces of shattered hopes, unfulfilled desires, a forced smile; these were not to be seen on Fr. Leonid's face. His face inspired openness and disposed cunning men to simplicity and unpretentiousness.

The Elder was gifted with a naturally strong constitution and extraordinary strength: he could lift over 400 pounds. When he was young his face was olive-colored, round and framed in thick, long locks of hair; in his old age his hair became a regular lion's mane of gray and blond curls which fell far below his shoulders. His eyes were rather small, gray and looked directly. Without examining a newcomer, without guessing what was concealed in his soul, from his very first glance Fr. Leonid knew what had brought a pilgrim to him from a distance of over a thousand miles. Fr. Leonid's hands were well-proportioned and comely with thick, long, elegant fingers. He was above average in height and had a pleasant gait; his manly and at the same time light, measured step indicated that he carried easily his 70-year-old and rather heavy body. No stooped or bent posture from old age was to be seen in this soldier of Christ who had been hardened in spiritual battles.

To complete the depiction of Elder Leonid, we will now recount some stories about him from his spiritual children and persons who knew him closely.

V

Stories About Elder Leonid

FROM HIS SPIRITUAL CHILDREN AND PERSONS WHO KNEW HIM[1]

1. The Account of Monk S.

THE MONK S. of St. Tikhon's Hermitage, a former disciple of Elder Leonid, related the following about himself: "While I was living at home, many people from our village came to Optina Monastery and were granted to hear wise Christian instructions from our Father Leonid; they praised him in their conversations with one another. I desired to see the Elder, and, should they accept me into the Monastery, remain there with him. I found a companion from our village who had a little education, but thought very highly of himself. As we were walking along the road I frequently reminded him of Fr. Leonid, saying, 'How do you think the Elder will advise us, to enter the Monastery or not?' To this my companion proudly replied: 'What do I need his advice for? I know how to read and write.' Finally we came to Fr. Leonid, who received us with warmth and humor. After living there a few days, we began to seek the Elder's blessing to remain in the Monastery. The Elder

---

1. We are printing these stories in their original form, as they were told to us.

blessed me to stay, but he told me to relate to my companion that he should return to the village. 'I do not advise him,' he told me, 'to enter the Monastery.' Offended by this, my companion began to grumble against the Elder, saying, 'What kind of an Elder is that! I do not advise you, brother, to listen to him.' But in spite of my companion's prideful advice, I remained in the Monastery with the Elder's blessing; and my companion set out for the village. But he did not heed the Elder's advice and entered a monastery. He lived in this monastery only a short time, as he saw his weakness and how the passions make war against and assault the lone combatant who has no help from the spiritual counsels of an experienced elder. He moved to another monastery, hoping to find something better for himself; but our passions are with us everywhere. Finally, he left this monastery after losing his fervor for the monastic life. Afterwards I heard that he married. This is what his stupid pride brought him: 'What elder? I myself am literate.'

"Now I will tell about myself. I went to the Elder every day, relating my bad thoughts and passions. But soon I lost this watchfulness over my soul. First I began to hide very insignificant thoughts (as I presumed them to be) from the Elder. Then I lost faith in the Elder and the fervor for living in the holy Monastery; I began to think about village life and marriage. Finally I came to the Elder with hypocritical devotion and asked to go home for a short time; but this deceit was not concealed from the clairvoyant Elder. With a severe expression on his face, and shaking his finger at me, he said, 'Watch out, brother; you aren't trying to fool me, are you?' I began to justify myself, 'No, Father, I only want to see my brother, and then I will come straight back.' Finally the Elder said, 'Go your way, brother, with God; you'll come running back here, where you don't want to stay right now.'

Merrily I left the Optina Monastery, with the intention of never returning; that is how fed up I was with my first efforts at forcing myself for the sake of the salvation of my soul. But things turned out contrary to my intention, and in accordance with the prophecy of the Elder. I came home to my village and began to work at the usual village chores. At that time one of the peasants in the village lost a horse. He began to suspect another peasant who had previously been caught for horse thievery, and he was not wrong in his assumption. But there was no evidence; the horse had been sold from one person to another. So he was unable to do anything to the culprit. Once this peasant was travelling home from another village after a feast day; he had had a lot to drink. Suddenly along a stretch of road in the forest he met up with the thief that had stolen his horse. In a fit of anger he jumped him, began to beat him viciously and then killed the poor man. That was my night to guard the horses in the field. The next day the villagers notified the local constable that one of our peasants was found lying dead on the road and that he had been murdered by some unknown person. The constable came and started an investigation. Who had been where at that time? A certain woman pointed me out, saying that at that time of night I had been out in the field with the horses. He began to interrogate me. I kept repeating the same words, 'I don't know; I don't know.' But our peasants asked the constable to lock me up and let me become worn out from hunger. They locked me in a closet and did not give me anything to drink or eat for three days. How I repented during those three days and nights that I had not heeded the good counsel of the clairvoyant Elder; and from my whole heart I beseeched the Lord that through the prayers of the Elder, whom I had deceived, He deliver me from by troubles! Finally they took me out, exhausted from hunger, for fresh interrogation. Our peasants suggested that the constable employ a torture still more cruel than the first: to heat up a big iron skillet and to put me on it. They assured the constable, 'He'll confess, if you do that.' I had no hope of being able to endure this cruel torment and made up my mind to bear false witness against myself. But by the prayers of the Elder, the Lord delivered me. The clerk told the constable, 'You'll have to answer for this if you go through with it; this is entirely in violation of the government's laws.' So he left me alone and began to question others. Soon he came to the guilty person, who became entangled in his own words and in a short time confessed his crime.

And I, overjoyed by my deliverance, immediately rushed back to the Optina Monastery. As soon as Fr. Leonid saw me, with a loving smile he blessed me and said, 'Ah, Dumbo[2] has come back. Did they show you a nice time? Tell us all about it.'

"I told the Elder everything, both my previous thoughts of not living in the Monastery and the trouble I had had at home because of the crime. From that time I was afraid to hide the least significant thought from the Elder.

"After I had lived awhile in the Monastery, the Elder wanted to send me back to my village. 'Get going,' he would say. 'Go home for a short while and then come back again.' I had no desire to go, and I asked the Elder not to send me, but the Elder said I absolutely had to go. I came home and found my brother had lost his mind from drinking too much wine. The peasants in our village were just going to send to the Monastery for me to come and look after our place, instead of my brother. What a sad state of affairs! I did not want to remain in the world and did not know what to do. Finally the idea came to me to go with my brother to St. Metrophanes of Voronezh; our peasants did not object. We came to Voronezh and offered a moleben to the Saint of God. My brother became better. The next day we asked another moleben to be served, and after this service my brother was completely healed. I brought him home in perfect health; everyone was amazed at the change in him.

---

2. This is what the Elder called this brother because of his good-natured simplicity.

And I was amazed at the clairvoyance of the Elder, how he had seen and told in advance about both of my trips home. After this I left my brother to continue his life by himself in the world. I rushed back to my Elder, coming to him now with faith and filial devotion.

"I also noticed while I was living in the Monastery that sometimes I would be assailed by grief, despondency and the bitter attack of thoughts. But as soon as I went to the Elder for consolation in my sorrow, the instant I entered his cell, in a flash everything would vanish and I would suddenly feel in my heart peace and joy. The Elder would ask, 'What did you come for?' And I wouldn't know what to say. The Elder would take oil from the lamp and anoint me, then give me his blessing; and I would leave his cell with a heart-felt joy and peace of soul.

"Afterwards, Elder Leonid told me to move to St. Tikhon's Hermitage. I did not want to leave the Elder, but did not dare to disobey him. Here I started to have a harder time; there was a lot of work and no one to provide consolation. The Elder came rarely. Finally, I decided to return to the Optina Monastery. At that time Fr. Leonid was visiting, and I told him of my intention. The Elder called me to the cell of Fr. Meletius; Fr. Alexius was there, also.[3] He told them to lay their hands on my head, and he himself also laid his hand on my head. He read the Trisagion and said, 'Live here and never leave.' From that time I have had no more thoughts about leaving this Monastery; I have been living here now for over thirty years."

---

3. Fr. Meletius, later Archimandrite and Ecclesiarch of the Kiev Caves Lavra. Fr. Alexius (Alexius Polycarpovich Bochkov), later Anthony, Abbot of the Chermenetsk Monastery.

2. The Account of the Novice of Optina Monastery, Alexius Ivanov Vasiliev, How He Profited from the Late Elder Fr. Leonid

"Once," he said, "I felt a coldness joined with a subtle uneasiness, and I thought to myself: this is the result of being scattered and self-willed. Three days had passed since I had gone to see my Elder, and I had not verified my actions or revealed my thoughts to him. One thought told me, 'There is no reason to go to him because during this time you have not done anything against your conscience'; but another thought urged me at least to receive his blessing, to strengthen me against the snares of the devil. At the same time I thought to myself, 'Out of the Lord's goodness, perhaps I can inform the Elder of my secret weaknesses, which I do not notice in myself because of my crudeness.' If I could receive some rebuke for them, with fatherly instructions, perhaps my previous calm of soul would return. Submitting to this idea, I forced myself to go to my instructor. When I entered his room the Elder was busy with guests; he saw me come in and asked, 'What do you need?' I came up to him, stood on my knees and said that I came to ask for his blessing and holy prayers. After giving me his blessing, I said, 'Thank you.' He asked how I was spending my time: was I busy with the obedience given me by superiors; was I painting the icons assigned to me in the icon studio? To this I replied, 'By your prayers, Father, I am keeping busy.' After a moment of silence, the Elder said, 'Fine, but I hear that you are making portraits also?' These words took me completely by surprise because the evening before, on my own, I had drawn a certain brother's portrait. Being a beginner I did not think to ask for forgiveness as I should have; and I said that I had just played around, thinking to justify myself that way. The Elder looked at the visitors and repeated my words several times, 'He was playing around!'

Taking me by the head and turning my face to the visitors, he said, 'Here, gentlemen, is a man over thirty years old; he already has a long beard. When he was a layman he was in charge of thousands of people, but he came here to the Monastery to play around. See, a lot of good is going to come of this person!' He sighed and said, 'Well, brother Alexius, so that you will be a little more precise in the future, make a few prostrations.' He told me that while I was making the prostrations to say these words, 'Although I am a proud person, I have to humble myself.' The holy Apostle Paul said: *Reprove, rebuke . . .* (II Tim. 4:2). After this, with a joyful spirit and warmth he gave his blessing and said, 'Now, my little child, you will be at peace. Go your way with God.'

"Once I wanted to learn about the difference in the kinds of prayer that are described in the *Philokalia*; I was especially eager to read the chapters of Callistus Cataphygiotes. But I doubted that the Elder would permit me to read them, since I was still a beginner. So I went to ask for this book from him when he had a lot of visitors, thinking that since he was busy with noteworthy people he would not bother to ask in detail about my reading. Beyond my furthest expectations, however, Fr. Leonid broke off his conversation with the visitors and with particular interest began to ask about why I needed the *Philokalia* and exactly what portions I wanted to read. When I explained to him, he gave me a stern look and said, 'How dare you take on such lofty matters? Lumpy,[4] your business is not reading Callistus Cataphygiotes; it is more profitable for you to clean up manure! Remember Simon Magus, how he climbed up so high and then fell down. The same will happen to you: if you don't humble yourself, you will perish.' At the time I was standing before him on my knees and felt as if I had been struck by lightning. Then the Elder told me, 'Let me

---

4. This brother had a bump on his forehead.

see your cheeks'; and after slapping me on the face a few times, he said, 'Go your way with God!'

"Once I happened to invite a certain brother for tea. While I was setting the table, I accidentally broke a tea cup; I came to the Elder to explain and found him sleeping in bed. The Elder woke up from the rustle I made, and when he saw me, he said, 'What do you need? Money?' I replied, 'I broke a tea cup.' Right away he called in his cell-attendant and told him, 'Congratulate Alexius Ivanovich; he has conquered a city.' I did not understand what the congratulations were all about. The Elder told me, 'Tell me, if you please, when are you ever going to straighten out? What good can ever be expected of you? In the world you were no good, and now you are living without correcting yourself. If you had fear of God, you would humble yourself and such things would not happen to you. It is apparent that because you became spaced-out, from being scatterbrained, you made it your business to play host; and that's why you broke it. And what is still worse, you came with a proud spirit to boast to your Elder: 'I broke a tea cup.' If you were a person worth his salt, you would have come with humility, saying, 'Father, forgive me for the Lord's sake; I accidentally broke a cup. What do you bless me to do?' But here you are boasting, as if you conquered a city. Get out!' When I got to the door, he heaved a sigh and in a gentle tone of voice he mercifully said, 'Alexius Ivanovich! Come back. I hope that you will make a beginning of straightening yourself out and that in the future you will be more humble.' And he told his cell attendant to give me a rouble."[5]

This brother assured us that he had never left the Elder in a state of distress, but always strengthened and consoled.

---

5. If any of the brothers who were under the direction of the Elder had any money at all, they did not keep it themselves; their money was always kept by the Elder. If anyone needed to buy anything, he always bought it with the blessing and permission of the Elder.

When he would show up weary with some sorrow, Fr. Leonid would greet him with indescribable fatherly love as soon as he noticed his arrival; and after listening to his deeds and thoughts, he would place his hands on him. Sometimes with a joke, he would take him by the head and press him to himself while he was reciting a prayer over him, and by this means bring calm and consolation to dwell in his suffering soul.

3. The Account of Alexander Smirnov.

"During the first year after my entrance into the Monastery, I came once in a disturbed state of soul to my spiritual father, Elder Leonid, and with tears I told him that the visit by my mother and my sister was upsetting me. The Elder, thinking that I was being overcome by the weakness of fleshly love for my mother and that I was sorry over being separated from her, came to such a state of zeal for God and indignation that, after giving me a hard slap on the cheek, said, 'You prefer love for your mother over love for God? And this is how you repay Him for bringing you into the world? You coward!' Even though I was not aware of being attached to my relatives, I rejoiced in spirit when I understood this action of my spiritual father, who was a true guide to God, Whom he obviously loved more than everything and to Whom he taught me to direct my steps without going astray.

"Then after some time, I was once standing in the Elder's reception room, knowing I would not be allowed to see him for a long time due to the crowd of pilgrims who had come to him from faraway places; he was busy with them. Being impatient, like an inexperienced beginner, I began to grow restless and finally started murmuring against my Elder. When his cell-attendant came out to me and did not close the door behind him, in disgust I said in a voice that the Elder could hear, these words which were extremely painful for him: 'The Elder is caring for strange sheep while his own go hungry.' These words of mine made the cell-attendant angry, and he reprimanded me for my audacity and impatience. But the Elder, on the other hand, called to me meekly and gently, 'Ah, Sasha, Sasha, you're upset? Jimmy, treat him to a cup of tea.' Then turning to me he continued, "Well, now, Alexander, have you settled down? Now aren't you ashamed of yourself to become upset because I receive others? After all, you want to receive food for your soul from me; don't you think others want to do the same? You are always here, but these people who upset you came from distant places to see me, to reveal their needs to me and to receive consolation from me: am I not supposed to let them see me? Is it right for us to love only ourselves? Quite the opposite — God wishes us to love others also and to wish all to be saved, as He does.' The truthfulness of his words and such meekness softened my heart, and with tears I asked for his forgiveness. I sensed his total guilelessness on this occasion and throughout the entire time I spent with him.

"When I compared this action of his with the first, I began to understand my Elder better. For the personal offense done to him, he did not show the least trace of dissatisfaction either in his face or in word. But for preferring worldly love to the spiritual, or love for God, he became angry and could not let me go without punishment."

4. From the Notes of Hieromonk A. B.

"A certain woman, a pilgrim, was with the Elder inseparably in St. Tikhon's Hermitage; and we were more fed up with her than the disciples had been with the Syro-Phoenician woman (Matt. 15:21ff). Her compliments, prostrations and the various contortions on her face, to me especially, seemed to be comedy and deceit. I dared to mention to the Elder that not only I, but all our brothers, were fed up with this pest, and that, according to her own words, she had been thrown out everywhere, from every monastery, because no elder could put up with her. 'Really? Are you telling me the truth?' 'I heard it from her own mouth.' 'Then if I throw her out, where will she go? She has a soul too; a human soul conceals much good in its depths. You just have to seek it out.'

"Fr. Leonid — so child-loving and all-compassionate for the repentant and who dedicated himself to serving his little brothers — was immovable in the presence of those worldly people who put their wealth, power or importance on the same level as the laws of the Church and who fearlessly violated the ecclesiastical rules, demanding of their spiritual fathers dispensation for public sins.

"There was a landowner who made donations to the Monastery but did not visit very frequently. He lived openly with one of his peasant women in his old age, even though his children by his first and lawful wife had grown up and married. After hearing about the famous Elder, Fr. Leonid, and that he received many people for confession, this landowner made overtures to Fr. Leonid through the Abbot: he would like to make his confession to him. Fr. Leonid refused, to the great offense of the landowner, who began to beg both the Abbot and Fr. Macarius to be his intercessors before Fr. Leonid. After repeated requests, the Elder against his will agreed, but stated that he would not be responsible for what might happen. The landowner made his confession; Fr. Leonid did not allow him to receive the Holy Mysteries. You can imagine the shame and humiliation of this gentleman, who looked down on everyone and who now had to humble himself before the entire Monastery, like a catechumen. To his even greater shame, his married daughter who was accompanying him was preparing to thank the great Elder for his decision. Once again the gentleman asked the Abbot and Fr. Macarius to intercede. They refused out of conscience and because they knew how immovable Fr. Leonid was in such matters. What happened? The landowner returned home and after less than a month broke off his years-long relationship with his mistress, to the mutual joy of his entire family. Apparently, in the depth of his soul the Elder prayed for this stray sheep and asked the Lord to soften the heart of his spiritual son.

"Another time a certain gentleman came from Vyazma and wanted to confess to Fr. Leonid. After confession the Elder blessed him to approach for Communion, but on the condition that he firmly resolve to correct his way of life. The gentleman promised to do this. 'If you don't keep your word, then don't come back to me,' the Elder told him. The next summer the gentleman from Vyazma once again came to Optina Monastery. When he approached the cell of Fr. Leonid, the Elder saw him through the open window and stopped him with the words, 'Stop! Stop! Did you keep your promise?' 'Father, forgive me. . . .' 'You didn't keep it? Then turn right around and go back; don't come to me.' And the man was thus forced to leave without even receiving the blessing of the Elder. Even though at the time these notes are being written more than thirty years have transpired since the death of Fr. Leonid, this event is remembered down to the present time in Vyazma and Smolensk Provinces. It became widely known right away and threw a salutary fear into many persons, giving them to understand that for those who want to profit from the counsels of the elders it is not enough just to ask them; one must also do what they say.

"A well-known archimandrite came especially to see Fr. Leonid. The guest was surrounded with every possible kind of attention, but Fr. Leonid did not interrupt his usual reception of the sick, pilgrims, nuns and his disciples on behalf of this person. In order to provide the archimandrite with the opportunity to speak with Fr. Leonid more freely, someone had the idea of inviting both the Elder and the guest to have dinner with the Abbot and some of his close associates. This was probably the suggestion of the guest himself. The fathers at Optina knew that Fr. Leonid never showed up for the Abbot's festive dinners, and he was never eager to have to put on his ryassa and kamilavka with veil; he regarded these hours as working hours for getting something accomplished and not a time for leisure; these dinners were the hardest kind of toil and torment for him. The Elder dressed up in his worn-out, coarse ryassa and for the sake of obedience went to the dinner. The archimandrite, at the end of the first course and after a period of appropriate silence, put the question to Fr. Leonid, 'Give us, Elder, some word of profit,' he said, imitating by his question the ancient monks (although they sought for a word of profit not over dinner but after mental prayer, surrounded by monastic poverty). Fr. Leonid frowned and replied bluntly, 'Everything profitable has been dumped out for the ladies; now there's nothing left.' His reply was taken as an expression of humility, and everyone kept quiet. The archimandrite turned bright red, aware that this was a reference to his own life, which he had spent among his lady devotees. We do not know whether the Elder said this with such an intention; but since he had been asked for a word of profit, the Elder's soul, on its own, spoke this word for the instruction of the archimandrite, an intelligent and spiritual person.

"Once the abbot of a certain monastery, while speaking about his brotherhood with Fr. Leonid, happened to say in passing, 'I have such-and-such a person who leads an exemplary life.'

"The Elder jumped out of his chair, threw down the belt he was braiding and made a big sign of the cross, striking himself powerfully on the forehead, breast and both shoulders. 'O Lord my God!' he exclaimed, 'How much insane pride is contained in little words! I have! I have! What do you have that belongs to you? Only your sins, only your thoughtless vainglory. The monastery is not yours; it belongs to the patron saint. The brotherhood did not come to you but to

Christ their Lord, seeking salvation from Him. What are you, some kind of contractor and they are your hirelings, so that you think you can recommend one of them to me? You could at least say: our brothers consider that such-and-such a person lives in such-and-such a manner. But you say: I have! You want them all to be your serfs? Don't you know why the brotherhood was scandalized with me at White Bluff? Not for my ostentatiousness, but because I conducted myself too plainly, because I travelled to Bryansk on a simple wagon and sometimes even drove the horse myself. That's why. But they wanted the same thing you do, that the abbot be like a big shot. Already the worm of love of honor had started gnawing away at the hearts of the brothers. That's why people similar to you come out from there. And do you think their positions of authority proved beneficial for their souls? No, brother, a big shot will never become a good abbot. You should imitate our Abbot Moses, at least by guarding your words and weighing them carefully. You remember what the Apostle says in his epistle: the person that can restrain his tongue is able to restrain his whole body. Remember these words of mine; otherwise you will never know restraint.' The abbot blushed but did not justify himself.

"A certain lady once brought Fr. Leonid a manuscript with an akathist to God the Father; she asked him to look it over. The book was written in uncial script and had a very luxurious binding with gold edging. The Elder sent this manuscript to the Superior of the Skete at that time, Fr. Anthony. After examining the manuscript, Fr. Anthony remarked that because the Church does not have any separate services to God the Father, he considered it would be dangerous to approve this.[6] Then Fr. Leonid said, 'Well, then, give it

---

6. Elders Anthony and Leonid expressed themselves in this manner because *no man knoweth the Father, save the Son and he to whomsoever the Son will reveal Him* (Matt. 11:27). Although there are prayers

here; we'll place it in the stove.' Fr. Anthony started to object, 'But what will the lady say?' 'She can say what she likes; we won't even look at her,' said the Elder, and he burned the book.

"The rector of a certain seminary came to the Optina Monastery. When he was invited to speak with Fr. Leonid, he said, 'What do I have to talk about with him? He's just a peasant.' But he went to the Elder anyway. As soon as he entered the cell, Fr. Leonid repeated his words, 'What do I have to talk about with him? He's just a peasant.' In spite of this unceremonious reception, the rector spoke with the Elder for two hours with great pleasure, and afterwards remarked about the Elder, 'What good is all our learning? His learning is from labor and grace!'"

* * * * * * *

In 1839, a young man named Michael, a townsman of Bolhov, wanted to enter monasticism; he set out for the White Bluff Hermitage. Here, among the various stories about the Optina Elder Leonid, he heard of the following incident. When Fr. Leonid was still the Abbot at White Bluff, there was a monk who lived in the forest as a watchman. He taught the peasant children who came to him how to read and write. Once a drunken peasant came to him and, for no reason, beat him so badly that the monk soon died. When Fr. Leonid was told about this, he said decisively, "Because this peasant without any just reason killed an

---

directed to God the Father, they commonly end in a doxology praising Him Who is worshipped in *Trinity*. There exists no separate feast day to God the Father on the Church calendar, and, although some iconographic representations of God the Father have at times been painted historically, they remain peripheral to the Orthodox Faith, which has suffered perennially from those who would sunder One of the Hypostases or Persons of the Holy Trinity. On two Great Feasts, Theophany and the Transfiguration, wherein the mystery of the Holy Trinity is so clearly revealed, the Father is manifest only through a Voice and not by means of any depictable image. —ed.

innocent man, he himself will die soon." And in fact three days later this man suddenly died.

From this and other stories testifying to the spiritual wisdom of the Elder, Michael's heart was enkindled. He wanted to spend his monastic life under the guidance of Fr. Leonid, and with this intention he set out from White Bluff for the Optina Monastery. The Elder, after speaking with him, blessed him to enter St. Tikhon's Hermitage under the direction of Fr. Gerontius. But Michael did not want to leave Fr. Leonid and asked permission to remain in the Optina Monastery. The Elder gave his consent. But some of the brothers explained to Michael that by remaining at Optina, he was disobeying the Elder and following his own will. Michael was upset by this and asked the Elder's forgiveness for his not going, as assigned, to St. Tikhon's. The Elder replied, "Don't worry! Stay here a while. But remember that St. Tikhon's is where you will be. You really will; yes, you will."

This same youth Michael, later the Optina Hieromonk Moses,[7] was appointed Abbot of the St. Tikhon Hermitage 18 years after this prophecy, at the direction of the diocesan authorities.

Once one of Fr. Leonid's devoted spiritual sons came to him and, after sitting in his cell for the entire evening, afterwards said to the Elder, "I saw how the brothers here came to you and how you received them. One came before the others but waited until they were finished; then he came to you last. Others came, waited a little, then came up to you and explained what they needed. Some of them did not want to wait at all; and as soon as they came in they pushed to the front, trying to get you to receive them right away. Is there any distinction in all this?" The Elder replied, "There is a distinction and a great distinction. The person who comes here and does not want to wait, who

_____

7. He was a disciple of Optina Elder Moses (Putilov).

pushes ahead of the others, will not be able to remember what I tell him for long. As soon as he leaves the cell, he forgets the instruction he received without much concern about doing what he was told. But as for the one who comes to express his needs but with patience and humility waits until all the others are through, giving them preference before himself: every word that he hears is stamped firmly into his heart, and for his entire life he will remember what he was told just once."

5. Account of the Monk N.

"During the initial period after I entered the Monastery," the Monk N. recounts, "I had an exceptional zeal for monastic asceticism. Sometimes after Matins others would go to rest, but during that time I would occupy myself with something in keeping with my obedience. When I was exhausted I would lie down for a brief rest, but in my thoughts I took care not to oversleep, so that I would be present at the very beginning of the early Liturgy. One morning someone came and woke me at the first sound of the bell; someone, it seemed, said a prayer at my door. I got up and looked around; no one was in sight. The next day the same thing happened. As soon as they started ringing the bell for the Liturgy, someone's voice said a prayer. I thought that it was our our monk, Fr. I., and I looked out; but no one was there. I told the Elder, Fr. Leonid, all about this. 'What do you think?' he asked me. 'Who is it that is waking you?' 'I think, Father,' I replied, 'that it might be an angel.' 'With little horns!' the Elder retorted. 'We'll see what happens next.' The next day no one woke me, and I slept through the entire service. The next day and the day after that I slept through again. So we were both put to shame, my unidentified caller and I, the gullible zealot."

6. Account of Hiero-schemamonk Th.

"When I was still a novice," the Hiero-schemamonk Th. relates, "on one occasion while I was standing on my knees before the Elder, Fr. Leonid, I was distracted by thoughts. I began thinking that a certain monk (who was well-acquainted with economic affairs) would make a good abbot. As soon as I thought this, suddenly the Elder slapped me rather hard on the cheek with the words, 'Mind your own business! You don't know what kind of a person he is.' I have to add that the monk I had been thinking about later left the Optina Monastery and passed through many monasteries, but never became an abbot."

* * * * * * *

A certain soldier, who was fervent for the salvation of his soul, put on chains. When he heard about the clairvoyant Elder, he wanted to see him. Upon his arrival at the Monastery, he found Fr. Leonid in church at the early Liturgy. After the service was over, he approached the Elder with the other people to ask for his blessing. The Elder, as he gave him his blessing, began to urge him to take off his chains. "Father!" the soldier said. "Bless me to wear them for just one more year, then I will come to you and you will personally take them off me." As they talked they came to the place where Fr. Leonid is now buried. In reply to the soldier's request, Fr. Leonid pointed out this place with his walking stick and told him, "A year from now, that's where I'll be. Take them off right now." And that is how it turned out; a year later Fr. Leonid was buried at the site he had indicated.

Once the young novice John came to Fr. Leonid, bowed at his feet and stood before him in a very humble pose. The Elder looked at him, shaking his finger, and said, "Oh, Johnny, you're not humbling yourself for anything good." These words which contained a prophecy could have served at the same time as a warning for John, if he had wanted to be instructed by them. Because he paid no attention to the Elder's words, the next day he fell into something which is not proper for monastics.

7. The Account of the Hieromonk A.

"A year after I entered the Optina Monastery," relates Hieromonk A., "I began to have a very strong desire to go live on Athos. At first I expressed my desire to Fr. Macarius. He replied, 'Live here in the Skete in the Athonite way; then the Skete will be Athos for you.' This did not satisfy me. I went to the Elder, Fr. Leonid, and began to ask him to bless me to set out for Athos. The noise he raised drowned me out. 'Where did you say you want to go?' he said. 'You good-for-nothing. You're just an inexperienced novice who has yet to grow steadfast in the monastic life, and here you think you're going to go to Athos. Make sure that you never have that thought in my presence ever again!' And so I left the Elder. But the desire to go to Athos did not abandon me. I came to the Elder on another occasion and asked him more insistently to let me leave Optina. The Elder was ready to raise another ruckus; but when he saw that I was unmoved in my intention, he suddenly came up to me, embraced me with both arms, pressed me to his breast and with gentle, fatherly love began: 'My dear little Arsenius, what are you doing? Here you are going off to a foreign land, and your Father is going to die here without you. How will you feel when you hear about this?' At that point I started to cry, fell at his feet and asked his forgiveness for my ill-considered request. I stayed to live in Optina. A year later our Father Leonid reposed."

8. The Account of the Kozelsk Citizen S. I.

S. I., who lived in Kozelsk and was one of the devoted disciples of Fr. Leonid, related this account: "In the 1830's,

I was in the pottery business, the same as now. My wife and I lived in our own little house. We did not have a horse, but we did have a fairly large wagon. So I would load up the pottery in the wagon, ask someone for a horse, and take the pottery to market. In those days I sometimes made a little extra money. At that time there was a soldier, a Pole, who was quartered in our house. (Later he left and came to no good.) Once when he saw a good chance, he sneaked into our yard and stole the wheels from our wagon. I told Fr. Leonid about my misfortune and said that I knew who the thief was and could locate the wheels. 'Leave him alone, my Simeon; don't go chasing after those wheels,' the Elder replied. 'This is God's chastisement. Endure God's chastisement, and through a little sorrow you will be delivered from greater ones. But if you don't want to endure this little trial, then you will receive greater chastisement.'

"I followed the Elder's advice, and everything turned out just as he had said. In a short time this same Pole again sneaked into our yard and took a bag of flour out of the shed. He threw it over his shoulder and was on his way to take it out through the garden, but my wife came out of the garden and met up with him. 'Where are you taking that?' she asked. He threw down the bag of flour and ran away. Soon after this there was another bad incident. We had a cow but decided to sell it. We found a buyer, made a deal and took the down payment. For some reason the purchaser did not come for the cow for several days. Finally he came and took it. That very night our thief came and broke into the stall where our cow had been kept, quite sure that he was going to take it away; but it wasn't there. So once again the Lord, by the prayers of the Elder, delivered us from danger.

"Many years after this I had a third experience along the same lines. Holy Week was coming to an end, and Pascha was on its way. For some reason I came up with the idea of moving all of our valuables from our little house over to my sister's, our neighbor. So that is what I did. As soon as the first day of the Feast arrived, I locked my house from all sides and went to church. Now I always experienced great joy at this Matins Resurrection Service, but this time — I didn't know why — there was something unpleasant on my soul. I came home from church and found that all our windows and the door were wide open. 'Aha,' I thought to myself, 'someone has been up to no good.' And that was the case; but since all of our valuables had been moved over to my sister's, whoever it was went away empty-handed. So on three occasions Fr. Leonid's prophecy was fulfilled in my life: that if I endured a little chastisement from God, then God would not chastise me further.''

* * * * * * *

A brother who was just a beginner once insulted an old monk; they both came to put the matter before Fr. Leonid. It was clear to everyone that the beginner was totally in the wrong. But the Elder regarded the matter differently. "Aren't you ashamed to put yourself on the same level as a beginner?" the Elder said sternly to the old monk. "He just came from the world; his hair hasn't even grown long yet. You can't demand very much from him for saying something wrong. Here you have lived in the Monastery for how many years, and still haven't learned to watch over yourself!" So they left. The beginner was triumphant, thinking that he had been totally acquitted. But soon after that, this same brother came alone to Fr. Leonid. The Elder took him by the hand and said, "What are you up to, brother? Here you just came from the world, your hair hasn't even grown long, and you're already insulting the old monks!" This unexpected lesson had a great impact on the brother, and he began to ask forgiveness. "God forgives," said the Elder. "But watch out now, brother; make sure you straighten out. Otherwise you will be in for a bad time.''

9. The Account of the Nun O.

"From my childhood I had a strong desire to live in a convent; and in 1837, when I was twelve years old, I asked my mother to leave me in the convent in Kiev where we were visiting. She did not agree to this, but promised she would arrange for me to live in the Borisov Convent when I turned fifteen. Soon after this, however, she died. My father did not want to let me go to a convent until I had reached the age of thirty-five. I grieved very much over this. In 1840, when I had already turned fifteen, I wanted secretly to run away from home as I was very afraid that my fate would be decided contrary to my desire. But one of my aunts, who was very sympathetic to me, took me into her home and later persuaded my father to go to the Optina Monastery to Fr. Leonid and let him decide my fate. My father agreed. When we appeared before Fr. Leonid, even though he did not know us he called us all by name and said that he had been expecting such guests for some time. We were so nonplussed by such a reception that we did not know how to reply. Then one at a time we went into his cell; and here the Elder spoke to each person as was fitting, speaking about the present, the past and the future. They made me go last. While waiting for the moment when I would have to go in, I became very much afraid; but I left his cell at peace and with great consolation of soul. He blessed me to go straight to the Borisov Convent. Through his prayers my father no longer detained me, but he gave me no money. When Fr. Leonid was asked how I was going to live, the Elder's reply was, 'She'll live better than the best.' The words of Fr. Leonid were fulfilled in every respect. In 1841 my father himself brought me to the Borisov Convent, where I am still living. I have always seen in my experience, and still see, the Providence of God over me in everything, by the prayers of the Elder.

"In 1839, a young lady from the nobility of the Schigrovsky region came to Elder Leonid for a blessing to enter a convent. He told her, 'Wait another year and then come see us.' She went home saddened that she had to wait for so long and afraid lest something might prevent her during that time. When she arrived home, she grieved and wept a great deal. In her sorrow, on two occasions she saw the Elder give her a piece of bread (the first time without salt, the second time salted) and tell her, 'Do not sorrow! I told you that you will live in the convent; only first come and see me.' After the year had passed she came to Optina; and as soon as she saw Fr. Leonid — before she could tell him anything — he said to her, 'So you were sad and cried? You know I gave you a piece of bread and you ate it; so now you can remain calm.' At the same time he gave her his blessing to enter the convent.

"At the same time that this young lady was present, six men brought a possessed woman to Fr. Leonid. As soon as she saw the Elder, she fell in front of him and cried out loudly, 'This gray-head is going to throw me out. I was in Kiev, in Moscow, in Voronezh, and no one expelled me; but now I have to go.' The Elder read a prayer over her and anointed her with holy oil from the lamp before the icon of the Mother of God. When they first brought her to the Elder, she resisted terribly and stomped on his foot. His big toe turned black and blue, and it gave him much pain for a long time after that. After the prayers of the Elder the possessed woman arose quietly and left. From that time, she came every year to Optina in complete health. Following Fr. Leonid's death she would faithfully take earth from his grave for others, who were likewise benefited thereby."

10. The Account of Abbot P.

"Soon after I entered Optina Monastery (about 1832)," relates Abbot P., "when Fr. Leonid's cell attendants were

Fr. Gerontius, Fr. Macarius Gruzinov and Paul Tambovtsev, a possessed peasant woman was brought to the Elder. During her fits of demonic possession she would speak in foreign languages. Paul Tambovtsev was a witness to this, as he knew some foreign languages. Fr. Leonid read the prayer over her three times, anointed her with oil from the vigil lamp before the icon of the Mother of God and gave her some of this oil to drink. The third time they brought her she had a completely different appearance. When Tambovtsev asked her to speak, as before, in foreign languages, she said, 'Father, how can I speak in foreign languages? I can barely speak Russian and can hardly walk. Glory to God that my former illness has passed.'"

* * * * * * *

Abbot Anthony (Putilov) told one of his spiritual children that the son of a certain couple he had seen visiting Fr. Leonid had a particular emotional defect, and that his facial features bore no resemblance to his father or mother. The Elder said that this was a chastisement to his parents for not observing the feast days.

A family from Karachev came to the Optina Monastery. They had suffered repeated family tragedies. The visitors looked up old Hieromonk Gabriel, the treasurer, who was from their same town, and told him their predicament. He had the idea that Cherubic incense would help them in their grief, but decided not to advise them of anything without the blessing of Fr. Leonid; he went to ask for the Elder's blessing. "What a funny fellow you are," Fr. Leonid told him. "Do you think fine Cherubic incense will help them in this case? Where the wrath of God is present, the Lord does not spare His holy things. Something else is required here, and that is sincere repentance for the sins for which the wrath of God has been sent and amendment of life."

Many of the lay people who confessed to Fr. Leonid did not undertake anything in their affairs without his blessing. They observed this rule especially in regards to marriage. For the most part it was people from some of the cities of the Tula Province who observed this, and it was noticeable that the marriages performed with the blessing of the Elder were happy ones. On the other hand, if those who would usually have observed this custom for some reason did not want to get a blessing for their marriage, it turned out that these marriages were not always happy ones. This distinction made some people ask his blessing for their undertakings even against their will.

When people asked his blessing for marriage, Fr. Leonid usually advised them to examine very carefully all of the favorable and unfavorable circumstances; for instance, to make sure that both the husband and wife were in good health, that they had a way of supporting themselves and that they were not from widely differing social backgrounds. He especially advised poor families not to take a rich bride, so as not to become her slaves. On these occasions he would repeat the simple, old proverb: "Let a fancy boot keep to a fancy boot and a moccasin to a moccasin." He also told those asking about how to select a groom to pay special attention to his father's personality, and those asking about a bride to pay special attention to the personality of her mother. He would say, "The apple can't roll very far from the apple tree." Finally, he advised the groom, bride and parents to examine their own hearts. When the final decision was to be made concerning the marriage, if the bride, groom and parents sensed a calmness of soul, then the Elder advised them to decide in favor of the marriage. If, on the other hand, at this point there was some doubt or inexplicable fear, unrest or distress, then Fr. Leonid would say that this was not a good sign and would advise them to look for another groom or bride.

Once a man who was not wealthy came to Fr. Leonid and explained that his daughter was being sought by three suitors: a craftsman, a factory worker and an wealthy farmer.

Fr. Leonid advised him to give her to the village farmer, saying that with him there would be plenty to eat. Afterwards there came a year of famine; and when it had passed the father of the bride came to thank the Elder for advising him to give his daughter to the farmer, who had also provided food for the father during the time of famine. He added that the craftsman and the factory worker had almost starved to death.

The widow of a certain merchant in Tula had a daughter. The mother wanted to marry her off and set out to get the blessing of Fr. Leonid. He told her to bring the girl to see him, mentioning that he had a wonderful husband for her. The mother brought her daughter to the Elder; he blessed her to take her daughter to the Belev Convent, where the daughter soon died.

Once Fr. Leonid's sister came to see him. He received her along with all the other visitors and gave her the same kind of help he gave to all others who were in need; that is, he gave her a five rouble note. On this occasion the Elder told certain people that if a monk gives one of his relatives a nickel more than to others, that proves he has yet to free himself from the bonds of blood relations and that he does not love all men equally; he makes distinctions.

Once the landowner P. came to the Optina Monastery, and when he saw the Elder he thought to himself, "How can they say that he is something special? He is just like everyone else; I don't see anything special about him." Suddenly, the Elder said to him, "All you care about is building your house: how many windows go here, what kind of porch over there." We must note that when this landowner arrived at Optina from Kaluga, he saw a very beautiful spot and took such an interest in it that he decided to build himself a house there. He was already formulating plans in his mind about what it would be like and how many windows it would have; the Elder exposed the man for this. And when P. began to make his confession before him, Fr. Leonid re-

reminded him of a sin he had forgotten long before, something which he had not even considered a sin. After that, P. agreed that the Elder was really an exceptional person after all.

11. The Account of the Nun N.

"After I entered the Belev Convent," relates the Nun N., "at first I lived in someone else's cell. My father had the means and could have purchased or built for me my own cell, but the Elder Leonid did not give his blessing for this; he told me to live in someone else's. After a time I received an offer to purchase a site for a cell in the Convent. Fr. Leonid gave permission, but told me not to build the cell for yet another year. The abbess at that time (who was not devoted to Fr. Leonid) and many of the sisters found this decision to be very strange and unintelligible. 'If you have the site and the means, why not build yourself a cell?' they told me. I personally was very eager to live in my own cell. Due to my lack of understanding, I employed some cunning; I went to my father and suggested that he build me a cell, as it were, on his own initiative. He agreed, and I told Fr. Leonid that my father by all means wanted to build me a cell right away. The Elder retorted, 'He wants to do so because you asked him to. Well, I guess you can put up the frame, but don't build the stove until next year so that you won't move in until then.' But I was overcome by my desire to have my own cell as soon as possible and was not satisfied with this. Again I convinced my father to build the stove without any delay. I told the Elder that that was my father's will. 'Watch out now,' said the Elder. 'This cell of yours is not going to do you any good. You'll have no consolation from it!' These words soon came to pass. As soon as I moved into my self-willed cell, God's chastisement came upon me for not listening to my Elder and for deceiving him. I lost my peace of soul, began to experience a joyless depression and finally came down with a terrible emotional illness. Or, more precisely, with God's permission, the spiritual enemies attacked me and my mind was darkened. For three years I suffered inexpressibly terrible sufferings; these sufferings taught me a lesson, and I came running to the Elder in repentance. 'I told you,' Fr. Leonid said, 'that your cell would not do you any good. Now you have suffered for your disobedience and deceitfulness, and you are going to have to suffer some more. Now you have only one way of salvation: sell the cell; without doing this you can't be healed.' After all that I had been through, this time I accepted the Elder's words with faith and made up my mind to show him obedience no matter what. My father was extremely indignant with me for deciding to sell the cell he had built for me. He was very much against this and threatened to abandon me for the future and leave me with no help. In spite of this I still sold my unhappy cell; and it was only then that I received some relief of soul, although, as the Elder foretold, my tortuous illness did not leave me right away. I endured many sorrows by living in other nuns' cells. I especially went through grievous suffering when I learned of the death of Elder Leonid. I almost came to total despair because I had not received permission from the Elder to live in my own cell and did not know how to arrange my life. But with God's mercy, bit by bit, everything worked out. In time Fr. Macarius blessed me to purchase a cell. I was afraid to carry this out, but Fr. Macarius put me at ease by telling me that the time of my trial had passed and the time when God willed me to live in my own cell had arrived. With his blessing I moved into my own cell where I have now lived for thirty years. After being taught through the bitter experience of my own life, I realized how destructive it is to disobey spiritual guides in anything. From that time no matter what the Elder told me, I made every effort, and still make every effort, to carry out his will precisely and without thinking twice about the matter. I would wish that my example could serve as a lesson for others, also."

VI

The Persecution of Elder Leonid and His Belev Nuns

1839 - 1841

DURING the Elder's final years he had to endure a trial prior to his death which was especially painful for him because it affected not just him alone — he himself was not afraid of any sorrows — but many of his spiritual children, also.

Among those who came to Fr. Leonid for spiritual counsels were young ladies of various backgrounds who had no inclination for married life and who had from their youth desired to unite themselves to the One Heavenly Bridegroom and Adorner of pure souls, Christ the King. They asked the experienced Elder for his advice; he received them with fatherly love and opened their eyes to a correct view of the monastic life. He taught them to walk the narrow path of cutting off their own will and understanding — not only to flee from the passions, but to pull them out by their very roots — and to purify their hearts from passionate thoughts and mental images through frequent revelation and confession of their thoughts to persons experienced and skilled in spiritual activity. For some of them who expressed a sincere readiness to walk this path, he advised entering the Belev Convent and entrusting themselves to the guidance of the Eldress there, Mother Anthia, who had grown up and matured in active spiritual life under the experienced guidance of Fr. Leonid himself. She referred to him for spiritual counsels and instructions even before the Elder moved to the Optina Monastery. Abbess Epaphrodite, seeing how Mother Anthia and the sisters close to her were visibly advancing in spiritual life, showed them a noticeable preference. The enemy made use of this in order to wound others who were careless; they accepted into their hearts the arrow of jealousy against Mother Anthia and the sisters devoted to her. Among the nuns who came to this Eldress for spiritual counsels were two sisters in the flesh, young ladies from the nobility. One of them, having become disgruntled with her sister, turned against Mother Anthia as well. First she broke off her spiritual relationship with her. Then, tormented by envy and suspicion, she told her spiritual father, the priest of this same Convent, Fr. G., that Mother Anthia was supposedly attracting sisters to herself and spreading some kind of "new teaching." She also said that Mother Anthia was hearing sisters' confessions and giving absolution in the name of Fr. Leonid. She made up other stories, as well, all based on distortion of the most simple, innocent words and actions of the virtuous Eldress.

Unfortunately, Fr. G. was already disposed to trust gossip against Mother Anthia, whom he did not like, because she (and following her example certain other sisters also) turned to Elder Leonid for spiritual counsel. He considered that he alone was their lawful instructor and thus regarded their turning to Elder Leonid as a slighting of his honor. The mystery of confession, which is the inseparable right of all those invested with the grace of the priesthood and who have the spiritual authority to loose and to bind, he confused with the revelation of thoughts. According to the rule of monastic life, the revelation of thoughts is the property only of experienced elders and eldresses, and those who have been perfected in the active monastic life. (Concerning this distinction, see the letter below of Elder Macarius to Mother Anthia.)

Fr. G. did not hesitate to label as heresy this kind of relationship, about which he knew so little; and, with his confidence bolstered by the testimony of one of his own spiritual daughters, he zealously went into action. He began by announcing his discovery to the Abbess and thereby greatly distressed this dear, elderly nun. In vain she demonstrated to Fr. G. that the Eldress Anthia — the victim of his slander — and the sisters of one mind with her were the best little lambs of the rational flock entrusted to her by God. Fr. G. would hear none of this, confirming with an oath that he had uncovered a heresy which had gone heretofore unnoticed and that it was the duty of his office, as he saw it, to adopt all measures against this evil.

He then began to spread various slanders and accusations against Fr. Leonid, both in the Convent and outside it. When news of this reached the humble Elder, being an experienced spiritual warrior he met the rumor of these slanders, which were not new to him, in a spirit of patience. But his co-struggler and spiritual friend, Fr. Macarius, wrote to Fr. G., who had *zeal not according to knowledge* (Rom. 10:2), a very convincing letter in order not so much to rebuke him as to instruct him. The letter breathes the spirit of meekness and condescension towards an erring brother. Here are the contents:

Your blessing,
   the most honored among priests, Fr. G.!

To my heartfelt sorrow, I hear from you that you have accepted a false opinion and have been persuaded by it to side against Fr. Leonid. Your opinion concerns not only his way of life, but even the matter of the Faith. You consider him to be some kind of sectarian or heretic; this I never expected of you. Because I retain deep respect for you in my heart I desire to help bring you out of this error, for you are falling into the sin of slandering an innocent person and are making others guilty of the same. No matter who it was that imparted this opinion to you, you ought to examine it very carefully: is it trustworthy or not? On what basis does the proof of it lie?

Believe not every spirit but try them, whether they be from God, wrote the holy Apostle (I John 4:1). The members of the Holy Synod know Fr. Leonid quite well, and the Eminent Metropolitans know him from his better side. The Metropolitan of Kiev has known him since the year 1807 when he was still Abbot of the Svensk Monastery in the Orlov Diocese. Fr. Leonid at that time was Superior of the White Bluff Hermitage, which was no more than twenty kilometers away, and they had frequent contact with each other. In 1837, during His Eminence's journey to Kiev, when he visited our Hermitage he accorded him a very merciful archpastoral blessing. The Abbot and Fr. Anthony have great sympathy and respect for him and take counsel with him on many occasions. Likewise, our other fathers and brothers trust and love him and profit from his instructions. Lay persons of various ranks also come to him and depart not without receiving consolation in their sorrows and problems of soul. Fr. Leonid spent almost twenty years with an Elder experienced in spiritual life, the Schemamonk Theodore. The Schemamonks Theodore and his co-struggler Cleopas are widely known for the correctness of their faith and the sanctity of their life; they were disciples of the Elder Paisius of Moldavia, and he (Fr. Leonid) was instructed by them in the spiritual life. The correctness of his faith is known to the Eminent Metropolitans of Moscow and Kiev and to our own Bishop, as to the presiders over the Church. We also know and firmly believe that he believes in the Holy Trinity, One in Essence and Indivisible, the Father, the Son and the Holy Spirit, as the Holy Catholic and Apostolic Greco-Russian Church commands. All [Her] dogmas and ordinances he rightly confesses and observes; and he has neither belonged to, nor does he at present belong

to, any heresy or sect. He dedicates his life, as far as
his strength and health permit, to abstinence; and his
life is not scandalous. Otherwise, how would it be
possible for his own brethren and for lay people to
receive benefit from him? Of course, there are persons
who come out of curiosity and deceit, seeking to
find a miracle worker, someone clairvoyant or a prophet; and when they do not find these qualities in
him they voice their slanders against him. Apparently these have reached your ears, also, and have distressed your spirit. If everyone spoke well of him,
then one should feel very sorry for him, for according
to the Word of our Savior: *Woe to him of whom
all men speak well* (Luke 6:26). Who of those who
lead a pious life has escaped slanders and accusations,
when even our Savior and Lord Jesus Christ Himself,
Who committed no sin but Who granted blessings to
the souls and bodies of men freely, was the victim of
loud cries and scandals? We are convinced of this by
His Divine words: *If they called the Master of the
house Beelzebub, how much more shall they call them
of his household* (Matt. 10:25); *if they persecuted Me,
they will persecute you also* (John 15:20).

It is no great puzzle that the enemy takes up arms
against him because he has established many through
his instructions in the firmness of the Faith and in a
pious life, to the destruction of the enmity which
exists between men. The enemy hates all of this and
raises slanders against him, thinking to shake him.
However, by the grace of God he is being preserved
and is not harmed in the least, nor does he lose courage
because of such things. Rather, he pities these souls
and eagerly forgives them and prays to God for them,
that He lay not this sin to their charge. And he has
great pity for you because you have stumbled in your
opinion about him to your own detriment. I feel sorry
for Fr. Leonid because of the false slander against
him, and likewise for you because you believe it. How
can your conscience be peaceful and calm when so

many souls are being falsely caused to stumble? The holy Apostle Paul writes to the Galatians in the fifth chapter, verse 10, *He that troubles you commits a sin.* This is how dangerous and woeful it is to spread false rumors that distress other people's consciences!

Furthermore, it is one thing when one is being accused only of some matter concerning his sinful way of life: this is something inherent in every person, for no one is without sin even if his life be but a single day (Job 14:4-5). But when the matter concerns the Faith, then he is obliged to defend and justify himself. St. Agatho was accused by certain people of various sins, and he replied to each one, "I am a sinner." But when they said to him, "Agatho is a heretic," he objected. And when they asked why he had suffered all the accusations with patience but did not endure this last one, he replied, "Those sins are inherent in a man, and we hope to receive forgiveness of them through the mercy of God; but a heretic is separated from God." You see how important this is; the Saint himself stood up against it. Likewise, we who love our father and know that he is right, are we not obligated to come to his defense and to demonstrate to you that he believes just as I have explained above? Moreover, his life is most virtuous and serves as an example for us and for many. All heresies, however, and teachings contrary to religious philosophy are developed in secrecy; yet we see nothing of the kind in him. If someone is convinced of the opposite, then let him judge as he pleases; but the judgment of God and the judgment of men differ widely. *Judge nothing before the time* . . . (I Cor. 4:5). At the Last Judgment, when we all shall stand before the righteous Judge, then not only the deeds but also the counsels of the heart of each will be revealed. Perhaps some will say: *Here is a man whom we once treated with mockery and scorn; how is he joined to the sons of God and has his lot among the saints?* (Wisdom 5:3, 5). I write this to you only because I feel sorry for you and want to bring you out of your erroneous opinion so as to put your spirit at ease. You see, I am certain that you have had no peace since you have accepted this opinion. I beg you, for the sake of the Lord and for your own benefit, to abandon it and not to believe those who are spreading it. I wish that the grace of God touch your heart, helping you to realize the truth of what I am writing.

Entrusting myself to your holy prayers, with the deepest respect, I remain Your Blessing's fervent co-intercessor, the very sinful

Hieromonk Macarius
January 24, 1839

We do not know what effect this persuasive and, at the same time, charitable letter of the humble Elder had on Fr. G. But the rumor Fr. G. had started — that he had supposedly uncovered a heresy in the Belev Convent — reached the local bishop during the course of that same year. Fr. G. and the Abbess were immediately summoned to Tula. To the questions of Bishop Damascene about the matter during the interrogation, Fr. G. did not hesitate to confirm his opinion about the supposed heresy, calling the Elder Leonid its "preacher" and claiming that the Eldress Anthia and Novice N. were spreading it in the Belev Convent. As proof of this he cited two of his spiritual daughters, who had reportedly been part of the heresy but who had then repented.

The Bishop was distressed by such unpleasant rumors about the Convent and worried that they might spread further, doing harm to his standing with the higher authorities. He hastily believed the words of Fr. G. and decided to cut off this evil at its very inception by strict measures, thus putting an end to the rumors which were unfavorable for both the Convent and the diocese in general.

The procedures were initiated by summoning Mother Anthia to Tula, following Fr. G.'s report. When she arrived in Tula, she was sent to Abbess Claudia of the Dormition Convent there at the directive of the Bishop, in order for her to be "dissuaded."

The Abbess acted with great fervor after hearing talk of a heresy and being frightened lest she herself get in trouble with the Bishop. She summoned Mother Anthia to her reception room, had her stand on her knees before the icons, and began to urge her insistently to admit to her errors with a pure heart, promising that if she did so she — the Abbess — would intercede for her forgiveness before the Bishop, and that he, being a child-loving father, simply wanted to learn the truth. Mother Anthia, who did not feel guilty of anything, simply and meekly replied to the Abbess that though she was sinful in general, she did not know about any heresy to which she supposedly belonged, and she asked her to explain to what it was she was expected to admit. Then the Abbess began to speak in a different tone. She began to describe the Elder, whom she did not know, in blasphemous terms, stating that he was a Mason and that he was seducing the innocent into his heresy.

Mother Anthia remarked that she did not know what the word "Mason" meant, but that she knew for certain that the Elder Leonid, whom the Abbess was slandering, was widely known as a person experienced in spiritual life: he taught nothing else but the correct path of monasticism according to the writings of the Holy Spirit-bearing Fathers who had shone forth in the monastic life.

The Abbess interrupted her with the question, "And what about these books of his he gave you to read?" "Yes," Mother Anthia replied, "I am now reading, at the Elder's advice, the book of Abba Dorotheus, which is the alphabet of the monastic life according to the words of the elders." The Abbess, however, who apparently had never read the book of Abba Dorotheus and who was eager to put an end to her unsuccessful "dissuasion," cried out, "There, you see, he's a Mason! A Mason, I tell you! You, my dear, have fallen into heresy; and if you do not repent, you will perish — you will surely perish. And in this life you will also be punished with exemplary severity."

Angered by her lack of success, the Abbess reported to the Bishop that Mother Anthia was a stubborn heretic who wouldn't admit to anything. The investigation regarding the other sisters accused of heresy (there were thirteen altogether) was entrusted to Abbot N. of the Novosilsk Holy Spirit Monastery. This investigator, even though he questioned each of the sisters individually, was unable to learn anything more than what had previously been known to the entire Convent: that these sisters went to the Eldress Anthia for spiritual counsel — something which neither she nor they had ever made any attempt to conceal. Because he did not want to accuse Fr. G. of jumping to conclusions too hastily, the investigator did not decide to absolve the sisters who had fallen victim to the Bishop's wrath, and therefore he reported that they were recalcitrant and refused to admit to anything.

After this investigation, which did not produce any concrete results, Bishop Damascene orally requested Abbess Epaphrodite to file a written report with him of all that had transpired in the Convent. The kindly but timid, elderly Abbess, seeing that in order to carry out this assignment she would have to accuse persons whom she considered innocent, decided through her own inward convictions that she would accuse them of being self-willed, rather than of heresy. In her report to the Bishop, dated November 24, 1840, she wrote concerning the accused sisters that she "had found no other heresy among them apart from the self-will of Mother Anthia alone."

Over two months passed before the final decision came concerning this report. During that time many sorrows visited the accused Eldress and the sisters devoted to her. But the Elders, Fr. Leonid and Fr. Macarius, themselves seasoned in sorrows, knew how to help those in the midst of temptation. Being themselves deeply convinced of the triumph of the truth which was under attack, they strengthened those in sorrows to persevere in expectation of a change for the better from *God, Who saves us from faintheartedness and the tempest* (Ps. 54:8), remembering that the Lord sends no one a temptation that exceeds his strength and that He does not hesitate to turn temptation into abundant profit. Of the letters written by the Elders to Mother Anthia and the sisters of one mind with her during these two years (1839-1841), we are printing one of them here below. It shows how the Elder regarded the essence of this matter:

Most Worthy in the Lord, Mother Anthia and M. N.!

We read your letter with no little astonishment. *O thou of little faith, wherefore didst thou doubt?* (Matt. 14:31), as our Divine Savior said to His beloved disciple Peter at the time that he was drowning. Now the same kind of drowning is happening to you; and with that same voice of the Savior we cry out to you: "O thou of little faith!" Do you mean to tell us that our frequent attempts to counsel you from the Divine Scriptures and the Holy God-bearing Fathers were unable to convince you of the true path to salvation on which the holy monastic fathers traveled and which we are trying to imitate, as far as we are able? Although we are unworthy and wanting in virtues, still we desire you, who seek salvation, to tread the path which they have shown us; for this reason your lack of courage grieves us. If it pleases you to listen to us, then *why do evil thoughts enter your heart?* (Matt. 9:4). Without making particularly subtle observations of the enemy of mankind, we see how he is making every effort, under the guise of truth, to deter you from your chosen path, from the path of virtue. We ask you, can a person who does not know a foreign language teach that language to someone else? There is a great difference between persons who have learned by experience and those who have knowledge from hearing alone. Let each person remain in the state wherein he was called. Experience is the best teacher. It is written: *Let your friends be many, but let one out of a thousand be your counsellor* (Sirach 6:6). If you doubt our advice and counsel, then why do you come to us? We draw no one to ourselves; you know that.

According to the rule of the monastic tradition, at the tonsure from the Gospel one is entrusted to an eldress, and not to a spiritual father, to whom [that is, to the eldress] the beginner must reveal her conscience in order to receive advice and instructions on how to withstand the temptations of the enemy; yet this is not confession but revelation of thoughts. In this instance the apostolic tradition is fulfilled, *confess your sins one to another* (James 5:16). Now the Sacrament of Confession is something entirely different and has nothing to do with revelation of thoughts; the duties of the spiritual father are entirely different than the relationship to an eldress. We remind you of a certain lady of the court who was entrusted to a certain eldress by the Bishop, and he asked the woman how she treated her. When he heard the reply that she was too kind, he then entrusted her to another, a stricter eldress. After some time he learned from her that this eldress had softened the lady's character somewhat. Is this not an example of the tradition we are discussing? Your Abbess is acting wisely and in keeping with the rules of monastic tradition by desiring that her sisters be taught ahead of time (prior to the monastic tonsure) to purify their consciences. By this means she is providing a genuine period of trial, in keeping with the tradition of the Holy Fathers who have shone forth in the monastic life.

The assertion that supposedly one is not permitted to pray in one's cell without a priest is something that deserves more amazement than belief. How many women saints do we see who lived in the desert and shone forth in asceticism? What did they do, if they did not pray in solitude? St. Mary of Egypt offered her prayers in the desert without any priest, and it was only in the last year of her life that she was granted to see St. Zosima and to receive from him the Holy Mysteries of Christ. The practice of not doing anything without the blessing of the eldress is not only beneficial, but it leads to salvation as well. From all the many examples to be found in the Patericon and the writings of the Holy Fathers, we remind you of the disciple who was sent by his elder on obedience into the city; he almost fell into fornication, but as soon as he remembered his elder, he was taken by an invisible force and found himself in his cell. As for eldership, in convents this applies to eldresses. Not all elders were priests; this is clearly to be seen in the life of St. Paphnutius of Borov, the Wonderworker (May 1). He had 700 brothers in his monastery, and not a single one of them was a priest; but every one of them was under the direction of elders. Thus it is better to conform to the rules of the monastic life and to remain calm.

In the *Philokalia,* in the epistle of St. Cassian to Abbot Leontius[1] there is written: "Abba Moses said, 'We reveal to our spiritual fathers not only what we do but also what we think, by never trusting our own thoughts and by following in all things the words of our elders, regarding as good what they have judged to be so. In this way not only does the monk remain unharmed, through true discrimination and by following the correct path, but he is also kept safe from all the snares of the devil.'" Having reminded your love of a little from much, and entrusting you to God's protection and the word of His grace, we remain your unworthy intercessors, the very sinful Hiero-schemamonk Leonid and the very sinful Hieromonk Macarius.

September 19, 1840

---

1. St. John Cassian, "On the Holy Fathers of Scetis and on Discrimination, written for Abba Leontios," *The Philokalia*, Vol. I, Faber and Faber Ltd., 1979, p. 103.

Finally, the following decision came from the Bishop, in response to the report submitted by Abbess Epaphrodite, in February, 1841. "Nun Anthia, after being deprived of the ryassa, is to be expelled from the Convent immediately. Her civil documents are to be sent to the authorities (in Belev) so that they can be returned to her. The novices who have not yet been officially registered with the authorities, but who are living in the Convent contrary to the directions of the authorities, are likewise to be expelled from the Convent. The Abbess, for her weak supervision over the persons living in the Convent and for failure to carry out the directives of the authorities, is forbidden to wear the mantia for two weeks, with the warning that in the future she be more attentive to the good order of the Convent and not permit distracting rumors to be circulated about it."

This decision, which condemned to expulsion Mother Anthia and all the sisters who came to her for counsel, was not enforced in full. The Abbess managed to persuade the Bishop to be satisfied with the expulsion of the two who were more guilty and stubborn: Mother Anthia and the young lady from the nobility, M. N. S. They were subsequently expelled from the convent. The rest of the sisters stayed there under intense suspicion and strict supervision.

Word of what had happened in Belev spread everywhere and provoked new suppressive measures concerning Fr. Leonid. His enemies depicted him as some kind of self-willed violator of monastic rules and a stubborn rebel against the authorities. The Abbot received a directive that the Elder move from the cell built for him at the apiary by Zhelyabuzhsky into another cell as far as possible from the gate and from visitors. This took place in 1840; it was the fourth time that the Elder had been ordered to move since 1835, and it was the last time. All of these forced moves Fr. Leonid accepted with a magnanimous spirit; he was not suppressed by them in the least. When he would be informed that he had been ordered to move to another place, the Elder would take the Vladimir Icon of the Mother of God in his hands and begin to chant loudly, "It is truly meet to bless Thee, the Theotokos"; and he would go to his new cell. As soon as he had put the icon in place and prayed, he would sit back down as if nothing had happened and continue what he had been doing: braiding belts and receiving visitors. Meanwhile, his close disciples would walk behind the Elder, carrying his books and the other furnishings of his cell. So he moved into his new home quite simply.

At the same time that Fr. Leonid was to move to another cell, the diocesan authorities also strictly forbade him to receive lay visitors; but this was not to to be in effect for long. In addition, the ailing Elder was ordered to attend the daily services in church, but in this way a triumphant procession was involuntarily arranged for him. The people awaited the moment he would appear; as soon as he came out, many would fall to the ground and kiss the hem of his garments. Others would loudly proclaim their expressions of sympathy for him. It took Fr. Leonid at least half an hour to make his way between two walls of people along the short distance between his cell and the church. He chased away by means of his walking stick and with humor those that pressed in on him. Everyone tried to grab his hand and receive his blessing. On the left cliros, where the Elder stood, a huge crowd of people would gather.

Meanwhile, there were rumors that Fr. Leonid would be exiled to the Solovetsk Monastery. Others were saying that he would be taken under supervision to the hospital of the Borov Monastery, and that no one would be allowed to see him. The disciples of Fr. Leonid at Optina, St. Tikhon's and at Maloyaroslavets spoke in horror about the possible fate of their 72 year-old Elder being imprisoned in a state-operated monastery. Fearing for the Elder, they were also afraid for themselves: in his absence, who could guide them along the path to salvation? As long as Fr. Leonid was alive, none of them could be called "elder"; and no one else was shown such complete faith, nor did anyone else's word have such great power. He was like a great oak; they were grafted onto him like weaker plants. If he were taken away, it would all come to nothing. It is true that after his death, Fr. Leonid, as it were, came back to life in Fr. Macarius; but at that time it seemed impossible to live without Fr. Leonid. His disciples suggested to the Elder to defend and justify himself and to write to Fr. Ignatius Brianchaninov, the Archimandrite of the St. Sergius Hermitage, to intercede for him before the members of the Holy Synod, and especially with Philaret, the Metropolitan of Moscow, who was then serving his turn in St. Petersburg. Having unshakeable faith in the Providence which protects us and permits no temptation that surpasses our strength, or perhaps having received some revelation from on high that the Optina Monastery would be his resting place, the Elder replied to all the worried and sympathetic talk about him with silence; he braided his belts and received those who came to him as previously. Finally Fr. Macarius, at the head of them all, made up his mind to convince Fr. Leonid to take care of himself, at least for the sake of his disciples. "What will come of us if you are taken to Borov?" "They won't take me," replied Fr. Leonid. "I'm going to die right here." "Father, we are fainthearted; we don't have your faith. Take pity on us and permit us to write to Fr. Ignatius; all you have to do is sign. We all beg you to do this!" For some time the intense entreaties of his disciples continued. In the end, Fr. Leonid gave in to these entreaties of his disciples when he saw that they were not going to let him be and that their fear for him was growing daily. He told Fr. Macarius in reply to this last request, "Write what you want; I'll sign without reading."

Fr. Macarius hastened to take advantage of this final permission given by the Elder; and in the Elder's name he wrote a letter, part of the contents of which are as follows:

"You desire to put me at ease in my old age and are seeking for measures and means to do so. . . . I appreciate this fully and, while accepting, offer you my sincere gratitude. As for the situation in which I currently find myself, I can tell you this: the circumstances that concern me personally, of which you may be aware, I accept magnanimously with God's help. While I do not dare to say, 'I can do all things through Christ Who strengthens me,' yet I know that the merciful Lord, knowing my weakness, sends such temptations so that I might endure them; and I believe that without His will, nothing will come about, and that whatever does come about will be for the profit and salvation of my very sinful soul. . . . Concerning my neighbors I am obliged to take an active part in their sorrows and sympathize with them with compassion when I see them ailing and still in need of protection from soul-harming circumstances; I am concerned lest such circumstances become for them a stumbling stone and a scandal at the expense of their spiritual disposition. . . . I do not oppose your fervor on my behalf. Whatever the Lord inspires you to do in putting my old age at rest or to speak in defending me against false accusations, I will be grateful for; especially because this applies not to me alone, but to all those who in God are kindly disposed towards me. Of course for all of this the Lord will not deprive you of His reward for showing compassion to your neighbor."

This letter, written by Fr. Macarius and signed by Fr. Leonid without his reading it, was sent to Petersburg. One of Fr. Leonid's disciples was living at that time in the St. Sergius Hermitage, as if sent there on purpose for a brief time to take part in this affair. Fr. Ioannicius sent the letter of Fr. Macarius and Fr. Leonid to this disciple for delivering personally to Fr. Ignatius and for participating in general. The letter was received in the evening; the next morning Archimandrite Ignatius visited the Metropolitan of Moscow.

After he had acquainted himself with the matter, this great Hierarch wrote to Kaluga that "there is no reason to suspect Fr. Leonid of heresy." Rumors of the Elder's being taken from the Optina Monastery were silenced. However, during his last visit with Fr. Leonid, Bishop Nicholas asked him, "Elder, are you going to keep bothering with all of these people for much longer? Isn't it about time for you to get some rest?" The truthful and forthright Elder retorted with the words of the Psalm, "*I will sing unto my God as long as I have my being*" (Ps. 103:35). The Bishop liked this reply very much; silently he left the Elder to live as before. Subsequently he cited these words of Elder Leonid for the instruction of others. When Fr. Anthony, the Abbot of Maloyaroslavets, petitioned for retirement in 1843, the Bishop in his letter of reply stated, among other things, "The elders of former times, in such instances, spoke with the Royal Prophet: *I will sing unto my God as long as I have my being. . . .* I recommend that you follow the example of men made wise by God."[2]

No matter what changes occurred in Fr. Leonid's situation, he bore everything with an undisturbed spirit.

"Our common and all-wicked enemy, the devil," he wrote to one of his spiritual sons, "although he does make a lot of trouble for us, can accomplish nothing if we put our hope in God, recalling this instruction: *Blessed are ye when men shall revile you and persecute you and shall say all manner of evil against you falsely for My sake; rejoice and be exceeding glad, for great is your reward in heaven* [Matt. 5:11-12]. And although there is some stain within us, nevertheless the Lord, being Almighty, has long preserved my nothingness, and hoping that he will do so in the future I entrust myself to His Providence." "You are anxious

---

2. See *Elder Anthony of Optina*, St. Herman of Alaska Brotherhood, 1994, p. 72.

about my wretchedness, as if I am being offended," he wrote to another person. "This anxiety proves your feelings of love towards me and for this I offer you heartfelt thanks. But as for me, thanks be to the Most High and All-good Providence over me! I see no sorrows which are unendurable. Even if such sorrows arise, I receive help from God to endure them also. It is impossible for us to be entirely delivered from them when our Lord Jesus Christ has left them for an inheritance. For He Himself suffered for us. The holy Apostles, also, in the midst of many teachings about patience and the necessity of sorrows, wrote that *we must through much tribulation enter into the Kingdom of Heaven* [Acts 14:22]. Therefore, without seeking for voluntary sorrows we have to submit to the will of God. Whatever sorrows it pleases Him to send us, we must accept with thanksgiving."

It was with feelings such as these that the Elder met and endured all the sorrow that came upon him; he took no care for his own fate. But he was unable not to sorrow over his spiritual daughters who had suffered many sorrows innocently. After their expulsion from the Convent, Mother Anthia and M. N. S. did not know where to lay their heads because wherever they showed themselves they were always received with distrust and suspicion. Mother Anthia went to Voronezh and wanted to find in the convent there a little corner for a time. When she met with a nun there she asked, "Has M. N. S. been here?" Fearfully the nun replied, "Yes, she was, and she stayed with us for a few days. But we are afraid to talk about it; we don't want to get into trouble ourselves. They say that she is some kind of heretic. We also heard there was some Anthia in Belev; they say she has been exiled to Siberia." When she heard this reply about herself, Mother Anthia, of course, had to leave Voronezh and live the life of a homeless wanderer until things changed.

The sisters of one mind with Mother Anthia who stayed in the Convent also became the victims of great sorrows and insults. But in all these sorrows they were supported by their mutual bond of love and oneness of mind. Common sorrows and persecutions bring people closer together, and the love and oneness of mind that ruled between their Elders and instructors, Fr. Leonid and Fr. Macarius, were reflected in their spiritual daughters, also. According to the words of one of the persecuted sisters who is now the Abbess of the Convent, Mother Paulina, their joys and sorrows were held in common. If one of their number was consoled this became a joy for them all. They knew of no envy; to the contrary, the sorrow of each sister was shared and relieved by the mutual participation and mutual love of all the sisters. A great source of strength and consolation in the midst of their sorrows was the fatherly love of Elder Leonid, who, during this difficult time for them, did not deprive them of his oral and written instructions. When the expelled Mother Anthia came to Optina Monastery, the Elder at the time was very busy with a pressing multitude of visitors; but when he learned of her arrival, he announced decisively, "Even if a sword were hanging over my head, I would still have to receive Mother Anthia." Possessing absolute faith in Divine Providence, the Elder in every way encouraged the sisters who had grown discouraged and were being slandered. In consolation he assured them, "Be patient for the Lord's sake; your sorrow will be changed into joy. I believe in the Lord," he added, "that to the same extent as the Belev Convent has now fallen into ill-repute, to the same degree will it later be glorified. I believe that the Belev Convent will be mine, that it will have an Abbess of mine." When Mother Paulina, the present Abbess of the Belev Convent, heard these words of Fr. Leonid she thought to herself in bewilderment, "How can this be? It must be," she thought, "that for the restoration of our Convent they will send some nun from Sevsk." She could not even imagine that these words of Fr. Leonid applied to herself because of the sad and disgraced position she was in.

The predictions of the great Elder soon began to be fulfilled. Metropolitan Philaret of Kiev came to the assistance of the expelled sisters of Belev. Fr. Leonid had asked for his defence in writing, not for himself, but for the nuns who were suffering such deprivation only because they wanted to benefit from his spiritual instructions and to lead a monastic life according to the precepts of the Holy Fathers. The Hierarch of Kiev, as was noted above, had known Fr. Leonid very well for a long time. He wrote to the Bishop of Tula, Damascene, in justification of the Elder and the slandered nuns. Metropolitan Philaret of Moscow also wrote on the same theme to Bishop Damascene, who soon was convinced that he had been deceived by Fr. G.'s misguided zeal. Towards the end of that same year, on October 4th, 1841, both of the expelled sisters were once again received into the Convent with the permission of the Bishop. Elder Leonid, who reposed on October 11th of that same year, was consoled and put at rest just a few days before his death by the news that the persecution against his spiritual daughters had come to an end.

A few years later, in 1848, the prophecy of the Elder was fulfilled in its entirety. Mother Paulina, one of the closest disciples of the Elder and of Mother Anthia, was elected and consecrated as Abbess of the Belev Convent. Mother Anthia herself, tonsured to the mantia with the name Magdalena, was appointed treasurer of the same Convent. Up to her very death she was a zealous assistant to the Abbess, especially in the inner, spiritual care of the Convent. Being an experienced Eldress she served as an intermediary between the sisters and the Abbess in their various needs: reconciling those who were at odds, humbling the obstinate, consoling the fainthearted and comforting the infirm and ailing. The Abbess revered her as a tender daughter honors her own mother. The respect of the spiritual authorities and the respectful attentiveness of all who had any dealings with the Convent or its Abbess served as a full reward for the sorrows the Eldress had endured during the beginning of her life at the Convent. Under Abbess Paulina and the treasurer, Eldress Magdalena, the Belev Convent began to flourish, in keeping with Fr. Leonid's prediction. Bishop Damascene erased in their hearts the memory of former sorrows by the trust and fatherly attentiveness that he constantly showed throughout the entire time of his administration of the diocese to those who had been innocently placed under suspicion. He earned their mutual love and a grateful memory for his personal attention to them — especially for his protection and approval of that very same spiritual relationship which had previously been presented to him in a distorted manner.

M. N. S., another close disciple of Elder Leonid who bore with Mother Anthia the greater share of sufferings, was named Macaria in monasticism. In 1862 she was made Abbess of the Kashira Convent, which she is governing successfully even until now [1875].

As for Fr. G., he realized his mistake and his guilt but did not make up his mind to offer public repentance before all for the public scandal and the distress of many persons. However, on many occasions he asked forgiveness in private of Mother Anthia (Magdalena) and others. Incidentally, by the mysterious workings of God's judgments he was taken from this life while still middle-aged.

VII

The Last Days and Repose
of Elder Leonid

THE ACCOUNT OF THE MONK PARTHENIUS

IN SEPTEMBER, 1841, the Monk Parthenius who was tonsured on the holy Mount Athos visited the Optina Monastery. He later became Abbot of the Guslits Monastery which he founded in the Moscow Diocese. In his account of his travels[1] he included the following curious narrative of his meeting with Elder Leonid.

On the fifth day, from the White Bluff Hermitage I arrived at the coenobitic Optina Monastery which is in the Kaluga Diocese near the city of Kozelsk. Many years before I had heard of the great Elder living at the Optina Monastery, Hiero-schemamonk Leonid; and for a long time I had longed to see him, to delight in his conversation and to receive guidance and consolation from him in my sorrows. After arriving at the Optina Monastery, I impatiently wanted to go to see Fr. Leonid in the hope of receiving some consolation for myself, and after asking where his cell was, I went to him without hesitation. When I came to the porch I began

---

1. *The Narrative of the Travels of the Monk Parthenius*, Moscow, 1856, Part 1, pp. 275-280 (in Russian).

to fear, partially out of joy that I was found worthy to behold such a great Father and partially at the thought of how could I, so unworthy, appear before so great an Elder. I stood on the porch a long time, afraid to open the door. Finally, his disciple came out. I inquired, "Is it possible to see the Elder?" He replied, "Yes, it is." Then I entered his cell; but then and there I feared all the more and began to tremble. Almost the entire cell was filled with individuals from various walks of life: landowners, merchants and simple folk. All were standing on their knees in fear and trembling, as if before a fearsome judge; and each one was waiting for his replies and instruction. I likewise fell to my knees behind everyone else. The Elder was sitting on his bed and braiding a belt. This was his handiwork, braiding belts, and he gave them as a blessing to his visitors. Then the Elder called out, "You there, the Athonite Father, why did you fall to your knees? What do you want: for me to kneel down, too?" I was struck with terror by this because he had never seen me and did not know me; I was wearing plain attire, but he called me an Athonite Father. I replied, "Forgive me, holy Father, for the Lord's sake. I am only observing the custom; I saw that everyone is kneeling, so I fell to my knees." But he said, "They are lay people, and, moreover, guilty ones; they can kneel. But you are a monk, and, furthermore, an Athonite one; stand up and come here to me." I arose and approached him. He blessed me, and told me to sit with him on the bed. He asked me many things about the holy Mount Athos, the monastic life of solitude and the communal monastic life, and about the various Athonite rules and customs. The entire time he kept braiding the belt with his hands. I told him everything in detail, and he wept from joy and glorified the Lord God that He still has faithful servants who have left the world and all worldly care, and who serve and labor for their Lord with faith and love. Then he began to dismiss the people. He tended to each one's ailments of body and soul: those of the body with prayer and those of the soul with fatherly love, meek words and instructions profitable for the soul — though some persons received a severe reprimand and some were even expelled from his cell.

Among these people kneeling before him was a certain gentleman who had come to worship at the Monastery and to visit the great Elder. The Elder asked him, "And you, what do you want from me?" With tears the gentleman replied, "I want, holy Father, to receive instruction profitable for my soul." The Elder asked, "And did you do what I told you to before?" He replied, "No, holy Father, I am unable to do that." The Elder said, "Then why did you come to ask for something else, if you didn't do the first?" Then he told his disciples in a stern voice, "Toss him out of my cell." And they removed him. I, and everyone else who was there, was frightened by such a severe action and punishment. But the Elder was not upset at all; once again he began to speak meekly with the others and to let people leave. Then one of his disciples said, "Holy Father, there's a gold coin on the floor." He said, "Give it to me." They brought it. The Elder said, "That gentleman dropped it on purpose, and he did well; it will come in handy for the Athonite father on his journey." And he gave me a half-crown (a five-rouble) gold coin.

Then I asked the Elder, "Holy Father, why did you treat the gentleman with such extreme strictness?" He replied to me, "Athonite Father, I know how to treat each person. He is a servant of God and wants to be saved, but he fell into a certain passion: he became addicted to tobacco. He used to come and ask me about it. I told him to stop using tobacco and gave him a commandment never to use it again and not to come to see me until he quits. But without fulfilling the first commandment, he came for another. You see, beloved Athonite Father, how difficult it is to uproot passions in a man!"

While we were speaking a sick woman was brought to him; she had lost her mind and reason. The three women that brought her were crying and begged the Elder to pray for the ailing woman. He put on his epitrachelion, placing the end of it and his hands on the sick woman's head. After he had read a prayer, he made the cross over her head three times and told them to take her to the guest house. He did all this while seated, and remained seated because he was unable to stand; he was sick and was living through his final days. Then each of his disciples, the brothers of the Monastery, came to him to reveal his conscience before him and the wounds of his soul. He tended to each one and gave them instructions. Then he told them that his end was approaching and said, "How long, my children, will you not be wise as serpents and innocent as doves? How long will you continue to ail? How long will you continue to need instruction? It's already time for you yourselves to be wise and to become teachers, but you still grow weak and fall every day. How are you going to live without me? I am living through my final days; I have to leave you and give what is my due to nature and depart to my Lord." When his disciples heard this, they began to weep bitterly. Then he dismissed them all, and myself as well.

The next day I came to him again, and once more he received me with love and spoke with me at length. Then the women from the previous day came. The sick one was with them, but no longer ailing; she was completely well. They had come to thank the Elder. When I saw this, I was astonished; and I told the Elder, "Holy Father, how do you dare to perform such works? Through human fame you can lose all your labors and ascetic struggles." But in reply he told me, "Athonite Father! I did not do this by my own power. The grace of the Holy Spirit imparted to me at ordination did this, and it happened according to the faith of the people that came; as for me, I am a sinful man." When I heard that, I was greatly profited by his good discretion, faith and humility. Then once again the gentleman from yesterday came in and begged for the Elder's forgiveness with tears. The Elder forgave him and told him to do what he had previously been told. Then he dismissed us all.

I spent an entire week at the Optina Monastery and celebrated there the Feast of the Nativity of the All-Holy Theotokos. There was a solemn all-night vigil. During the polyeleos all three psalms were chanted verse by verse, and all the brothers and people stood with burning candles. Many times I visited the quiet and hesychastic Skete, which is about half a kilometer from the Monastery in the midst of the forest. Many times I spoke there with the fathers; with Hieromonk John, who had been converted from the Old-Believers; and also with the spiritual father, Hieromonk Macarius. I also spoke often with the hospitable Abbot of Optina, Moses. Then I set out on my way. Elder Leonid reached the end of his life and departed to his Lord a month after my visit.

It was not without sorrow that the Elder approached the end of his labor-filled life; he sensed its approach or he received some revelation from the Lord. In June, 1841, he visited St. Tikhon's Hermitage, where, with his blessing, the construction of a new refectory had begun. Speaking about the new building, the Elder told the Abbot, "I won't see your new refectory, I guess." The Abbot objected, "Maybe the Lord will prolong your life, and you will console us once again with your visit." Again the Elder said, "No, I will scarcely live until wintertime, and I will not be here again." When he had returned to the Optina Monastery he told many people, "I will not live until winter"; and he gave several of them a final solution to their problems.

To a certain famous person who visited the Optina Monastery during the summer of 1841, the Elder said, "Stay here, if you want, until November so you can bury me." But this person decided not to stay. Later when the

THE CHURCH OF ST. JOHN THE FORERUNNER AT THE OPTINA SKETE

news of Fr. Leonid's death reached him, he was very amazed at how his words had come to pass.

From the beginning of September, Fr. Leonid's health began to fail and he was sick for five weeks. He felt a sharp pain in his right side, his chest became congested and he was extremely constipated. The people who surrounded the Elder wanted to summon a physician, but he would not agree and did not want to take any medication. Until September 15, the Elder still moved about his cell. On the Feasts of the Nativity of the All-Holy Theotokos and the Exaltation of the Holy Cross of the Lord during the all-night vigils, which were served in his cell due to his illness, he himself censed and chanted the Magnification at the appointed times, being supported by the brothers.

On the 15th he received Holy Unction in the midst of a large gathering of the brethren who loved him. At that time Abbot Anthony of the Maloyaroslavets Monastery and Fr. Leonid's disciple, the Abbot of the St. Tikhon's Hermitage, Fr. Gerontius, both arrived as if they had been informed. They performed the Mystery of Holy Unction together with the Elder's co-struggler, Fr. Macarius; Abbot Barlaam,[2] who was living there in retirement; and others. From that day, the Elder began to prepare intently for death. He bid farewell to the brothers who came to him and blessed them: giving one a book, another an icon and leaving no one without some consolation. On September 28, after he communed of the Holy Mysteries of Christ, he wished that they would chant the Canon for the Departure of the Soul. The brothers around him were distressed and, at the thought of becoming orphans, began with weeping to entreat him not to leave them in sorrow. When he saw and heard this, he was afflicted in spirit and, with tears welling up in his eyes, he said, "Chil-

---

2. Fr. Barlaam was formerly Abbot of Valaam Monastery (1830-33) and a friend of St. Herman of Alaska. He retired to live a life of seclusion and settled in the Optina Skete.

dren! If I find boldness with the Lord, I will receive all of
you where I am going. I am entrusting you to the Lord. He
will help you to finish your course here; only cleave to Him.
He will preserve you from all temptations. Don't be distressed that you have chanted the canon; maybe you will
chant it six or seven times." And in fact, from September
28 to the day of the Elder's repose on October 11, the
canon was chanted a total of eight times. He took no food
at all during this period, apart from a little water. He was
strengthened only by the heavenly Bread, the Most Pure
Body and Blood of our Lord Jesus Christ, for during these
final two weeks he was granted to partake of these Mysteries
twelve times. After October 6, the Elder was unable to
stand up. Lying on his death bed he would call out in a
compunctionate voice, "O, Ruler of All Things! O Redeemer!
O All-Merciful Lord! Thou seest my illness; I can endure
no longer. Receive my spirit in peace." And then, "Lord,
into Thy hands I commit my spirit." Likewise he called out
to the All-Blessed Mother, the All-Holy Theotokos, imploring
her for help. He told the fathers and brothers who came,
"Pray that the Lord shorten my sufferings." But then once
again, submitting to God's will and entrusting himself to His
Providence, he called out, "Lord, Thy will be done! Do
what is pleasing in Thy sight."

When Saturday, October 11 arrived, Fr. Leonid partook
of the Holy Mysteries in the morning. That same morning
the Fool-for-Christ Basil Petrovich Braguzin, who was well-
known in that area, arrived at the Optina Monastery to
bid farewell to the dying Elder. He had been over 180 kilometers away from the Monastery at the house of the Dubro-
vins when he beheld in spirit the repose of the Elder; and
with this news he had alarmed his hosts, who themselves
hastened to Optina by the post road. When Braguzin entered
the Elder's cell (he had always maintained spiritual unity
with the Elder), he said, "It's time to change your clothes";
by this he signified the approaching death of the Elder.

"Basil Petrovich, pray that the Lord deliver me from eternal death," the Elder said quietly. "Hopefully, He'll deliver you," Braguzin replied very slowly to this humble request of the great ascetic.

About ten o'clock Fr. Leonid began to cross himself, saying, "Glory to God!" He repeated these words many times; then he fell silent for a while. He then told those present, "Now the mercy of God will be with me." About an hour after these words, he began to rejoice more and more in spirit and to be gladsome in heart. Although he was suffering great physical pain, still, because of his hope in the approaching blessings, he could not hide the spiritual joy he was experiencing: his face began to grow brighter and brighter. The bell for Vespers rang; the Elder blessed his disciples to read Small Vespers, but he was unable to hear it to the end. When he told them to stop reading his disciple, the Novice James (later Hieromonk Joachim) said compunctionately, "Then rest, Father; you will probably finish over there, in the assembly of the Holy Fathers." The Feast of the memory of the Holy Fathers of the Seventh Ecumenical Council was beginning, as appointed for the Sunday after October 11. It was on the eve of this day that the Lord was pleased to receive the soul of His faithful servant, as if in rebuke of those who out of their ignorance had called him a heretic. The dying Elder called out several times, "Glory to God! Glory to God! Glory to Thee, O Lord!" To those who asked questions, he replied with divinely wise answers filled with great benefit. Then bidding farewell to all that were around him, he hastily dismissed them. Only one disciple remained with him, who shortly noticed that his breathing became less frequent and that he quickly glanced at the icon of the Most Pure Theotokos; he called in the others. The Elder no longer spoke. When he saw his disciples he lifted his right hand, crossed himself, then blessed them all and glanced once again at the icon of the Mother of God, as if asking Her intercession for his disciples. After this, at 7:30 in the evening, he closed his eyes, quietly surrendered his spirit and departed from these present sorrows and pains to eternal rest.

Many who were devoted to the Elder in distant places had mystical and consoling revelations concerning his blessed repose.

His body lay in the church for three days without exuding any odor of death; it warmed his clothing and even the bottom plank of his coffin. His hands remained soft, as if he were alive, and had a unique whiteness. During his illness the Elder's body and hands had been cold, and he told many who loved him, especially his beloved cell-attendant James, "If I receive God's mercy, my body will heat up and stay warm."

Up to his burial, the church was full from morning to evening with people who came to pay their last respects to the one who had been the spiritual father and unmercenary physician for all who came to him. At his funeral, which was celebrated on October 13 by Abbot Moses together with all the hieromonks and hierodeacons who were present, the crowds of people were enormous — as if for a great feast. Although in the Monastery the custom of kissing the body of the reposed was not observed, still, overcome by their great love for the deceased, during the entire Liturgy and funeral people in an endless stream kissed his hand with tears. When the time came to carry out his body, the crowds began to press more and more around the coffin of the Elder. Immersed in grief over the loss of their beloved Father, the brothers rushed in a crowd to carry his coffin; lay visitors were unable to draw near because of the multitude of brothers. Basil Petrovich Braguzin was in a triumphant spirit during the funeral, but when he bade the Elder farewell, he wept.

Elder Leonid's body by the common wish of the Abbot and brotherhood was buried next to the Catholicon of the Entrance of the Theotokos, opposite the chapel of

St. Nicholas the Wonderworker. The site was alongside the grave of his spiritual son and friend in the Lord, Alexius Ivanovich Zhelyabuzhsky, who had died a few months before Fr. Leonid on June 11 of that same year, 1841. During his lifetime Fr. Leonid had told him jokingly, "Old man! We're going to lie down together side by side." These words of the Elder were recalled later, and people were amazed at how precise they were.

At the graves of Fr. Leonid and A. I. Zhelyabuzhsky two tall memorials of cast iron were erected, identical in form, gilded and surrounded by an iron fence. On the memorial of Fr. Leonid the visitor could read the following inscription:

1. What man is there who shall live and not see death; but blessed are they who die in the Lord: yea, they find rest from their labors.

2. This monument covers the body of Hiero-schema-monk Leonid (Leo) who reposed peacefully in the Lord; he bore the good yoke of Christ in monasticism for 46 years. He was born in Karachev of the family named Nagolkin.

3. He fell asleep in the hope of resurrection and life eternal. He left his memory in the hearts of many who received consolation in their sorrows.

4. He died on October 11, 1841. In all, his life spanned 72 years.

5. Fervor and love for him erected this monument.

After Fr. Leonid's death, his orphaned spiritual children were in great sorrow over losing their spiritual father and guide. But this sorrow was mixed with the good hope that the Elder had found the mercy of God and was interceding on behalf of all his children. Here is how these common feelings were expressed in letters to various people by his closest disciple and successor, Fr. Macarius: "Our beloved

Father Leonid is no longer with us. His body has been hidden by the moist earth, and his soul has surely departed into the hands of God. . . . You will probably grieve over our being left orphans, but at the same time console yourself in spirit over his rest, which he undoubtedly will find with God. . . . Apparently the time appointed for him by God's decision had come, and it was necessary for the soul to depart from the flesh to be set free from the sorrows and pain here in order to pass into eternal rest. . . . One cannot doubt that he was vouchsafed mercy by the Lord and surely will intercede for us sinners who still wander in this vale of tears, assailed by passions of soul and body."

"Your feeling of love for our honorably blessed and beloved Father Leonid," wrote Fr. Macarius to Abbot Anthony of Maloyaroslavets, "found beautiful expression in what you wrote to me on October 17, together with your sympathy over his departure from us. You and all the brothers gathered around; you poured forth tears free from deceit, tears of sincere grief over being separated from such a Father. Yes, it seems that there are few among those who knew him who do not offer him this tribute. *The memory of the righteous is with praises* (Prov. 10:7); this proved true of him. And what tidings I receive from the Convents! O what happened there when they received news of his death — weeping and lamentation and great mourning! In Sevsk they instituted the reading of the Psalter for 40 days and thought that only a few of the most devoted would do the reading. But instead they all came running to honor his memory with the doxology of God and prayer for him without interruption — up to 200 people are reading voluntarily. The Abbess in Tver writes that she cannot stop her tears after she delayed her journey and thus deprived herself of seeing him and receiving his blessing. She instituted like commemoration of him there and made donations to several of the churches for his commemoration. From Borisov, M. T. writes that all that were devoted to our Father were extremely grieved over his death; it is only the hope that he has found eternal blessedness that encourages them and thus scatters the darkness of sorrow. . . . In truth our Monastery is fortunate that the Lord granted us so virtuous an ascetic to be in our midst. Although the dark grave has concealed his body from our gaze, mentally we remember and behold his fatherly love for us and believe that in spirit he abides with us."

In 1842, the Optina Monastery was visited by His Eminence, Metropolitan Philaret of Kiev and Galits, on his way from St. Petersburg to Kiev. Wanting to honor the memory of the blessed Elder Leonid whom he so deeply respected, he served a Lity at his grave. The next year, 1843, Bishop Nicholas of Kaluga came to the Optina Monastery. He served a solemn Panikhida and then a Lity at the grave of Elder Leonid. In speaking with the Abbot and the brothers, Bishop Nicholas expressed his reverence for the deceased Elder. At the same time he openly stated his regret that, because of misunderstandings, he had not appreciated the Elder during his lifetime but had believed unjust rumors about him. "I am also human," the Bishop stated, "and I can thus err by believing what some people had told me." Bishop Nicholas also expressed the desire that information on the life of Fr. Leonid be gathered and that his biography be published. Thus the humble Elder was accorded honor by that same Archpastor who had previously regarded his ministry of benefiting suffering mankind with doubt and distrust.

But above all, it was time which vindicated Fr. Leonid. The dignity of every teacher and the correctness of his teaching is known above all by its fruit. The teaching of Fr. Leonid and his personal influence, wherever it extended, wherever it was and is accepted with fervor, found and still finds a warm reception, always produced and produces the most beneficial effects. Many are indebted to the labors of Fr. Leonid for the prosperity and flourishing of three monasteries in the Kaluga Diocese and five convents in other dioceses, where worthy disciples of his were appointed abbots and abbesses — some during Fr. Leonid's lifetime and some after his death. Who can count the great number of private individuals, monks and laymen who found the sure path to salvation of soul through the fatherly care of Fr. Leonid and who always blessed with thankfulness the memory of the Elder? The voices and echoes of Fr. Leonid's opponents have long ago fallen silent; his name has become known throughout all Orthodox Russia and is spoken with reverence by all advocates of monasticism. At the grave of Fr. Leonid one frequently hears "Memory Eternal" proclaimed by the ministers of the Church, due to the fervor and love of the numerous devotees of the Elder. The word of Holy Scripture was fulfilled in him, that *the name of a pious man abideth unto the ages, and his glory will not be wanting; the people will shew forth his wisdom, and his praises will the Church declare* (Sirach 44:13-14).

Spiritual
Counsels
of Elder Leonid

I

A Disciple's Questions
and the Replies of the Elder

THE DISCIPLE'S questions and the Elder's replies we
are providing here are the personal notes of one of Fr. Leonid's
disciples, Paul Petrovich Tambovtsev. Born in the Kursk
Province, in the city of Belgorod, he was the son of a wealthy
merchant. He received a very inadequate schooling for his
natural abilities, but educated himself by diligently reading
the Holy Scriptures, the works of the Holy Fathers and,
above all, by the counsels and encouragement of Elder
Leonid. He occupied himself with copying out the books
of the Holy Fathers and for a time he wrote down Elder
Leonid's replies to his numerous spiritual children, through
the dictation of the Elder. In all instances where there was a
problem or lack of clarity, he sought the solution from Elder
Leonid. The Elder replied to them with the clarity and
experience which distinguished him from all others. This
was the fruit of the countless sorrows he had endured, of
his keen observation and of his exceptional memory which
retained all that he had read and heard. He did not cast
out those who came to him, in keeping with the words
of Christ. He explained to his disciples the hidden mysteries
of God's wisdom. Paul Tambovtsev was one of his fervent
and zealous disciples; he caught the drops of grace from the

lips of the Elder, preserved them in his warm heart and related them in his own words, in a somewhat exalted manner. However, he was unable to express himself in any other way, due to the gifted disposition of his mind.

The life of this youth was short; it came to an end in his 26th year (on August 4, 1835), if not in victory over all of his passions, at least in opposition to them. His death came after he had been bedridden because of a tragic occurrence — his father, for whom he had enormous respect, died by suicide. For believing Christians, what can be more terrible than the thought that the soul of such a close person has perished? This thought which pursued the suffering youth exceeded his strength. First he fell into depression from this spiritual conflict; then an emotional fire inflamed his organism and, in the end, a fever cut short his days. Apart from the dream (see below) which told of his approaching sufferings, he also had a significant vision. At the Skete of the Optina Monastery, according to the rule of services the reading of the Psalter is performed day and night for the commemoration of the reposed and the health of benefactors. Paul read during the midnight shift; and once when he began to commemorate the reposed and to make the usual bows, he beheld his own likeness on the right cliros. He looked at this appearance for a long time. Finally he decided to go to the cliros; but as soon as he came up to it, the vision vanished and he was seized with fear. Paul locked the church and left; he went to the Elder, woke him up and told him what he had seen. Fr. Leonid calmed him down and sent him back to finish his hour.

Paul died fully conscious during the celebration of Holy Unction over him. Just before his repose he quickly looked up and glanced from side to side in the air. Then he closed his eyes, convulsed and once again looked attentively at something which no one could see. But everyone noticed that he could see the enemies of his soul who were disturbing him at the terrible hour of his departure. Then he firmly closed his eyes, made the sign of the cross, heaved a sigh and his life was extinguished. On that same day he had made confession and communed the Holy Mysteries.

Eternal memory to you, Elder worthy of blessedness and obedient disciple!

GUARDING THE TONGUE

1. Disciple: How should I act when I am in the company of other brothers and am not able to refrain from speaking, and then when I speak I offend someone by what I say?

Elder: You should remember this cry offered by the Church to God, *Set, O Lord, a watch before my mouth and a door of enclosure round about my lips* (Ps. 140:3). Moreover, you should consider that those who are speaking are doing so with spiritual understanding and that they are worthy of this, but consider yourself unworthy of conversing with them. When they ask you a question, reply with reverence.

When you are carried away into the opposite, repent and make every effort to correct yourself. You should also conduct yourself so that the brothers will notice that you are making an exceptional effort to correct yourself.

JUDGMENT OF OTHERS

2. Disciple: How am I supposed to act when I see others freely expressing their thoughts and I am scandalized? Likewise, in regard to you, Father, I don't always see the meekness of an elder in your conduct with others, and then I also become offended.

Elder: It seems that way to you because of your lack of attention and lack of understanding. You must not judge anyone since you don't know the reason for his actions. Neither do you know the purpose behind the way I treat some other person. Such actions can more quickly bring out the internal character of a person, and this is needful for those who breathe conceit. Thus, you are not being fair. Try to pay better attention to yourself and try not to figure out the actions, conduct and dealings of others. You have come to the school of self-denial in order to do what you are told; and you don't have the right to make judgments about when, where, how and with whom other people have their dealings.

BROTHERLY LOVE

3. Disciple: I don't see love among the brethren, and I don't find anyone with whom I can discuss questions about the Holy Scriptures.

Elder: It is impossible that there not be love among them. That is what you should think, and that is the correct conclusion at which you should arrive. If you don't see love among them that is because you do not have any love yourself. You yourself must first manifest the characteristics of genuine love, and then you will see that love dwells among them and is abundantly preserved within you. Moreover, we have a commandment of God to love our fellow man with a pure heart, but for us to seek love from them is nowhere mentioned. If they are unable, or better to say, if they do not have the audacity to discuss the Scriptures with you, then don't zealously seek this. Where one has humility one also has simplicity, and this divine sprout does not scrutinize the judgments of God. It simply submits with faith and, until the proper time, is satisfied only with those concepts which faith reveals to it. God is not going to demand of the novice why he did not become a theologian, but rather why he did not tend to himself. God will not abandon him in regard to salvation. If it is pleasing to Him, He will reveal to him also the mysteries of His dispensation. The mind that is enlightened with the Light of God, in keeping with its measure of faith, is above any book learning because, obviously, the mind discovered learning and not learning the mind.

SPIRITUAL GROWTH

4. Disciple: Why is it that after five years of living in this desert Monastery and trying as hard as I can to correct myself, I sense the opposite: that in fact I've become worse, as my inconsiderate actions, coldness of heart and lack of courage testify?

Elder: Very few have flown up in a short time on the wings of faith and virtue into the spiritual heaven or have sensed in themselves the undying pledge of hope and the betrothal of future glory. Very few after prolonged labors have sensed mystically the consoling reward or the blossoms of sincere activity in the Lord that promise a harvest of fruit in the vineyard of Jesus Christ on high. And there are others who will never sense this during their whole life on earth; they will not sense it according to the dispensation of our heavenly Protector, God, who always provides what is best for us. For we, infants in our understanding of the judgments of Him that directs the world, often ask of Him such tools which in their own right and power are for our salvation, but we would put them to entirely detrimental use because of our inexperience. Therefore the loving Father of Lights hides from certain pious people the gifts which are for the salvation of some, but to others bring perdition. What would happen if God, Who knows all things, completely fulfilled our every wish? I think, but I'm not saying for certain, that everyone in the world would perish. Even though He does not reject the prayers of His chosen ones, God still does not at times fulfill their desires. And this is only in order to arrange everything in a better way, in keeping with His divine intent. You should also note that people who live without attention to themselves are never found worthy of the visitation of grace; and if they are found worthy of such things because of the goodness of God alone, this is just prior to the end. Just because you see yourself making no progress does not mean that you are not making any progress at all. Such feelings can plant sincere humility in your heart. And when you have the genuine awareness that you are deprived of spiritual fruit, then make an unfailing effort to force your striving for God. When we find that we are deprived of the virtues and therefore have no high opinion of ourself, then this by itself can attract God's favorable gaze, which will strengthen us with hope against the deadly spirit of despair. When we have had no success in the virtues, there is no closer means for salvation than humbleness of mind. Haughtiness, even when joined with the virtues, is offensive to God; but a meek thought will not be forgotten before God.

LOSS OF FAITH IN ONE'S GUIDE

5. Disciple: How has it come about that I have lost faith and reverence for your counsels and that your instructions have ceased to have an effect on my heart and everything seems difficult to do?

Elder: You have lost faith because of suspicion and have lost reverence because of familiarity. My instructions have no effect on your heart because you listen with some sort of curiosity; you think that I jump very suddenly from one subject to the next and answer all your questions with simple expressions. Leave off curiosity; observe moderation in your boldness; and have faith that it is God Who is instructing you through other persons. Do not be high-minded; keep to the simplicity of obedience, and then you will feel something very different in your heart. If you do not have a discerning simplicity, acquire it by not trusting yourself and by remembering your intention in coming here. Recall the fervor and the disposition of soul which you felt at the very beginning of God's visitation of your heart, the sacred change wrought by the right hand of the Most High. For the person who is truly under obedience, with God's help nothing is difficult to do. True self-denial will always feel that the yoke of salvation is easy. If temptations do not exceed God's gifts, the person who desires to be saved can do anything by the power of the Name of the One who gives strength to all — the Lord Jesus. And this is such a sacred truth that anyone who has any kind of living faith will never doubt it. For a person of little faith, even a particle of dust seems like a mountain; likewise for the person who believes it is very simple and easy to move the mountains of temptation.

LAUGHTER

6. Disciple: What am I supposed to do when I'm in the presence of the senior fathers of our Monastery, and they insert something in their conversation which makes it difficult to refrain from laughter?

Elder: Concerning their words you should think this way: I don't understand, due to my dull wits, the reason why they said this. Since I don't know the reason, I should not laugh. If, unexpectedly and involuntarily, you do laugh, reproach yourself, remembering the true teachings of the Holy Fathers that nothing breaks the chain of virtues and evangelical love like laughter and joking. Just as conversing with filthy thoughts in your internal feelings takes away the presence of grace, so the practice of laughing and the inclination toward it drive away one's Guardian Angel. The virtues are made void when each one is combined with some vice in the soul; the bastion of success is thus destroyed. The Savior of the world has ordained eternal shame for those who immerse themselves in joking: *Woe unto you who laugh now!* (Luke 6:25).

CARNAL SENSATIONS

7. Disciple: How can I be delivered from the extremely powerful sensations of carnal passions, not only in the presence of women, but even at the thought of them?

Elder: On seeing them you must guard your mind and feelings, and, in particular, not say anything without circumspection. Make every effort to get away as soon as possible. At the thought of them, restrain your thoughts. Continence is beneficial, but even more reliable is discreet measure in everything. But first of all you have to beg the Almighty Lord for deliverance from the attacks of this fiercest of passions, because a man on his own will never uproot it. When our intention is good, the most merciful God extinguishes the bursts of this fire.

WARFARE AGAINST THE FLESH

8. Disciple: When enticing carnal thoughts drag the mind by force, how can I be delivered from them?

Elder: Descend with your mind into hell and through the mirror of the Sacred Scriptures gaze on the flesh-pleasers. Are you sure that you want eternal perdition in return for the ephemeral sweetness of sin? Remember that you are mortal. Humbly beseech God, for He is the Vanquisher of passions, that He deflect those mental arrows of the flesh, this enemy that unremittingly rebels against the law of the mind and the spirit — for without the Most High we cannot do the least good thing.

REMEMBRANCE OF WRONGS

9. Disciple: What means should I employ against thoughts that powerfully force me to judge my neighbor — especially one who painfully insults me, whose actions seem audacious and out of keeping with his calling in Christ, and who is obviously offending other brothers? When I see this and share in their dissatisfaction, I become even more

irritated and am unable to be at peace; and when I am not calm in spirit, I bear a burden harmful to my soul.

Elder: At the appearance of thoughts that arouse you to judge your neighbor for some offense that he has done you, when the storm of thoughts is blown to gale force and rushes for revenge, then compare your state of sorrow with the former state of sorrow of the Savior of the world. He, the Angel of Great Counsel, the Son of God Who was without sin, magnanimously endured the very greatest sorrows; how much more so, then, must we not endure grievous circumstances, we who are sinful people and deserving of chastisement. We must also further condemn ourselves. In this case, with the weapon of self-condemnation we can do battle with the provoker of our soul, the invisible Philistine who steals the God-like ark of our soul. On the other hand, we should regard the person who is heaping offenses on us as our benefactor; he is nothing but an instrument with which God constructs our salvation.

In this way we will respect our offenders as benefactors, and when we begin to teach ourselves self-condemnation we will unnoticeably advance in our inner condemnation. Then our heart, with help from above, can become soft — meek in the spiritual sense; a person will become the vessel of grace and spiritual peace. The soul will then feel such peace that even in a state of sorrow we will feel it, or, better to say, partake of it. It is this peace that will enlighten the mind of the ascetic. The dawn of spiritual meekness will extend its rays into his mind, speech and intellect; then he will more easily repel evil, submitting and dedicating his heart to all that is solely unto salvation. His dissatisfactions will then seem joyful and pleasant.

INSENSITIVITY

10. Disciple: When no sacred thought or image is able to take effect on my heart while irritated or given over to insensitivity, then what must I do to soften myself?

Elder: You must seclude yourself, forcing yourself to prayer, to pouring out your soul before God. When the waves of insensitivity subside somewhat, then seek out the cause of this coldness. If some passion has risen within you, chase it away from yourself. But when such a grievous hardness has settled in for reasons that you cannot fathom, ask the Omnipresent One all the more that He dispel by His grace all the causes of unbelief, the evil offspring of insensitivity.

WARMING THE SOUL

11. Disciple: How can the soul be warmed after it has grown cold?

Elder: By the Word of God, by prayer, by a humble, grateful feeling of heart toward God in all unexpected changes, not only in your outward state but in your inner state as well.

VAINGLORY

12. Disciple: I sense within me not only the inclination, but also the actual movements of vainglory; and I want to be delivered from it. How can I be successful in this?

Elder: If you continue your obedience with sincerity, if you will not persistently try to incline your seniors to agree with your will in anything or seek out their special attention to you and if you lay your nothingness totally before God, then through His almighty grace you can with time be delivered from vainglory. This passion frequently continues from youth unto old age and even to the very grave. It torments not only the passionate and those who are advancing, but sometimes even the perfect. Therefore no little circumspection is needed. The passionless Creator alone can uproot it. Oh, how difficult it is to avoid this poison which kills the fruit of even the ripest virtues!

READING THE SACRED SCRIPTURE

13. Disciple: When I read the books of Sacred Scripture, I note the most edifying passages. Should I do this or not, and is it profitable?

Elder: My Elder, to whom with the help of the Almighty I submitted for twenty years, forbade me to do that. The notes you make will unnoticed give birth to traces of high-mindedness in your heart, the feature of all-destructive pride. This is known from experience. When the God of peace causes the true light to dawn in your memory, then you will remember without notes where certain passages are to be found and what their purpose is. The intellect that is enlightened by grace will show you in the Holy Scripture all that is needful for your salvation. Holy Scripture, while in general granted to us by God as a kind of guide for progress, still has its divisions. For example: some sections apply to those in authority, others to those who submit to them; some apply to those advanced in years, others to the middle-aged and the young; some are for monks, others for lay people; for those who are married, for virgins, and so on. But you must read books simply. You must ask the all-wise God to inscribe His holy will in your soul; then you will fulfill it humbly. Then you will be divinely wise and possess a sharp memory in the Lord.

CORRECTING ONE'S BROTHER

14. Disciple: When I see a beginner who is careless in some of his actions or doing something improper, should I correct him?

Elder: If you are obliged to be attentive to your own self, if you do not have a blessing from your superior and if you realize that you are the victim of the passions, then do not become involved in any way in matters and occasions which are not your business. Keep silent. All either stand or fall before their own Lord. Make every effort not to become your neighbor's tempter. Physician, heal thyself.

THE CELL-RULE ON SATURDAY

15. Disciple: On Saturday, must I do my cell-rule?

Elder: You must, except on the feasts and those days when there is a vigil. Make bows from the waist [rather than prostrations].

THE CELL-RULE

16. Disciple: When, because I have been absent or because of my obedience, I have no other time for my rule except very late at night, what should I do?

Elder: If you have been away and are tired, then get your rest. Set aside your rule, humble yourself and do not worry about it. But when your obedience is average, make an effort to complete your rule and you will receive no little benefit from this. Keep to this rule up to ten o'clock. But if it is later then attentively read the prayers before sleep and get your rest, saying the Jesus prayer until you fall asleep; you will then be better prepared for Matins and to continue your obedience on the following day, if it pleases God to raise you up. But this only applies to novices.

OVERCOMING THE PASSIONS

17. Disciple: I want very much to correct myself, but I keep getting distracted by the yearning of the passions. What can I do to overcome them?

Elder: Persist in your desire and the Almighty God will grant you according to your heart; for the beginning of the virtues and their source is one's disposition, one's desire for good in the Lord. A person cannot overcome the passions on his own. This is the work of the right hand of the Most High, the action of the power of God. On our part we have only to preserve intact the holy disposition given us by God, and, in keeping with it, offer our efforts to attain the land of passionlessness. The Most High, beyond doubt, will perfect the effort of the one who desires this. So, if you desire to rise from the tomb of the passions, then always keep your mind attentive to this; take care for this, and have unwavering action and zeal. Hope in God, Who can manifest His power in our weaknesses through His grace, and you will be saved.

SCATTERED THOUGHTS

18. Disciple: How can I be delivered from the scattering of my thoughts during the time of prayer?

Elder: When you pray with your lips, pray also with your mind; that is, enclose your mind in the power of the words of the prayer.

If you are distracted by a thought about something, as soon as you realize your carelessness in this, redouble your attention to the prayer. Do this all the time and you will sense benefit.

Constancy of the mind attracts special actions of grace.

SLOTH

19. Disciple: Laziness has a strong grip on me; how can I be delivered from it?

Elder: If you fight against laziness indecisively, you will never overcome it. But as soon as you rise up against it with a firm resolve, with God's help, although not without inner suffering, you can gain the victory. To resist even though you are being attacked is the sign of a faithful and good soldier; but to turn your back all the time is the characteristic only of an indolent bearer of arms. A person must watch over himself right up to the grave when it comes to this vice, lest he hear on the last day that most terrible sentence of the Knower of hearts, "Thou wicked and slothful servant!" (Matt. 25:26).

In the Scriptures it is said, "To him that overcometh" and not "to him that has overcome" because without the help of the Most High we cannot overcome the enemy entirely; we can never get any advantage over him. It is only to him that overcomes that the crown is given, and only to the person who goes forth into the contest with a firm resolve to wage war to his very last breath — to the person who never abandons his weapons at the moment of the greatest danger, who, even if he be in involuntary captivity, does not surrender his heart to the enemy. Such a person, while he may be beaten at times, never lessens his sacred zeal; he sacrifices himself undeterred with the spirit of hope. For this reason he advances and is crowned for his intention alone, for being courageous and worthy of heavenly honors.

DESPONDENCY

20. Disciple: How can I be delivered from the stifling spirit of despondency?

Elder: You are probably being attracted to something by your own will. If you leave off directing yourself and undertake everything with God's blessing, then with this blessing you will reap peace of soul and the other fruits of the Holy Spirit. If you completely abandon your own will, you will never feel the heavy darkness of despondency. The fiercest waves of the passions will subside; in place of them there will arise clarity of mind, stillness of thoughts, meekness of spirit and undeceiving peace which will bless you from above and will come to dwell in your soul. If you maintain unbroken attentiveness and watchfulness over yourself, you will become like the wise virgins and will enter into the bridal chamber of the immortal Bridegroom. The Bridegroom comes at midnight! Watch then, that you do not burden your heart with despondency. Give glory to your Lord God before sunset begins. Come in the Name of the Lord by the path of self-denial if you truly want to be saved. Despondency torments everyone; it destroys the salutary fruits of sobriety in even the greatest men. But it has no place in the simple and genuine novice. He who has denied himself with hope in God, over what can he be despondent? For such a person, *the swords of the enemy have failed unto the end* (Ps. 9:6).

THE MONASTIC TONSURE, MONASTIC RAIMENT

21. Disciple: I have heard about the presentation of the names of certain brothers to be tonsured, and specifically about some who entered the Monastery after me. I too want to receive the angelic habit; and because I do not have the blessing of my superior for this, I am very upset and feel that I am not attaining my goal. How can I regain the calmness of spirit that I lost through this?

Elder: First, you must humbly and without any further consideration submit to the will of God. The decision of the superior is the will of Him that rules over all. For this reason whoever does not submit to the superior does not submit to the will of God, Who governs everything; and whoever does not submit to God's will bitterly afflicts himself with the deprivation of grace, the corrupting spirit of sorrow, disorder, woes and all manner of ill-considered undertakings. Those who were recommended for the tonsure ahead of you should probably be considered more worthy. While you want to receive the external angelic betrothal, take care in advance to become an angel internally. Without inner monasticism, the external on its own will not save you. In keeping with your calling and your intention, imitate to the extent that you can the way of life of the ancient Holy Fathers, and believe that Almighty God rules over all of us. Respect the superior as the one who fulfills His holy and clairvoyant will, for he mystically bears the image of Jesus Christ. If you believe this, of course you will not approach the superior indiscriminately. Also, dare we to keep a disturbed spirit against the Lord Jesus Christ when we are obliged to be at peace with those who never seek peace, to be meek and humbly submissive? But I am not going to speak any more about this. If God beholds the heart and intention and looks down upon the works of each person, if He sees all our future actions and the end of our life, then ought we to have any doubt that He, being all-good, is arranging all things to the better for us? When God simply wills, the usual order of nature is overcome; for grace by itself, without doubt, is above all the wisdom and power of this world. What God has ordained no human counsel can annul. Of course it is not pleasing to God that you be received into the monastic order. If you become worthy of this, then be certain that either before your death you will be granted this or after being released from your body the angels will present you before the Lord in the monastic habit. This is true. And if you only had a little faith in your soul, faith that passes understanding, you could accept this; but if you do not have such faith, then take care to cry out with the Holy Apostle Peter, "Lord, grant me faith."

God looks upon the intention. Take the example of Blessed Thais who, having been an unworthy woman, in an instant through resolute self-denial alone became a perfect nun. She conceived the resolve to be the handmaiden of God alone and absolutely surrendered her heart to the guidance of Jesus Christ. When amidst this resolve physical death found her on the road, her companion St. John, who had converted her with the help of the Most High from the paths of depravity to the saving path of repentance, to his great astonishment beheld with his pure soul how the angels snatched Thais' soul, which had found peace with God, into light unapproachable. She had not yet reached the desert; she did not know in what the monastic life consisted; she was not clothed in the habit she desired. But by means of turning to God, by despising the world and her own self, she was granted instantaneously the most merciful judgment of God and was brought to dwell in the divine mansions not made by human hands. Had she not become a perfect nun? It pleased the hidden will of all-supreme Compassion to cut her days short at the moment of her decisive intention, and thus a mere good intention was crowned equally with the deed itself. A heart that is broken and humbled, God will not despise. If you want to have an even clearer proof of this, then look with the eyes of humility and faith at that novice who for his good intention and worthy way of life immediately after burial was clothed in the schema by the angels, as we have seen in the lives of the Holy Fathers of the Caves. But woe to that schemamonk from whom God's judgment decreed that the external habit be removed as proof of his inner barrenness!

If you clothe yourself in Christ in the habit of the inner monk, then you won't worry much about your external habit — even though it is not sinful at all to desire this. The Beholder of hearts, Who always orders everything profitable for us, will provide for you in correspondence to your faith and deeds which please Him. Remember St. Pimen the Long-suffering. A great many turn out to be monks only in their intention, although in this world they were unable to be tonsured by mortal hands due to the judgments of the Ruler of the world. St. Pelagia knew the true faith and thus desired to offer fruits worthy of repentance as soon as she received enlightenment. By the might of indescribable ascetic exploits she became saintly, although she was not clothed in the monastic mantle by men. The mantle signifies physcial affliction, the vow of voluntary poverty, of purity, of obedience and monastic humility. But the mantle of inner raiment has been pre-ordained by the Most High as an eternal reward in the heavens; this is the all-sacred attire of the garments of the Holy Spirit.

FAITH IN DREAMS

22. Disciple: Are we supposed to believe in dreams that (apparently) vividly portray the future?

Elder: No, we are not, even though in their own way they may turn out to be true; through believing in dreams

many have been deceived. The wisdom-loving Elder Theocter-
istus, who composed the Paraclesis to the Most Holy Theotokos, by believing in dreams finally became so deluded that
he perished. And so that person is very adept who does not
believe even the most realistic representations.

A VISION OF CRUCIFIXION

23. Disciple: What then does this dream I saw mean?
Does it contain anything deserving credence? Maybe it deserves no attention, but I am obliged to reveal it to my Elder.

I suddenly beheld a light so radiant that it surpassed
the light of the sun many times. From this radiant shining
there came a loud, gentle voice which commanded, as it
were, some beings in submission to it: "Place him (that is,
myself) upon the cross." With these words (I don't know
who it was), they took me, stripped off my clothing and
dragged me. as it were mentally, to a cross which quite
clearly stood before me. It seemed to me that it was made
of some very pleasant, yellow wood used for construction,
and it was large enough for me to be crucified upon it.
But who was it that was doing this to me? When I looked
around, I could not see anything but noise and very hurried
activity. When they lifted me up on the cross, the one who
was doing this to me said quietly, but distinctly, "Give me
the nails." Four nails were presented, each one no less than
seven inches long; and with one of them they began to
nail my right hand to the cross. At this point I felt extreme
pain, although in my soul I wanted to be crucified. On account of the pain I was agitated in spirit, in spite of this
desire of my heart; and I almost cried aloud the pain I
felt. But with God's help, I know not how, I restrained
myself. When the nail had pierced my hand, after a few
minutes I sensed some alleviation of the pain; and afterwards I hardly felt it at all. Then they took another nail
similar to the first and began to drive it into my left hand.

This time, while I sensed pain, it was incomparably less than the first time. Then they took the third nail which was for nailing my right foot to the cross. When I saw that this nail was directed at me, I was shaken in spirit and wanted to cry, "Have mercy!" Yet I was restrained by the weariness of my own spirit. I sensed my lack of patience. After this, however, an even greater desire to endure entered my heart. In my mind I turned to Almighty God, having on my soul an inexplicable confidence that He could help me. With this hope I mentally asked God for strength. I trembled; I wanted to endure, but I was afraid of giving in out of the weakness of my unstable spirit. In fact the compassionate Lord, although He allowed me to feel terrible pain in my entire being, yet He marvelously strengthened me out of His lovingkindness. They drove in the nail. In spirit I was extremely weak. However, after involuntarily enduring the pain, I soon began to sense relief, then moderate pain or just weakness. They took the fourth nail and drove it into my left foot with such exceptional speed that I did not have time to imagine or think anything. I assume that this was due to the weakness that I felt, but the pain at that time was moderate so it seemed that I could endure it. A little later for the second time there thundered forth out of the light from above, the loud voice, far clearer than the first time, but still accompanied by a spirit of love, gentleness and good will: "Pierce him" (as if pointing to me with a spiritual finger); "drive a nail into his heart." Hearing this decree and knowing my weakness, I was extremely distressed. My resolve was shaken. Clouds of terrible thoughts weighed upon me; my heart would burn with desire and then become numb from fear. Finally, the resolve to consecrate myself to long-suffering tipped the scales; all my conflicting thoughts scattered, and my mind soared to God with prayer for help. After this I prepared myself to withstand the execution of this terrible sentence which had flown from the bosom of the unseen voice, although with a certain amount of trepidation — yet at the same time with love and gratitude to the mighty Name of the Knower of hearts, Who is greater than the heart and knows all things; I sensed in my heart a promise from the Lord that He would help me. (All this happened so quickly; it takes longer not only to describe it in writing but even to narrate it in words.) They brought a fifth nail which was stationed right opposite my heart. Judging by its size it could pierce all the way through me, and it seems there would be over a foot projecting out each side. When the nail was still approaching my chest I found myself prepared to hope in the power of God; when it drew right next to me I suddenly changed my intention and wanted to cry out. "Have mercy! What is this for?" It appeared to me that as soon as this sentence was carried out, I would lose my life from excessive pain. They began to drive the nail in against my heart with hammers; I felt extraordinary pain -- such unendurable pain that my spirit was totally overwhelmed. My soul left me without feeling on the cross, as if gathering into itself my shattered, weak powers. When it parted from my body it was detained for a few minutes by some invisible and unexplainable being. My eyes went blank and rolled back. My head sagged to, I don't remember, which side.

It was a terrible spectacle! My soul was in me, but it seemed to be outside my body. Soon though it seemed to me that I had simply been extremely exhausted, but that my soul was still within me. The pain began to subside, and then suddenly I could not sense a trace of it.

My eyes opened immediately; yet I sensed nothing, except that I was on the cross. But my poor heart was seized and filled with such a sweetness that neither a thousand great minds nor even I myself, who experienced it, are capable of describing such gladness. This sweetness, I think, is the cup of the offering of sweetnesses beyond this world from the most-sweet Ruler of the world, Our Lord Jesus Christ. He alone can have such a vessel of this kind of manna and out of the impenetrable mystery of His compassion grant it to mortals. But why should I, mad man that I am, begin to speak about what my entire life is insufficient to express! Forgive me! My heart rejoiced unspeakably and then my eyes, aflame with the spirit of peace, dropped down. I beheld myself, all covered with blood, nailed to the cross. Sweetness seized my spirit; in my heart there remained the traces of this astonishment which awakened me from my sleep.

It was now the first hour after midnight. I thus came directly to you. I am bewildered, perplexed; I rejoice and am horrified. My heart trembles without fear due to the traces of sweetness and astonishment. Tell me, what does this unusual dream mean?

Elder: St. Barsanuphius the Great[1] writes that the Lord Jesus Christ, an angel or another person can be portrayed by the demons, not only in sleep but when a person is awake — for satan can transform himself into an angel of light. But the Cross of the Lord, upon whose power, as the Church chants, the devil does not even dare to gaze — for he trembles and is convulsed being unable to behold its power — this he cannot represent. The cross you saw in your dream signifies in advance some enormous sorrow, and the sweetness signifies intercession. The more prepared you are, the more easily you will be able to endure, for *I made ready and I was not troubled,* cries St. David (Ps. 118:60). If you were shaken in your sorrow, then keep to the rule: *I was troubled and spake not* (Ps. 76:4). If your sorrow is beyond measure, then remember the following: *With patience I waited patiently for the Lord and He was attentive unto me* (Ps. 39:1). Thus, let the will of the Lord be done! Go your way, do not worry; God is faithful.

---

1. Sts. Barsanuphius the Great and John, *Guidance Toward Spiritual Life,* University Press, Moscow, 1855, Answer 413, pp. 367-368.

Several days after I had seen this dream I was informed of the unfortunate violent death of my father, and I asked the Elder:

Disciple: I sense that my dream was a prediction of this present, ineradicable sorrow, although I do not dare to apply it to this matter. The unfortunate death of my father is a heavy cross for me, the cross that I saw. Now I am on the cross, and its pain will accompany me to the grave. When I think of how terrible eternity is for sinners who have yet to repent, I am tormented by the sight of the eternal torments that await my father who died without repentance. Tell me, Father, how can I console myself in this grief?

Elder: Entrust both yourself and the fate of your father to the will of the Lord, which is all-wise and almighty. Do not probe into the wonders of the Most High. Strive through humbleness of mind to strengthen yourself within the limits of measured sorrow. Pray to the all-good Creator, fulfilling thereby your obligation of love and the duties of a son.

Disciple: But how can I pray for such persons?

Elder: In keeping with the spirit of virtuous and wise men, pray thus: "Seek out, O Lord, the lost soul of my father, if possible; have mercy! Thy judgments are unfathomable. Do not account this prayer of mine as sin. May Thy holy will be done."

Pray simply, without pondering, entrusting your heart to the right hand of the Most High. Of course, such an unfortunate death was not the will of God for your father, but now he is entirely in the will of Him that is able to cast both soul and body into the fiery furnace and Who *bringeth low and lifteth high again, slayeth and engendereth life, bringeth down to hades and bringeth up again* (I Kings 2: 7, 8). Moreover, He is so compassionate, almighty and full of love that the good qualities of all the earth-born are nothing before His supreme goodness. For this reason you should not grieve to excess. You say, "I love my father and therefore I grieve unconsolably." That is right; but God, incomparably more than you, loved him and still loves him. That means that the only thing left for you to do is to leave the eternal fate of your father up to the goodness and loving-kindness of God, Who, if He is pleased to show mercy, then who can withstand Him?

II

The Questions of Another Disciple[1] and the Replies of the Elder

CONDEMNATION OF OTHERS

1. Disciple: What is condemnation, and why do the Fathers compare the person who condemns to Antichrist?

Elder: Condemnation is when you see or know of a sin or shortcoming of your brother and you say in your heart, "In my opinion he deserves torture, execution or illness." Then you become like a judge over your neighbor and want to seat yourself on the throne of the only Judge, Christ; so for your proud madness you become like the Antichrist. Speaking evil and vilification are something else, but are not yet condemnation. Scandal is something different: when involuntarily, out of natural feelings, your soul is scandalized at some shameful action or word. The silence of the Fathers, occupied with inward activity, knew not the sins of their neighbors but beheld only their own falls.

SPEAKING OF THE SINS OF OTHERS

2. Disciple: In confession, may I tell about another person who sinned with me in word or in deed?

---

1. Alexius Polycarpovich Bochkov, later Anthony, Abbot of Chermenetsk Monastery.

Elder: Do you want to repent in his place? If he doesn't want to admit to his sin, just speak about your own: I sinned by speaking evil or in lewd conversations or some such thing.

THE SINS OF OTHERS

3. Disciple: Can I suggest to a brother that he go in repentance to his elder about a sin he committed verbally?

Elder: (The Elder smiled.) You have too much anxiety about your brother's salvation. I think it is better to pray that the Lord Himself inspire him.

CONFESSION OF CARNAL THOUGHTS

4. Disciple: The Fathers say that a detailed description of carnal thoughts and actions is vain, that it is enough to explain them with a general expression, that the recollection of them defiles the lips and thoughts. Is this so?

Elder: That is so. The Fathers were more experienced than we in the matters of the soul. But each person has his own rule. One elder can listen to your confession without passion or harm; and you yourself, let us suppose, could make a detailed confession without much passion, with contrition and abase yourself for humiliation. For this reason a detailed confession (on rare occasions) can be beneficial. But apparently the elders knew the great mercy of God which does not desire our extreme humiliation; thus they found it better to abbreviate confession of evil thoughts. Sometimes it is the devil that inspires them, so you will be revealing not your thoughts but his suggestions; and he will mock you in doing something good. Sometimes the elder, not being very steadfast, cannot quickly blow your thoughts out of the ear of his heart.

THOUGHTS AGAINST THE ELDER

5. Disciple: Is it better, therefore, to keep quiet about evil and blasphemous thoughts against the elder, against his life and his weaknesses?

Elder: That depends on the elder. It is better to keep quiet about the details of the thoughts and to speak only in general that "I had blasphemous thoughts against you." Sometimes the devil wants to mock and blaspheme the elder with your lips, and you will be entertaining the devil by becoming his mouthpiece. If the elder is experienced, without agitation he will explain all of this to you. But if he is weak he will be troubled, especially if such warfare becomes prolonged. The elder could reject you out of his own and your own lack of experience. It is only very rarely that the Lord allows someone younger to rebuke an elder, although we ought to love those who rebuke us.

DISCRIMINATION OF THOUGHTS

6. Disciple: How can we discern which thoughts are our own and which are from the enemy?

Elder: A certain desert-dweller at Konevits told me that after he had occupied himself with mental attentiveness for no little while, he still could not discern his own thoughts from those of the enemy. When the enemy distracts your thoughts to something, he does not say, "Go do this or that." He seems to be thinking in place of you, and he tells you with your own thought, "I would like to do this or that. I think this is a good thing, but that is harmful; I made up my mind to do such and such." Frequently all this is not your thoughts, but the thoughts of the enemy camouflaged under your own or his "I." You suppose these are your thoughts, but no; you are just hearing the enemy's suggestions.

LENGTH OF CONFESSION

7. Disciple: Certain priests with theological training require very detailed confessions for the cleansing of the soul.

Elder: Leave them alone, that's their business. But can they keep to this practice if, for example, they have to hear 500 confessions in three hours?

MENTAL PRAYER

8. Disciple: Is mental prayer granted to everyone?

Elder: Whomever the Lord visits with a grievous trial, with sorrow or with the deprivation of a beloved neighbor: such a person will involuntarily pray with his whole heart, with all his thoughts and with all his mind. Consequently the wellspring of prayer is in everyone; but it is tapped either by gradually delving deeper into oneself in accordance with the teachings of the Fathers, or instantaneously, by God's drill.

LOVE FOR THE MOTHER OF GOD

9. Disciple: Some of the Fathers that I know have great love for the Mother of God, and they boast of this; but why does this fervor of theirs seem dubious to me?

Elder: Yes! Whoever sets forth his own virtues is in a dubious state. Sometimes we boast of our prayers, but at the same time we are far from the Heavenly Queen. Let us praise the Mother of God by having her virtues within us — purity, humility — and not by the praises we voice.

READING THE WORKS OF THE HOLY FATHERS

10. Disciple: Which books of the Holy Fathers is it better to read: that of Climacus, or Isaac the Syrian or of Abba Barsanuphius?

Elder: Read the words of the saints by your actions.

AKATHISTS

11. Disciple: What do you have to say about the akathists that some people use to fill out their rule?

Elder: The person who understands the words of the akathist like their hymnographer and who penetrates into each word prays through the akathist and offers praises that are not irrational — that is, as long as he does not attribute to his own self and mind another's labors and another's words, psalms and hymns. We are just their readers. All are not Davids who read the Psalter, and all are not Damascenes who read canons. The simple prayer of the publican is better and is closer to all of us.

THE PATH OF SALVATION

12. Disciple: What is the easiest way to be saved? On what path? I'm just asking for myself.

Elder: Imagine that the Lord Jesus Christ is walking about the earth in all His human, evangelical simplicity. Walking together with Him, would you be any better than you are now?

Disciple: After thinking a moment, I replied to the Elder: I suppose I would remain the same as before, without any special grace from God. After all, were there not many who followed Christ and then fell away?

Elder: And what is it that attracts the grace of God more than anything else?

Disciple: I don't know, Father.

Elder: If you would be simple-hearted like the Apostles, would not conceal your human shortcomings, would not pretend to be especially pious, if you would walk free from hypocrisy, then that is the path. While it is easy, not everyone can find it or understand it. This path is the shortest way to salvation and attracts the grace of God. Unpretentiousness, guilelessness, frankness of soul — this is what is pleasing to the Lord, Who is lowly of heart. *Except ye become like children, ye shall not enter into the Kingdom of God* (Mt. 18:13).

CONTRITION OF HEART

13. Disciple: Why is it that I become disgusted with the people — because of their stupidity and ignorance — who come to you, even though I know that many of them receive benefit from you?

Elder: Because your heart is not contrite. Whoever is pained by love for his neighbor does not notice their stupidity. Rather, he beseeches the Lord with fear that he be shown what to say for his neighbor's profit, and he fulfills the task of giving counsel reverently as the work of God. Sometimes even after prayer you cannot find a useful reply; here you are put to shame and should rebuke yourself. Having this awareness of your own unworthiness, not of the stupidity of men, you are ready to tell everyone: pray for me, a slave of God.

DISPOSITION TO THE ELDER

14. Disciple: How is it that sometimes I love you, like right now (at this point I had tears in my eyes, and my voice quivered), and at other times I am irritated with you because of the multitude of people who come and bother you?

Elder: Will you ever understand me? It is because you are still not a monk, but a passer-by; you have yet to separate yourself from the world. You want to catch my words on the fly; you want to find salvation in passing, to learn in a hurry. That is why there is this exaltation, this kissing your Elder's shoulders or hands. But with Fr. Theodore, without fanaticism[2] I was mentally prepared to fall down at his feet on my knees in filial devotion. Look at Abbess Anatolia and Mother Arcadia.[3] They do not envy the people who come to me. They are ready to give way at any time and place. At the same time they love me more than you because they fulfill my words through their actions. When will the Lord finally free you completely from the

---

2. The Elder frequently used this word.

3. Anatolia of the Borisov Convent was a woman of exceptional kindness, with a very warm heart. Arcadia of the Sevsk Convent, because of her bearing and dignity, was humorously called "the Queen" by the Elder.

world? Maybe you too will someday love your neighbor as yourself. Furthermore, besides that, I don't wish Tabitha's disposition on you.

Note: The Mother Tabitha mentioned here lived in the Borisov Convent and was not only a nun of strict, ascetic life, but also a very spry old lady; she had great concern for many other persons and gave instructions to many. But she herself had an ecstatic disposition of soul, and she sought for the lofty things in spiritual life without completely scorning human fame or cleansing herself of other passions. She judged the weaknesses of other persons strictly, probably due to the lack of her own humility. Although she was much enlightened by the elders, she did not leave off her improper striving and ecstatic disposition. Due to this she fell into the delusion of the enemy and died in a state of insanity, or partial insanity.

The words of the Elder to Fr. Anthony that perhaps he would come to love his neighbor as himself came to pass thirty years later, after the death of Fr. Leonid. Fr. Anthony (Bochkov) in 1871 settled in the Skete of the St. Nicholas Ugreshsky Monastery near Moscow after he resigned as Abbot of the Chermenetsk Monastery. In that year there was an epidemic of cholera in Moscow and for that reason the Abbot of the Ugreshsky Monastery was asked to send hieromonks to Moscow to assist the Muscovite priests in administering the last rites to the sick and the dying and to serve funerals for the deceased. It was then that Fr. Anthony, on his own, expressed his desire to dedicate himself to this work of philanthropy. At the beginning of 1872 he moved to a Moscow hospital for common laborers, where a special cell was prepared for him. For two months the 70-year-old Elder daily heard confessions and administered the Holy Mysteries to many of the sick, and he himself communed each day. He would also administer Holy Unction to three persons each day, and on occasion would serve funerals for six people in a single day in the winter-time in an unheated chapel. While he was doing this, Fr. Anthony said of himself that he had never enjoyed such health or such a peace of soul as during that period. Finally, on March 17, his former name day (St. Alexis, the Man of God), he was stricken with typhus and died on April 5. He was buried in the St. Nicholas Ugreshsky Monastery.

СХИМОНАХЪ ѲЕОДОРЪ.

SCHEMAMONK THEODORE, ELDER OF SVIR
(1756-1822)
Commemorated April 5/18

The Life of
Elder Theodore
of Svir

ST. PAISIUS VELICHKOVSKY
(1722-1794)
Commemorated November 15/28

The Manuscript Life
of Elder Theodore of Svir

In the Optina Monastery Manuscript Library I chanced to find a true pearl: the Manuscript Life of Schemamonk Theodore, disciple of the great Moldavian Elder Paisius Velichkovsky. Paisius Velichkovsky was for Russian monasticism at the end of the eighteenth and in the nineteenth centuries, as well as for contemporary monks living a true monastic life, the same as St. Anthony the Great was for the Egyptian monks and the desert dwellers of the Levant. From him stems also that great tradition of Optina Elders, headed by Hieromonk Leonid, in Schema Leo. Schemamonk Theodore was the teacher and fellow struggler of Elder Leonid. It is understandable what interest I had towards the manuscript which I found and with what love I transferred from the sheets, already yellow with age, its precious text into my spiritual journal (On the Banks of God's River, Vol. I, 1916).

S. Nilus
St. Sergius Lavra, Sergiev Posad

ELDER THEODORE OF SVIR
A portrait from Valaam.

1. A LONGING FOR THE OTHER WORLD

THE SON of pious parents, Theodore first opened his eyes upon the world in the town of Karachev, a district town in the province of Orel, in the year of Our Lord 1756. His father, whom he lost in his infancy, was of the merchant class; his mother was from a family of clergy. The orphaned child was given by his mother to live in the house of the archpriest of Karachev to be schooled in reading, writing and singing. Soon he revealed exceptional abilities which led him to advance rapidly in his studies. He was particularly gifted in singing, for which he had a remarkable voice. The boy's heart, childlike and not yet sullied by passion, was readily disposed to receiving divine impressions. As he sensitively sang the church hymns, their language of holy mystery imperceptibly penetrated his heart. In learning to read and write, he was given the key to a treasury which held a precious pearl: the books of Holy Scripture and patristic texts. At the same time, good deeds, obedience, simplicity and the reading of spiritual books taught Theodore wisdom and cultivated feelings which he later was to offer as a sacrifice on the fragrant altar of piety.

He was already a young man when he returned from the priest's home and, at the insistence of his mother, opened a little store in the village of Karachev. He spent about two years in this occupation. But his heart, having once tasted the sweetness of spiritual life, could not be reconciled with the vain attractiveness of the cares of the world. Forcibly compelled to a way of life contrary to his inclinations and thoughts, Theodore longed in the depths of his soul for some quiet refuge; he decided to leave the world and take upon himself the light yoke of monasticism. Unable to resist the lawful demands of his conscience and the feelings in his heart by which God Himself often calls a man, he left his mother's home. Leaving Karachev at night and telling no one of his plan, he set out for the Ploshchansk Hermitage, which lay sixty miles from Karachev. Here Theodore concealed himself from the snares of the care-ridden world.

At that time Ploshchansk Hermitage was under the skillful guidance of the virtuous Elder Serapion. It was adorned by the good conduct of the brethren and the well-ordered rule of church services. There the young Theodore entered the arena of monastic obedience in order to gain inward freedom by outward slavery, to earn inner nobility of spirit by external abasement. To obedience he tried to join patience, which strengthens and unites the entire building of virtues. He founded patience on humility.

Not much time had elapsed before his mother discovered that her son was living in the Ploshchansk Hermitage. She hurried there and snatched the youth away from the protected and peaceful monastic life, casting him into the stream of worldly clamor with all its temptations. Oh, fleshly love, love without reason, you are unworthy of the holy name given to you by God Himself! You often arm blinded parents with unjust fervor, and those who received from them mortal life lose spiritual and true life!

Theodore returned to the shop, and thoughts of a higher calling once more agitated his soul. Taking advantage of the darkness of night he ran away again from home, away from the town and reached the White Bluff Monastery, which at that time was still relatively unknown. From White Bluff Monastery he directed his steps once more to Ploshchansk Hermitage, from which he was again forcibly abducted by his mother who was inflamed with the desire to make him friends with the world — a desire hardly natural to the soul of man.

Exhausted by such hindrances and thinking that his engagement in mental warfare was not pleasing to God, Theodore wanted, at least, not to be deprived of the sweet, life-giving commandments of the Lord. They were like a thread by which he hoped to find his way out of the labyrinth of worldly life and, with the sword of deeds, to slay that monster which devoured all those lost in the labyrinth, those who did not follow the shining gold thread of Christ's commandments. Thus his doors were open to pilgrims; the poor did not leave his window without the joy of receiving alms. The sick were comforted by his compassion and the service he rendered them; thieves could not say of him that he repaid evil with evil. He devoted free time to reading, endeavoring to embrace unceasingly the sweetest Name of Jesus, both with his lips and with his thoughts.

But a man is subject to change; it is not only youth filled with wind and passion which is tossed about on the stormy seas of life, but even old age, which prides itself on its steadfastness and experience — often imaginary. Deprived of the quietness of the wilderness and the guidance of the elders and troubled by the unruly desires of youthful flesh, he began to sink into the darkness of sinful thoughts. Little by little his heart was overtaken by sensuous feelings, and he fell.

Let us proceed to the moving and instructive account of his grievous inclinations and show the pit of sin into which he fell; we will come to know the great power of repentance when we see him on the highest step of the virtues. The shipwreck of a righteous man, says the divine Chrysostom, becomes a refuge for the sinner. When a righteous man falls from heaven, then I no longer despair of my salvation. Those crippled by the wounds of battle are deemed by the king to be deserving of special honor. Likewise, those

who struggle in unseen warfare receive shining crowns when
they appear before the face of the King of Kings, stained
by the blood of their falls and through these same falls
having conquered their vanquisher by means of repentance.

At the time that Theodore was continuing to occupy
himself in his small business, an opening as a merchant's
clerk was made available in the town. The sensible and
talented young man was offered the position. The master
of the house had passed away. His widow, an honest and
simple-hearted woman, was well-advanced in years and
not capable of taking on the management of the house
herself; she entrusted it to Theodore. It was in this house
that the nets were laid, and his foot became entangled.
The widow had four grown daughters who were very at-
tractive. Theodore, carried away by the passions of the
flesh, sank into an illicit relationship with the oldest
sister, then with the youngest. For a long time he floundered
in this quagmire of depravity — lust blinds man's higher
sentiments , and, at last, desiring to close his sinful wounds,
he united himself in marriage to the youngest daughter. But
this did not untangle the burden of his sin. His conscience
was awakened: he became aware of the value of the treasures
he had lost, and his heart was wounded by the desire for
their return. He began diligently to visit the churches of God.
In a word, he doubled his efforts to fulfill, as much as lay in
his power, all the duties of a Christian. But the light of his
monastic striving which had previously shone in him did not
regain its original brightness.

2. WITH ELDER PAISIUS

Deeply grieved, Theodore experienced a lack of fulfillment in all he did. He felt that everywhere the world was
strewn with obstacles towards leading a God-pleasing life.
Lacking the strength to endure the grievous wounds inflicted
by the loss of spiritual warmth and not finding any comfort

in worldly pursuits, he at last decided to leave the country, his estate and his wife and young daughter. Stripped of earthly cares, he entered once again upon that joyous path which he had previously trodden. Concealing his true intentions, he told his wife that he wanted to go to Kiev to venerate the holy relics of the righteous Fathers of the Caves Monastery. With her consent, he set out for that city taking with him only four roubles and fifty kopeks. There he entrusted himself to the prayers of the righteous ones and then quickly directed his steps to the borders of Russia and Poland, crossed the border and set out for Moldavia where at that time shone the great luminary, Elder Paisius Velichkovsky, Archimandrite of the Niamets Monastery.

This Monastery is situated seventy miles from Jassy at the foot of the Carpathian Mountains. At that time the Monastery had about 700 brethren. The harmonious ordering of the church services and the quality of spiritual instruction were in full flower; the Turkish yoke and the poverty of the brethren greatly contributed to the spiritual progress of the inner man. It was to this flock, guided by a truly wise shepherd, Elder Paisius, that Theodore wanted to join himself. Archimandrite Paisius was at that time already ill and seldom left his cell. Theodore begged those close to the Elder to accept him, but he was refused. They cited the great number of monks and their insufficient means. The young pilgrim Theodore found himself in dire straits: the money which he had brought from Russia had been spent; the summer coat in which he had left Karachev had become threadbare; winter was approaching. Far from home, lacking the basic necessities of life and turned away by those close to the Elder, Theodore asked that he might at least be admitted to the Elder to receive his blessing. This was allowed, and he presented himself before the earthly angel.

Elder Paisius, seeing the ragged and despairing state of the youth, wept tears of compassion, comforted him with strong words of love and joined him to his blessed flock.

From that time the holy man strictly forbade that anyone should be turned aside in the future without his knowledge.

The overjoyed Theodore was taken to the bakery; there were no available cells. He was entrusted by Paisius to Elder Sophronius, who was to be his spiritual father before whom he was to reveal his thoughts and receive spiritual instruction. In accordance with the tradition of the Monastery, Theodore confessed to him all his sins from his very youth and was forbidden for five years to partake of the Holy Mysteries of Christ.

Having spent several days in the bakery, one night he saw in a dream a crowd of people who seemed to be on trial; among these he saw himself. Before them raged an enormous fire. Suddenly from somewhere there appeared some unusual looking men who led him out of the crowd and into the flames. And he began to think: why is it that out of the whole crowd I am the only one thrown into that terrible fire? In answer to his thoughts those men replied: "It is thus pleasing to God."

Upon awakening he related this vision to his Elder and received the following explanation: "This fire represents the fiery trial which awaits you in the monastic arena."

From the bakery Theodore was placed under obedience to a very strict elder who looked after the Monastery bees. Here Theodore carried beehives about on his shoulders and dug the earth. In a word, he occupied himself with hard manual labor to which he was unaccustomed. It is difficult to describe the patience with which he bore these bodily hardships and the rebukes of the elder; he ceaselessly reproached himself with the humble thought that he deserved such punishment for his many sinful falls. The sweat of labors, the cup of dishonor which he drank continually and his humble nature bore the fruits of meekness and tears. This blessed sorrow which afflicted his heart gave a special strength to his prayers. He cried out with deep sighs and unhypocritical knowledge of his weakness, and the Lord

Jesus gradually cleansed his mind, chasing away the darkness of passions and making glad the disciple of Archimandrite Paisius' monastery with feelings of unearthly sweetness never experienced by men buried amid worldly cares.

Nearly two years passed thus. For his immaculate life Theodore was released from his difficult obedience with the bees and was assigned to the prosphora bakery in the Monastery of Sekoul, a dependency of Niamets located about seven miles away. We shall not detail his labors in this obedience, but rather pass over to those circumstances by which God led him to the height of virtues.

In a deserted wilderness near the stream Polyana-Vorona, two miles from the Skete of that name, dwelt the Elder Onuphrius, adorned with not only the gray hairs of his advanced years but also with divine wisdom. Born of a Russian merchant family, Onuphrius loved Christ from the early years of his childhood. While still a young man he spent six years as a fool-for-Christ's sake. He then went to the Ukraine with a friend who later became a hieromonk, Nicholas; there he was clothed with the angelic habit. Onuphrius and Nicholas together walked the royal path of temperance and mutual counsel. Hearing about the high spiritual attainments of Elder Paisius, they were overjoyed and moved from the Ukraine to Moldavia, where they entrusted themselves to the care of the great Elder. Nourished by the pure wheat of his teachings, they received from him a blessing to settle in the wilderness of the Polyana-Vorona and there to partake of the waters of divine contemplation.

In the prosphora bakery, Theodore increasingly acquired inward compunction and zeal of heart. The more one partakes of spiritual food, the more one thirsts for it. Such was Theodore's experience. His soul thirsted for a life in the wilderness; and he conveyed this longing to Elder Sophronius, asking his blessing to go and serve Onuphrius who was already physically weakened with age. Elder Sophronius approved of his intent. Then Theodore presented his idea to the great Elder Paisius, and with love and joy the Elder blessed his intention and sent him to Onuphrius.

3. DESERT DWELLING ACCORDING TO THE ROYAL PATH

Having moved to where Onuphrius was living, Theodore entered upon the path of total and unreserved obedience. Cutting off his own will before his spiritually-experienced and holy Elder and confessing to him all — even momentary — thoughts, he gradually died to the world. He cast off from himself the dark garments of the old man and put on the resplendent robe of the new man, which shone with the holiness of dispassion. The blessed tree of obedience bore its customary fruit: Christ-like humility. "To the humble," says St. John Climacus, "God grants the gift of discernment." Not only outwardly did the meek Theodore possess the fragrance of this gift of discernment, but it also graced his heart inwardly.

These three ascetics — Onuphrius, Nicholas and Theodore — had the blessed custom of partaking each month of the holy, glorious and life-giving Mysteries of Christ and were thus cleansed, enlightened, strengthened in their spiritual struggles and enkindled with the fire of divine zeal. Onuphrius and Nicholas lived as brothers. Crowds of men who were oppressed by doubt and despondency streamed into the cell of Onuphrius, who was abundantly endowed with the gift of discernment. Nicholas watched carefully over himself and, not having tested the thoughts of his heart in a life of solitude, served as a sacrifice of purity to Him Who is all-pure. Theodore occupied himself with that which the Holy Fathers [St. John Climacus, for example] placed on the same level as that of a confessor — holy obedience. These three earthly angels shone forth to the glory of the life-giving Trinity not only in number, but by their very lives. I will not speak of their patience, meekness and temperance — it would make their story too long; it is enough to make mention of the queen of virtues, that virtue whose name is that of the Lord Himself — most holy Love. Like a precious chain it united these three heavenly men with God and with one another. They burned with the flame of pure love, willingly bearing the infirmities of the weak and rejecting any thought of pleasing themselves. Nicholas and Theodore forgot themselves in serving the needs of Onuphrius, whose bodily weakness permitted him to partake only of very bland food, and even that in small quantities. Onuphrius would forget his infirmities in lightening their virtuous labors by his spiritual wisdom. Truly in their midst the unutterably sweet Jesus dwelt unseen, according to His faithful promise.

Their oneness of spirit provoked the evil one, and a great trial befell them which clearly testifies to the good will of the Master of the house Who said, "Whom I love I chastise." Theodore went once to the Skete for confession and Holy Communion, and in his absence during the time of the vigil some robbers broke into their forest cell. Before making off with the small supply of provisions found in the cell, they laid their criminal hands on the two Elders and left them severely beaten and barely alive. The solicitous Theodore lovingly attended to them and helped them to recover. Then Theodore was himself struck by an illness that nearly carried him into the grave, but God preserved the days of the righteous one for the benefit of many sinners.

Then there came a new sorrow — the death of Elder Onuphrius. Twelve hours before his death, the eyes of his heart were opened: there appeared before him the tribunal that awaits each soul departing from the body, and this tribunal was [presented, after a fashion,] to Onuphrius' two companions. The righteous Elder, tormented by beings invisible to those surrounding him, suffered and gave answers which clearly indicated that the stern judgment of his sins was the cause of the frightful torment. Onuphrius reposed in the spring, in March.[1]

Returning the remains of his spiritual Father to the earth, Theodore continued to live with Nicholas. But the desert without the presence of Onuphrius was no longer so dear to him. He was allowed to experience despondency, no doubt so the candle would not remain hidden under a bushel. He left the wilderness, where he had lived for five years with Elder Onuphrius and another half-year with Nicholas. Upon his leaving, Nicholas made him promise to return for him the following spring, when they would go together to Niamets Monastery.

Theodore was joyously received by Archimandrite Paisius, and he entered upon various monastic obediences. He copied out books of the Holy Fathers which Elder Paisius had translated from Greek into Slavonic; he sang on the cliros where later he was made canonarch; and, under the guidance of Elder Paisius, he learned the art of all arts — mental prayer, the Jesus prayer of the heart.

From this time he began to be assailed by the jealousy of others towards him, and this jealousy followed him to the grave.

At the end of winter with the blessing of the great Elder Paisius he turned his steps towards the Polyana-Vorona, where he was greeted by the meek and silence-loving Nicholas. Together they returned to Niamets Monastery. But infirmities and old age began to drain Nicholas of any physical strength; the great Nicholas died in Theodore's arms, and his relics remained incorrupt.

Theodore stayed in Niamets until 1801 and was present at the deathbed of the renowned Elder Paisius. The successor of Paisius as Superior of the Monastery, Elder Sophronius, blind and bent over with years, was already approaching the sunset of his days.

---

1. His incorrupt head and arms bear witness of his unquestionable salvation and holiness.

Meanwhile Tsar Alexander I had ascended the Russian Throne. The manifesto which he issued granted all those who had fled abroad to freely return to the fatherland. Elder Sophronius, seeing the upheaval in his Monastery and prompted by some kind of foreknowledge, advised Theodore to take advantage of the Monarch's decree and return to Russia. Theodore obediently left Moldavia and returned to Russia after being clothed in the angelic schema by Elder Sophronius, who cherished a special love for him.

4. IN WHITE BLUFF

Having returned to Russia, he went to Hierarch Dositheus of the city of Orel and chose as his dwelling place the Cholnsk Monastery, in accordance with his wishes. Here he worked in bringing the church services into harmony, dug a cave and, most importantly, began to share with those close to him the spiritual treasures which he had gathered in Moldavia. But envy and jealousy soon raised their heads against Theodore, and he moved to the White Bluff Monastery. Hieromonk Leonid was Abbot there; he had lived under Fr. Theodore for a time in the Cholnsk Monastery and had been nourished by the manna of his teachings. But even here Fr. Theodore did not escape jealousy, for, according to the sayings of the God-bearing spirit-filled Fathers, he rose in spirit to spiritual perfection without bounds. There was a constant stream of brethren weighed down by the burden of the passions who came to his cell and who received healings from him as from a skilled physician. He did not hide from them the precious pearl preserved under the humble covering of obedience — this pearl of which he had not only heard of with his ears but had experienced in very deed. He did not ignore the mystery of the frequent and attentive invocation of the fearful Name of Jesus, by which a Christian first burns up the tares of the passions, then becomes inflamed with love towards God and enters upon the ocean of heavenly visions.

At that time an epidemic of fever struck the White Bluff Monastery, and many monks became ill. The merciful and loving Schemamonk Theodore looked after them and nursed them. Then he too came down with the disease. He became very weak. For nine days he ate nothing; everyone thought that the hour of death had come for the righteous one. Suddenly all his senses became numb; his eyes were wide open, his breathing barely noticeable. His features became motionless, but on his lips remained a heavenly smile and a soft blush glowed upon his face. For three days he remained in such a state, and then he came to himself.

Fr. Leonid ran up to him: "Batiushka, are you dying?"

"No," answered Fr. Theodore, "I was told that I am not going to die. Look, do dying people have such strength?" With these words he gave him his hand.

Just then Fr. Theodore's favorite disciple came running up to him. "I considered you to be great," Fr. Theodore said to him, "but God showed me that you're altogether small."

After this he got up from his bed, dressed only in a shirt. Supporting himself on crutches and with the help of his disciples, he went to the sick about whom something had been revealed to him while he was unconscious.

It is impossible to describe all that was opened up to him during his illness. Earthly language cannot accurately describe what lies in the spiritual realm, and thus one can only speak figuratively and imperfectly about this. Furthermore, many of those concerning whom he had received revelations are still taking the opportunity offered by this temporal life to repent.[2]

This visionary state commenced in the following way. Once in the evening several days before his illness, Fr. Theo-

---

2. This was written approximately during the 30's of the last century.

dore was reconciling one of his disciples with the Abbot. Suddenly he felt in his heart an unusual feeling of great consolation. Unable to hide this feeling of extraordinary sweetness, he hinted at this to Fr. Leonid. Then began the illness, which took a strange course. For almost its entire duration Fr. Theodore was fully conscious, but his face shone with the abundant activity of interior prayer of the heart. The bodily sickness manifested itself, however, in both fever and extreme weakness. When he began to enter a state of unconsciousness and his soul seemed to leave his body, there appeared to him a certain invisible youth, who could be sensed and seen only with the perception of the heart. This youth led him along a narrow path to the left. Fr. Theodore, as he himself later related, felt as though he had already died and said to himself, "I have died, and it is not known whether I will be saved or will perish."

"You are saved!" said an unseen voice answering his thoughts. Suddenly a force like that of a whirlwind seized him and carried him over onto the right side.

"Taste the sweetness of the heavenly nuptials which I give to those who love Me," an unseen voice informed him. With these words it seemed to Fr. Theodore that the Savior Himself had placed His right hand upon his heart and that he was transported to an indescribably wondrous dwelling altogether unseen and which no human can describe.[3]

---

3. Our Savior calls them *many mansions of His Father's* house (John 14:2) — the noetic levels of those who dwell in that land — that is, the differentiation and variety of spiritual gifts in which they noetically take delight. It is not according to the variety of place, but according to the gradation of gifts that there are "many mansions." Just as everyone enjoys the material sun according to the measure of clarity and perceptiveness of his strength of vision, and just as from one lamp in the same house the illumination varies, although the light is not divided into many lights, so also in the future age all righteous ones will individually abide in one land, but each in his own measure will be illuminated by the mental sun and, according to his worthiness, will attract to himself joy and happiness, as

From this feeling he went to another still more wondrous, and then to a third; yet all these feelings, according to his own words, he could remember only with his heart but could not comprehend with his mind.

Then he saw what seemed to be a church and in it, near the altar, some sort of pavilion in which there were five or six people. "For these people," said the mental voice, "the hour of your death is postponed. For their sakes you will live."

The spiritual stature of some of his disciples was revealed to him then. Afterwards the Lord indicated to him those trials which were to disturb the evening of his days. In this vision he was even shown the people who later heaped upon him all manner of evil. But the divine Voice assured him that the ship of his soul would not suffer from these tempestuous waves, for its invisible helmsman was Christ Himself.

In a short time, without any medicines, the Elder regained his health.

5. A TIME OF TESTING
AT PALEI-OSTROV MONASTERY

Desiring a more solitary and silent life, Fr. Theodore informed the Abbot and brethren of this desire; they built him a cell in the forest about a mile from the Monastery. Fr. Theodore settled in this cell with the virtuous Hieroschemamonk Cleopas. Within a short time Fr. Leonid joined

---

if from one air, from one place, one altar, one sight and image. No one is shown the measure of his friend as higher or lower, lest he should see his friend's superlative grace and his own inferiority, and this become the cause of his sorrow and grief. (St. Isaac the Syrian, "On the Heavenly Mansions," Homily Six.) [See *The Ascetical Homilies of St. Isaac the Syrian*, trans. by Holy Transfiguration Monastery, Boston, Massachusetts, 1984, Homily Six, pp. 55-56.]

them, having voluntarily resigned from the honorable position of Abbot.

A city set on a hill cannot be hid. Soon the reputation of Theodore's saintly life spread far and wide. Numberless crowds of people formed a constant stream to the door of his cell and disturbed the silence of the desert dwellers. Theodore and his fellow strugglers, wearied by all the interruptions, began to beg God that He would arrange things according to His holy will. Soon they were all struck in the heart by the same inspiration — to move to the northern regions of Russia. For three years they were unable to bring this to pass. Providence decreed that Theodore leave White Bluff before his companions. He took with him for the road fifty kopeks which had been given to him by the abbot of Svensk Monastery[4] and set off on his journey. Knowing the disdain of the righteous one for money — a disdain which was born from a strong trust in God — one of his followers, Schemamonk Athanasius, secretly placed in his sack a five-rouble note. Having traveled about thirty miles from White Bluff, Theodore met an old beggar woman along the way and gave her this note.

Theodore headed for New Lake Monastery, situated in the eastern part of the province of Novgorod. Its Abbot at this time was the well-known Theophan. After they welcomed him with love, they proposed that Theodore restore the St. Nilus Skete and live there with his like-minded companions. Having received from Theophan a letter to Metropolitan Ambrose, Theodore set off for the Metropolitan's residence. But the Metropolitan did not agree to Theophan's proposal and sent Theodore to the newly-restored Palei-Ostrov Monastery, located on a northern island of Lake Onega.

Here Providence decreed that Theodore enter the fire of cruel temptations. The Abbot of the Palei-Ostrov Monastery was a certain Belousov who was of the merchant class.

---

4. In the city of Bryansk, in the Orel Province.

He had bought his way into the nobility and then into monasticism. Having no understanding of the principles of true Christianity and monasticism, Belousov was seized with jealousy towards Theodore and began to persecute him. Not being content with this, he went armed with various slanders to complain about him to the Metropolitan.

Belousov returned from the Metropolitan with a decree that "Schemamonk Theodore is forbidden to go anywhere or leave the Monastery under any circumstances. If he does anything unseemly, not befitting his rank, he is to be deprived of his rank and sent to civil prison." This was read aloud in the refectory, when Belousov also forbade the righteous Elder to enter the cells of the other monks, to receive them into his own cell or to talk with pilgrims.

"All this came about," said the humble Theodore, "as a result of my grievous sins, my pride and my loose tongue. Glory to Thee, my most merciful Creator and my God, that Thou dost not forsake me, a wretched sinner, but that Thou visitest me and chastenest me for mine iniquities by Thy mercy and Fatherly kindness!"

After some time Theodore asked that a request be sent to transfer him to Valaam, but he was refused. "It is evident," he said, "that it is thus pleasing to God. Blessed be the Name of the Lord from henceforth and for evermore."

Once again came a directive which said: "Schemamonk Theodore is not to be allowed out of the Monastery gates and is not to give any counsels."

"O, most merciful Lord and my Creator," said Theodore, "grant that for the sake of my sins I may graciously and with thankfulness endure all this and whatever might happen in the future. Grant that from henceforth I may at least lay a beginning for a life according to Thy holy will and out of love for Thee, my merciful God, Creator and Savior."

Soon after this decree, Belousov sent him an order to go to the fields and rake hay. "I cannot leave according to the decree," answered Theodore.

Belousov became angry and shouted, "I'll send you to sit in the cellar, and I'll feed you grass."

"Do as you wish," said Theodore. "I trust only my merciful God. Only that which He allows for my sins can happen to me, and that which He allows I myself desire. It is better to be chastened in this life than to be tormented in the life to come."

This persecution from the Abbot lasted for two years. During this time, deprived of shoes and clothing, he wove for himself a crown of patience. At length, seeing the disharmony of the Palei-Ostrov Monastery and the implacable hatred of the Abbot, he decided to go himself to the Metropolitan for an explanation.

6. VALAAM AND THE END OF HIS LIFE

Theodore was transferred to Valaam Monastery and settled in the Skete of All Saints; but because it was of his own will that he left Palei-Ostrov Monastery, he was for a year deprived of wearing his monastic hat and veil [kamilavka]. Before him Hiero-schemamonks Cleopas and Leonid, with many other close disciples, had already moved to Valaam from White Bluff Monastery.

Theodore spent about six years in this renowned Monastery and drew to himself almost all the brethren. This aroused the envy of those in charge. An assembly was convoked similar to the reprehensible sanhedrin which sentenced to death the Son of God. Those in Valaam whose righteousness did not exceed that of the Pharisees wanted to erase from the face of the earth one who was truly righteous. At this time the revelations he had received in White Bluff came to pass in deed, as did the promise of the Savior that he would be kept from harm. These events are recent, and to say more on this subject is not wise.

Having commended Cleopas to the Lord while he was still living in Valaam,[5] Theodore now moved to the Monastery of St. Alexander of Svir with Fr. Leonid. His days were linked by a chain of trials. For a year and a half before his repose, he was severely ill. During the heavy attacks of his sickness he repeated over and over again the words: "Glory to God! I have crossed the stormy sea of life and endured many troubles, but now the end is in view."

The day before his repose he had a vision. He saw himself in the midst of a magnificent church in which everyone was all in white. From the midst of the right cliros, he heard the triumphal voice of his deceased friend Hieroschemamonk Nicholas, "Theodore! The time has come for you to rest from your labors and come to be with us."

This took place on the Friday of Bright Week, 1822. A nine o'clock in the evening a joyful smile was seen to play on Theodore's lips; his face shone and his features were transformed by a wondrous divine change. The disciples surrounding his bed forgot their tears and lamentations and became immersed in the realization of this glorious and

---

5. The chance discovery of the relics of Fr. Cleopas was thus described by the Abbot of New Valaam Monastery in Siberia, Fr. Sergius:

"I came to the holy island of Valaam on October 13, 1893, and was soon received as a novice at the Skete of All Saints.

"The novices who had come before me told me that not long before my arrival at the Skete, there reposed a monk by the name of Fr. Arsenius who was a photographer. When they were digging a grave for him behind the altar of the church, about four and a half feet down they began to smell a wonderful fragrance. Not trusting their senses, they at first said nothing to one another; but as they dug deeper the fragrance became stronger and finally was so apparent that it was noticed by everyone and they began to speak about it amongst themselves. When they had almost finished their work, a human skull fell out of the neighboring grave. The fragrance became even stronger. The brothers sent for the Elder, Fr. Theophilus, who was at that time the Skete superior. The latter came and gave orders to send for Fr. Alexius and the other elders of the Skete. (Continued on p. 231.)

ALL SAINTS' (GREAT) SKETE ON VALAAM
at the beginning of the 19th century.

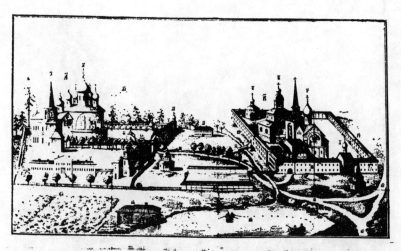

THE MONASTERY OF ST. ALEXANDER OF SVIR
in the 18th century.

extraordinary departure of his soul. Godly fear, sorrow, joy and wonder suddenly gripped their senses. On their Elder's face they could clearly read the ecstasy in which his soul had flown into the embrace of the light-bearing angels.

The death of a righteous man is the birth of a new and most joyful life. It is the sweetest harvest of an abundant ear of corn sprouting from the seeds of trials and struggles, the majestic exodus of the soul which has cast aside by activity and vision (theoria) the passionate fetters of the prison of the body. This soul on its path to heaven will not be afraid of meeting the evil demons. The death of a righteous man is the flight of the soul, swift and spontaneous, on the wings of love to the Source of love, the Lord Jesus.

O holy Father! You are now dwelling in the heavenly bridal chamber, and you insatiably partake of the heavenly bread. Pour out before the King of kings a prayer for us. Hand not your children over into the jaws of the enemy. Be our helper in the terrible hour of death, and present us before the Face of the Most High, that we may join our weak voices to your voice of exaltation and that we may be worthy with trembling to praise unto the ages of ages the Tri-Hypostatic Godhead glorified by all creation. Amen.

"Approaching the grave, Fr. Alexius took the fragrant skull into his hands and, making the sign of the cross, reverently kissed it. Then he informed all those present that this was the head of the Elder Father Cleopas of blessed memory, a disciple of the famous ascetic of the 18th century, Schema-archimandrite Paisius Velichkovsky.

"They immediately served a Panikhida for the righteous Elder, after which the skull was reverently returned to its place.

"Hiero-schemamonk Cleopas, as is known, moved to Valaam in 1811 and reposed in the Lord in 1816.

"Give rest, O Lord, to the soul of Thy departed servant Hiero-schemamonk Cleopas and by his holy prayers have mercy on me a sinner."

Abbot Sergius

(Michael Janson, *The Great Skete at Valaam,*
Tallin, Estonia, 1940, pp. 70-71.)

HIERO-SCHEMAMONK ANTHONY (MEDVEDEV)
Disciple of Elder Leonid and father confessor of the
Kiev Caves Lavra. (He is not to be confused with Fr.
Anthony Putilov, Optina Elder and Skete Superior.)

7. MEMOIRS OF FATHER ANTHONY (MEDVEDEV)[6]

I had long desired to venerate the holy relics of the Saint whose name I had borne in the world, St. Alexander of Svir. I frequently begged Fr. Leonid during his lifetime to permit me to make a pilgrimage to the Svir Monastery; I specifically wanted to see there the grave of Schemamonk Theodore. But Batiushka would grow silent and did not bless me to make a pilgrimage there during his lifetime. It was after Fr. Leonid's repose that I succeeded in obtaining a blessing from Abbot Moses to go on pilgrimage to the Svir Monastery. I also wanted to see Valaam, about which I had heard many good things from Fr. Leonid.

I left on foot, with staff and knapsack and with five roubles in my pocket, which Fr. Anthony, the Skete Superior, had given me for the road. From lack of habit, at first it was difficult to walk. My legs rubbed until I had blisters and sores, but eventually I became accustomed to the journey. [In those days] the Russian people were simpler and more kind; almost everywhere I received free lodging, food and drink and bread for the road. When I offered money to spend the night, people would become offended and wouldn't take it under any circumstances. Rarely would I lodge in the monasteries, save to venerate the holy relics. I was at the relics of St. Nilus, the Wonderworker of Stolbensk, in the St. Nicholas Monastery, which is located in the Tver Diocese on an island in the great Lake Seliger. I spent three days there resting from my journey and then headed toward Great Novgorod, but not everything there appealed to me. There were many churches and monasteries, but almost all of them were in a state of neglect. The monasteries had few people; yet there were many ancient holy shrines everywhere, and this gladdened my heart. I spent more than a week in Novgorod.

---

6. Bishop Nikodim of Belgorod, ed., *Biographies of National Ascetics of the 18th and 19th Centuries* (Moscow, 1908), October, p. 304.

One hospitable merchant sheltered me there, a pious old man who was so kind that even now I remember him. He fed me, gave me to drink, took me to the bath and provided me with clean clothing. He also gave me money for the rest of the journey; but I didn't take it for I had my own, given me by Fr. Anthony, which I had not yet used. From Novgorod I went to Tikhvin to venerate the Queen of Heaven. She consoled me, a pilgrim, with grace-filled feelings from Her wonderworking icon. In the church, directly across from this very icon is a window through which one can look from an open porch, and there She almost continually greets pilgrims who pray through the window towards the wonderworking icon of the Theotokos. That is where I too was first granted to venerate Her.

As soon as I saw from a distance the wonder-working icon of Our Lady, there came upon me a joy and tender contrition, which neither before nor afterwards have I experienced in such a way. This was about mid-afternoon. The catholicon was closed; the monks were resting. There were also a few people next to the window. All of the two or three old village women were Old-Believers, as it seemed to me then. The neighboring Old-Believers also revered the Tikhvin wonderworking icon of the Mother of God. They came to the porch in front of that window to pray to her during the periods between the church services, which they tried to avoid. The old women were clearly displeased by my arrival and glanced at me in an unfriendly way, but I didn't pay attention to them. With deeply reverent feelings I knelt down before the window through which the wonderworking icon of Our Lady was visible and began to read her akathist quietly. I read with inner sweetness; my heart trembled so much that it was about to jump out of my chest, and the tears involuntarily welled up in my eyes. When I finished reading I looked up. The old women also stood behind me on their knees and prayed. One of them approached me and gave me a five-kopek copper coin, saying, "Although you are not one of ours, you read so well that tears came to our eyes hearing you read. Here, take this for a large bagel." I treasured that five-kopek piece for a long time in memory of those spiritually-sweet moments whereby the Queen of Heaven consoled me in Tikhvin.

When they opened the catholicon for Vespers, I was granted to pray and be present before the heavenly-revealed Tikhvin Icon of the Theotokos. It is large in size and dark of countenance, richly adorned with a gold covering with precious stones. I spent two days in the Great Tikhvin Monastery and walked to the monasteries surrounding Tikhvin — to Besedny and to the Monastery of St. Anthony of Dymsk. The monasteries were small, isolated and poor.

From Tikhvin I went straight to the Svir Monastery of St. Alexander. I first saw there the local Karelian people. They were most kind, and I dearly loved them. Their morals and hospitality are of the highest calibre. You can freely enter into the house of a Karelian, take anything you want, do anything you wish and no one will interfere. The host himself or his wife is the first to serve you in all things. Their huts are also clean and tidy; in this they far surpass our Russian homes.

I came at last to the St. Alexander of Svir Monastery and was very puzzled, seeing side by side two monasteries standing a short distance from one another. Their locale was secluded, beautiful. The River Svir rapidly and pristinely flowed alongside the Monastery; the people crossed over her on rafts there, for then there were no steamers. I first arrived at the Trinity Monastery, thinking that the relics of St. Alexander rested there. But it turns out that they rest further on, in the Transfiguration of the Savior Monastery where the monks now live.

In the Transfiguration of the Savior Monastery, which is 200 yards from the Trinity Monastery, I found several former disciples of Batiushka Leonid, who received me as one of their own kin and put me to rest in a cell by myself with brotherly love. I went to the Saint not without trembling, for at last the long-standing desire of my soul to venerate his holy relics was fulfilled. A tall and completely bald elder, the hieromonk in charge of the sepulchre, opened for me the ancient, silver coffin of the Saint; and there perceptibly drifted towards me from the coffin such a sweet fragrance that I staggered back. The elder who cared for the sepulchre noticed this, supported me and with fatherly love said, "Fear not, my little dove; this is the grace of God. The Saint himself has given this to you. Turn to him with faith and love." I fell to my knees before the holy relics of the God-pleaser, who was so dear to me. For a long time I could not tear myself away from them. All my sorrow, all my longings, as a heavy burden I laid down upon his sacred reliquary. No one was around me. The attendant elder was patiently waiting for me while I finished praying, and I freely poured forth my feelings before the Saint. Since that time I have grown ever closer to him.

I experienced no less consolation in the cells of the monks who received me. I began to question them about the Elders Theodore and Leonid: where had they lived here and in which cells? "In these very cells in which we presently find ourselves," the monks replied and showed me the very place where Schemamonk Theodore reposed. These cells seemed to me then like a sanctuary, and I was ready to kiss the very walkway which they walked through — my beloved, and now departed into eternity, Elders Theodore and Leonid! It was pleasant to share reminiscences of the Elders with their disciples in Svir. They remembered details of life with both blessed Elders in the Monastery. They spoke of the righteous repose of Father Theodore and the incorruption of his body. The grave of the Elder, his clothing and body were uncovered intact when, after a considerable time, they dug a grave for his closest disciple (his name appears to have been Hilarion), who had desired to be buried unfailingly next to Elder Theodore. From his body there exuded a fragrance to which my conversers, as eyewitnesses, testified in the name of God. I also related as an eyewitness the details of the life and many sorrows of Elder Leonid in the Optina Monastery and about his blessed repose. I involuntarily cried, remembering that Batiushka had now left us orphans and departed to eternity. My fellow conversers wept also, having known him well and having deeply honored him.

They led me to the Monastery cemetery and to the grave of Schemamonk Theodore. Next to him his disciple also rested. We prayed and wept there. I grabbed a branch from the nearest tree and took a little earth, too, from the grave of Father Theodore for a remembrance and blessing. I stayed for more than a week in the Svir Monastery with my kindly disposed hosts and co-brothers, by virtue of my Elder. They showed me around the Monastery; they also walked me throughout the Hermitage where St. Alexander labored and where he was deemed worthy of the visitation of the Holy Trinity. Not without melancholy did I part from the Svir Monastery and from the kind monks who offered me shelter there. But I needed to go to Valaam, as well, where the footprints of St. Alexander can also be found.

8. HIS DISCIPLES IN THE SVIR MONASTERY

In the St. Alexander of Svir Monastery together with Elder Theodore, the renowned ascetic, are buried four of his disciples, likewise distinguished by their holy life. Testimony of the details of their life has not been preserved. But deeply interesting inscriptions are upon their tombstones, which we will present here:

1. "On this spot is buried the body of the slave of God, Hiero-schemamonk Meletius, who reposed on the 23rd of May, 1877, in the 76th year from his birth."

2. "Pause, ye passers-by and hearken. Behold, here rests in the earth beneath this stone the sacred body of Antiochus,

who from his youthful years until his last breath was like an Angel faithful to God and converted many to God. Hiero-schemamonk Antiochus reposed in the year 1832, on the 27th day of October. Being born of Orel merchants, his entire life from birth was 60 years; in his 17th year he entered the monastery."

Additional information: This Elder was noted for the gift of clairvoyance. In the Svir Monastery they also have his portrait painted upon a board.

3. "Here is buried the body of the slave of God, Monk Ignatius."

The first three graves are located alonside the grave of Fr. Theodore, and the fourth lies twenty feet away.

4. "This memorial was erected to the memory of Hieromonk Bartholomew.

"Passers-by, pause and cross yourselves and flee from the vices. Commemorate me in your prayers, and, for the fact that I have reminded you, forgive me, for you will also come to an end. This earth conceals the remains of Bartholomew, who passed into eternal life in the year 1864, on the 4th day of June, in the 97th year from his birth. The time of his earthly sojourn passed in sickness and sorrow. At first he settled in Valaam and was tonsured into monasticism in the year 1802 in the Moldavian Niamets Monastery. He finished his life in the St. Alexander of Svir Monastery."

Appendices

APPENDIX I

A Letter of
Elder Theodore of Svir

TRANSLATOR'S PREFACE

SCHEMAMONK THEODORE of Svir is scarcely known to the Orthodox faithful. His spiritual father, St. Paisius Velichkovsky, and his disciple Elder Leonid, have now both been canonized. The relics of his spiritual brother Elder Cleopas were discovered incorrupt at the turn of the century at Valaam. Of the actual words and thoughts of Schemamonk Theodore almost nothing has been preserved save the following epistle written in 1820 to a spiritual son, a monk and — as is evident from the text — a priest as well, who had drifted far from monastic life. The letter sets forth the perennial monastic teaching on repentance and renunciation of the world, the core of monastic life, as pertinent today as when it was written. It is in itself a patristic text of recent times and can rightly be placed alongside the writings of the Holy Fathers. The teaching of St. Isaac the Syrian, as expressed in his tenth homily, is referred to many times throughout the text.

Such cautious monastic teaching became the direct inheritance of St. Ignatius Brianchaninov, who as the young novice Demetrius joined Elder Leonid in the St. Alexander

of Svir Monastery about five years after the death of Fr.
Theodore. St. Ignatius later compiled the first Life of Elder
Theodore and more importantly developed this teaching
of Elder Theodore on repentance and renunciation of the
world in very eloquent, beautiful speech, setting it forth
for his contemporaries.[1] This in turn contributed to the
flowering of sanctity in 19th and 20th century Russia.

The similarity between this letter of Fr. Theodore
of Svir and the two epistles of St. John Chrysostom "To the
Fallen Theodore" should be noted. In fact, the individual
who edited the Life of Schemamonk Theodore for publication in 1839 so as to pass the ecclesiastical censor, made
use of these very same epistles of St. John Chrysostom to
provide a dramatic character for the young Father Theodore's repentance. The author of this second edited version,
most likely the respected Archimandrite Ignatius, at that
time Superior of the St. Sergius Hermitage not far from the
Imperial capital, writes: "It is grievous to behold a young
champion falling under the blows of the enemy! It is grievous to behold a stain on a bright lamp, a dark cloud in the
clear sky, and the stain of vice in a pure soul! *But do the
fallen not arise, or he that has turned aside does he not turn
back?* (Jer. 8:4). According to the teaching of the great
doctor of the Church, Chrysostom, 'There is nothing strange,
(beloved Theodore) in a wrestler falling, but rather in his
remaining in a fallen condition; neither is it a grievous thing
for the warrior to be wounded, but rather for him to be
stricken with despair after the blow has been struck and not
to care for healing the wound.'"[2]

1. Chapter Five of Bishop Ignatius Brianchaninov, *The Arena: An
Offering to Contemporary Monasticism,* Holy Trinity Monastery,
Jordanville, New York, 1983.

2. *The Life and Labors of Schemamonk Theodore,* reprinted in
Father Clement (Sederholm), *Elder Leonid of Optina,* St. Herman of
Alaska Brotherhood, Platina, California, 1976, pp. 235-236. See also
"Letters to the Fallen Theodore" in Schaff, Phillip, ed., *Nicene and Post-
Nicene Fathers:* Volume IX, pp. 95-96, 111, 115.

Following the teaching on repentance of St. John Chrysostom, the future Elder Theodore ponders: "Truly you have beheld, Theodore, the shipwrecks of those who sail upon the sea of this present age. Wherefore, I beseech you: flee the waves, and climb to that lofty place where catastrophe cannot reach you."[3]

About Elder Theodore we then read:

"And thus, following the teaching of the Hierarch of Christ, Theodore determined once again to withdraw in flight and settle in the wilderness (Ps. 54:8) — in a desert place further withdrawn from the world and from the bonds of flesh and blood. . . . And he set out for the ancient monastery of the ascetics of Christ."[4]

The instructive life and writings of Elder Theodore manifest the practical nature of patristic teaching and the lives of the God-pleasers who spoke not from the point of view of opinion but rather from grounded ascetic experience handed down as a priceless treasure to our own day.

Prefatory Note by Hieromonk Euthymius (Trunov),
Secretary to Archimandrite Moses,
Preceding the Letter of Schemamonk Theodore

Having prayerfully called to mind the memory of the great Elder Leonid on the day of his blessed repose, I involuntarily recall him who was no less great than Elder Leonid, the one who was his guide, instructor and teacher in spiritual activity. I have in mind Schemamonk Theodore, whom I mentioned while describing the repose of Elder Leonid (Leo). Beneath my hand I have a remarkable letter of his found in the manuscripts which belonged to Elder Leonid. It was written to a certain disciple on the occasion of his fall.

---

3. *Ibid.,* p. 237.
4. *Ibid.,* p. 238.

What wisdom, what power of words and what love! And just think, this letter was written by the hand of an "uneducated" man, a simple citizen of the city of Karachev! (Schemamonk Theodore came from the same city and same class as Elder Leonid.) Ye wise and prudent of this age, can you find an explanation, as to whence such inspiration came in one of those whom you accuse of darkness and ignorance?

I have copied down this treasure word for word.

Most honorable Father!

I, together with my spiritual friends and children, inexpressibly wish you the heavenly Kingdom in the One and only Ruler of the World, Jesus Christ!

Because of our lowliness we have not been accounted worthy to receive a reply to the letters that we sent to you, nor have we received from you any news about your situation, about anything that might actually have taken place with you, whereby we might have been reliably informed. Nevertheless, for this reason we have been even further compelled to write to you once again. The cause for this is that I, although a wretched sinner, am also your spiritual father, and not simply your spiritual father, since I acquired most importantly this responsibility in front of the Holy Gospel: It was I who embraced you as sponsor when you solemnly vowed to preserve purity, obedience and austerity of life, receiving upon yourself the angelic habit, entering in your heart upon the path of self-denial.

Therefore, I am obligated to edify you even at this remote distance, to inspire in you everything from which a kindly disposed son might derive immediate profit for his soul; and not only for you and for your salvation, but also for the calm of my own spirit and conscience.

I wish to bring to mind the High Priest, Eli, who had no contrition at the contempt of his sons Hophni and Phinehas in the performance of their duties of piety, for which reason not only did his house perish, but, through the wrath of

God towards the transgressions of his sons, the Ark of the Covenant of the Lord was given over into the merciless hands of the Philistines. Along with this most pitiful plight of the holy things, the sons of the virtuous Elder were stricken dead. By their wretched life they wrought for themselves a lamentable end, for alas, their souls perished as well. Contemplating this grievous event, I tremble, lest we too become ensnared in such a fate.[5]

And now, therefore? I have heard that you are bound to your mother through your taking care of her, as if you were one of the sons of this world who have an obligation to devote themselves to the composure of their mothers, not only as the law requires, but also as vanity dictates. You allow her to be often present in the monastery where you dwell. But this is absolutely incompatible with your vows. Heartfelt contrition must be your mother; with such a mother are we obliged to continually divide our time. But that mother from whom you were born, her you must honor inwardly — but do not have recourse to her frequently. It is shameful and disastrous for a monk to comply with the demands of the world, since it is vain and can be ruinous. In a word, I will tell you this: correct yourself.

I further hear from many that you very often leave the monastery and your cell, return late to your place of seclusion, and, apparently, travel during that time to unspecified or, it is better to say, to suspicious locales. Finally, in conversation with several people you have said, "I have lost here such a thing, of more value than the entire city!"

I have come to recognize that in this instance you have actually said the truth: not only the city, but even the whole world is not worth one's soul, the value of which the Savior of the world sacredly indicated, *What can it profit a man, if he gain the whole world and lose his own soul?* etc. [Matt.

---

5. A free rendering of Homily 10 of St. Isaac the Syrian, Section 2.

16:26]. If you have lost your soul, then indeed you have lost that treasure which all the resplendent beauties of nature truly are not worth.

However, most beloved father, so long as your life has not reached its end, by the true awareness of your sins and by firm hope in the blessings of Christ, this inestimable loss can be overturned. And further, when with most humble contrition of heart you will call in a spirit of faith on the help of the Most High, then you will lay in the temple of your soul a firm foundation, so to speak, not to again follow lightmindedly the yearnings of the flesh. The noetic Dinah, your soul, will not go unto Shechem or corrupt teachings [Gen. ch. 34]. True is the following promise: "There is no sin too great for the mercy of God," which can encourage even the most dejected spirit. But one must discern that this holds true only for those who, as I said, truly repent with the intention of soul never to return to sin, who do not imitate the dog by returning to his own vomit. . . . Perhaps you are waiting for a later opportunity? But who can declare unto us what tomorrow will bring? Are not the flowers of the field like a man? Listen, therefore, to what the most wise and holy Isaac the Syrian writes to this end. "Whoever," he says, "trusting in repentance, sins, such a one walks before God on a path of insidiousness, for such a one will not attain the goal of repentance" [Homily 10]. Consequently, he will be unexpectedly razed by the hand of death and carried away from the face of the earth by the spirits of the underheaven; and they will settle him in a dark land of merciless citizens, the abode of hellish spirits whose food is fire, whose drink is envy. Take heed, son: you are consecrated to God! Are you not moved, hearing the following examples?

Many people honored and respected a certain priest-monk who had the appearance of being a pious man but inwardly was secretly given over to the vile lusts of the flesh. Once, celebrating the most holy Divine Liturgy, during the Cherubic Hymn as he bowed his head in the usual manner and read the prayer "No one who is unworthy" and the rest of the words, he suddenly died. In what state did his soul depart?

Again, one priest-monk well-known to me, inclined to catering to his passions, dared unworthily to celebrate the Divine Services: he contracted a horrible illness and drew nigh to death. All efforts to ward off the illness were in vain; on the contrary, the illness intensified and became extremely dangerous. His awakening, troubled conscience suggested that he would be given over to death for his unworthy priestly activity. Coming to such a realization, he resolutely promised never more to celebrate the Divine Liturgy. Together with his abdication of the priesthood, his former state of health returned in such a way that no traces of the illness were noticeable.

Actually, the rank of priest and the majestic vestments also represent the inner beauty of the soul. When she grows dark out of carelessness, when the conscience which severely reproaches one of impurity is neglected, then darkness takes the place of light and opens the path to eternal darkness and the fire eternal — if one does not stray from this path onto the path of virtue and humility which leads to the Kingdom of Glory. Thus writes St. Theognostus in Chapters 51, 54 and 55.[6]

But one pious father told me further of the following incident which he had heard from his elder: Two brothers, akin in spirit and disposition, eventually became recluses,

---

6. These are not to be found in the Slavonic *Philokalia* but rather in a rare Paisian anthology entitled *Selected Ears for Food for the Soul*, published in a limited edition by Optina Monastery in 1849, pp. 196-197. (These same chapters are to be found in the recent translation of the Greek *Philokalia*, Volume II, pp. 370-372.) This testifies to the fact that Elder Theodore most likely brought this manuscript with him from Moldavia and bequeathed it to Elder Leonid, whence it arrived at Optina.

dedicating themselves to the solitary life. This occurred in
the Ukraine at the end of the 18th century A.D. They
lived in different cells, and after some time had elapsed one
of them was drawn aside by concupiscence into which he
fell headlong. Knowing of this, the other, a lover of purity,
humbly and lovingly persuaded him to cease this perilous
habit; but through the enslaving passion of impurity, there
being, evidently, something insatiable in his heart joined
together with pride as well, he replied: "It is characteristic
of angels not to sin; of demons not to repent."

Who could not agree with this? But it is necessary that
this not result to the furtherance of iniquity, for the Divine
compassion is a hidden mystery. Although the Triune compassion has triumphed and now triumphs over righteous
judgment, this, it seems to me, deals more with what takes
place by accident than with that performed with intent;
it touches upon the weakness of men upright of heart and
humble, but not with those who hopelessly deceive themselves, having a proud mind, or those carried away by the
dark teaching of Origen on the absolute compassion of the
Immoveable One, who in truth abides unto the ages of
ages.

Having waited a certain length of time, the aforementioned chaste brother, once having finished his appointed
rule of prayer, sitting on a bench and leaning upon the table,
dozed off accidentally into a light sleep. He beheld in that
state, at the side of a small river thereabouts called the
Irdic, two Ethiopians[7] which in the customary manner were
casting a fishing line into the water. While they were so
doing, they greatly spurred each other on to fish. One of
them cast his hook to catch something, but caught nothing.
Seeing this the other said, "You are helpless! Watch how I
cast it." With these words he sank his hook into the deep
and suddenly pulled out of the water a monk in complete

---

7. Or demons.

attire, proper to his rank. Beholding this, the brother vividly noticed that this was his own friend who had carelessly enmeshed himself in licentious impurity. Awakening in fear, he quickly went to inform his brother whom he had seen hooked by the Ethiopian. He reached his cell and woe! — a frightful and lamentable spectacle presented itself to his gaze. What did he find? He found his brother, already dead, lying in a pitiful disarray. A woman, with whom he had had intercourse sinfully, sat in utter grief, bewilderment, fear, revulsion and wailing; and he realized that the scythe of death that haunts the earthborn at every moment had harvested this brother in the very act of fleshly defilement.

Woe! Woe! Woe! Who shall give to our eyes tears fitting to weep over the lost fate of the miserable lover of the flesh? Oh! How fearsome that all such evil men, more so than other people, are pursued by the sudden hour of death.

Hearken once again to the following lamentable incident, which the very same elder told me:

One monk, an offspring of the Sophroniev Hermitage, clothed there in the angelic habit by the honorable Archimandrite Theodosius, left the Monastery and, by his striving solely according to his own will, joined a certain monastery in the Chernigov Diocese. Here he was elevated to the rank of hieromonk. Having lived in this way for a certain time, he fell headlong, so to speak, into the clutches of the shameless passions of the flesh, and, beating back the safeguard of his conscience, he repeatedly dared to celebrate the Divine Liturgy. I call his vile passion a river of lust, for as difficult as it is to curb the flow of a river, still more difficult is it to curtail the foul habits of carnal lust. As in the troubled waters of a spring nothing can be observed besides the dark chaos of the two elements of water and earth, so in the lost conscience nothing can be spotted besides the miserable orientation of his heart in relation to the truth, for the man *no more does what he wisheth, but sin dwelling in him does it* [Romans 7:17, 20]. He lightmindedly meditates all lawlessness, heedless of the riches of God's goodness, and that is why he quite easily sinks at last to murder. And thus, once preparing to celebrate the awesome mystery of the Holy Eucharist, this monk came, as usual, to the holy temple. And what happened? There appeared to him a most horrible demonic vision. As soon as he beheld it, he became troubled, his heart trembled, all his senses shook as if in a fever, his facial features were changed; he spoke in a strange voice, expressing his darkness of soul and his despair. This attracted the spiritual eagles of the monastery to the living corpse; the brothers gathered around him at the sound of his extraordinary howl. Although they flew around him they did not disturb him, but removed him from his misery and downfall, soaring with him to the throne of God's compassion, but — woe! they could not fulfill their intention. To the question of the brothers, the miserable and hideous discloser of his secret transgressions, in horror, trepidation and fear declared in detail all his vices for which cause he had been stricken by a glimpse of the indescribable spirit of hell. Confessing his falls, regretting his audacity in regards to the sacred ministry, he finally concluded: "If my gaze continues to meet such a frightening spectacle, then my spirit will hardly be able to remain within me!"

Having pronounced these last words, looking at them with an unusual countenance, he fell to the ground dead.

How insensitive must an unworthy sacred minister be, if he is able to indifferently behold such a frightening picture of eternal torment.

This event was related to the aforementioned elder by a hieromonk who had known his unfortunate fellow-server. The elder on occasion visited the hieromonk's cell, where the unfortunate one revealed to the hieromonk his spiritual wound about which his conscience was always tormenting him, making him bewildered in this matter and irreconcilable. Though his conscience had been defiled and wounded, yet it had suggested to him in every way to stop serving.

At the same, however, the vices also persuaded him in their own way; and he, either out of fear or faintheartedness or the passion of self-love, did not make a decision until the time that bitter death cut short his days. The reproach of the conscience is the secret voice of God; and if one does not respect God, how can one expect from Him deliverance in time of misfortune?

Wishing thee salvation in the Triune God, I will set forth here a third event which occurred in our day, namely what one devout man related to me:

"In one of our Russian monasteries there was a certain priest, at the same time a monk, who due to the duty of his rank began once to celebrate the Divine Liturgy, which he continued to do, and reached the reception of the Holy Body and Blood of the precious Redeemer of the world, our Lord Jesus Christ. During that time, as was customary, the choir was singing the communion verse, while the priest was to approach the holy sacrificial table for mystical union with the unblemished Lamb of the Apocalypse in uprightness and humility of heart with pure feelings. In contrast to this, he, with a tainted envious spirit and conscience, drawing near, sensed a horrible tremor, so that he could hardly keep from falling to the ground; but stepping aside, he sat down on a chair. Then, somewhat confident in his own strength, he approached a second time the sacrificial oblation and was again stricken with feebleness. Then, having rested, he gathered his strength a third time, but he had already become extremely weak. The Superior, the treasurer and the brothers, standing outside the altar and wondering at the unusual elapse of time, were compelled to enter the altar. Finding the priest in utter exhaustion, barely breathing, they asked the reason for this. Convicted of the punishment of the unfailing lovingkindness towards him of the Right Hand of the Most High, he confessed that he, having become enslaved to the passions of the flesh, heeding neither the natural law nor the Law of God, without fear, repentance or reverence

had attempted several times to serve in church. Upon confessing and explaining his falls, he then with the deepest
fear, contrition of heart and the firm intention of amendment, was barely able to finish the Divine Service. Upon
his reporting this to the higher ecclesiastical authorities,
and upon the conducting of an inquest, on account of his
full confession and unhypocritical humility of spirit, it
was decided that he be sent to one of the secluded, strict
monasteries under the severest penance.

Glory be to God, that he punishes the unworthy and
spares them. But one must not place one's trust in this.

Beloved son in Christ! Presenting to you the circumstances of these terrible events, I implore you before God: if
because of our pride you have, as a man, fallen, then "arise,
save yourself, and Christ will enlighten thee!" Let us fear
the terrible judgment and wrath of God which hangs over the
heads of unfeeling sinners unto their destruction, to their
merciless destruction. Let us turn our gaze to the land of
eternal fire, which mercilessly devours all unrepentant evil-
doers, plunges them into the eternal abyss, and covers them
with impenetrable darkness, where the fire is not quenched
and the worm dieth not.

Let us endeavor to cast off from ourselves the vile raiment of impurity, that is, to leave, I say, the destructive
habit of abominable lasciviousness. Fear God, my son!
If you will, then not only I, your insignificant father, but
also the angels in heaven will rejoice over your return. But
do so as soon as you can, or listen to what follows:

*Know ye not that ye are the temple of God? If any man
defile the temple of God, him shall God destroy* [I Cor. 3:
16-17]. Is not this frightening which has been decreed? Have
you fallen? Then arise! Have you violated chastity? Then
make amends for this through repentance and sorrow in a
godly manner [II Cor. 7:10] to the extent that you can!
Have you defiled the temple of God? Then you can cleanse
yourself through repentance for the compassionate God is

always ready to forgive you and reward you. Furthermore, let us listen to the advice of the Holy Fathers: what do they advise in such an instance? This is what: you must absolutely flee from that place where your fall occurred and with a heartfelt disposition to amendment move to another remote monastery. I beg this of God: may He thus grant you the means and the strength. O, when will you wish to come to my unworthy embrace! What kind of joy would then fill my soul! Ah! beloved son. For you I often weep bitter tears, and sometimes, harboring no bitterness in my heart, I sing in a like voice, the words which the holy David sang, weeping over his beloved Absalom, "My son! my son! my son! . . ." I write this not according to knowledge, but according to the prompting of my heart. But although you have left me, nevertheless, I still nourish the hope that the compassionate God will give you the wings of discrimination, like those of a dove, that you may fly through repentance to the land of piety-rest. If you should not obey, then I, with heartfelt sorrow, will entrust you to God's Providence "free of your blood," and you yourself will bear your own burden and "by your own works shall you be judged." But when such news about you proves unjust, then I, being informed of this by your disclosure and sympathy, will ever more rejoice in your chastity, thanking God to Whom I entrust you, and will greet you again in Christ in a spirit of sincerity. I remain your well-wisher of earthly and heavenly good things, your unworthy father, the insignificant elder, Schemamonk Theodore.

1820

St. Alexander of Svir Monastery

SOURCE: *Holiness Under a Bushel: Mysteries of the Orthodox Monastic Spirit.* St. Elias Brotherhood, Forestville, California, 1977, pp. 86-96.

RIGHTEOUS ANTHONY IVANOVICH
(†1832)
Commemorated June 7/20
A portrait from Valaam.

APPENDIX II

Righteous Anthony Ivanovich

FOOL-FOR-CHRIST OF VALAAM

RIGHTEOUS ANTHONY IVANOVICH (Zenoviev) was originally a citizen of Petersburg. He settled in Valaam on April 5, 1816, and lived there until his repose on June 7, 1832. Living in the Monastery, he always behaved as a Fool-for-Christ's sake, at first laboring at various obediences which he performed with great zeal and self-denial. Later he was sick much of the time. He was bedridden and in pain, and always laid in bed on his back, not touching the pillow with his head, so that his head was always, so to speak, hanging. Many, observing his much-laboring and much-suffering life, considered Anthony Ivanovich to be a holy one and would come to him for advice. In his always-jumbled answers, they found meaning corresponding to their inward quest, and for this reason they concluded that he had the gift of clairvoyance and foresight. Concerning his life the late Metropolitan Philaret of Moscow was well informed.

Anthony Ivanovich died in the 76th year of his life, adorned with gray hair and handsome features.

One Moscow merchant, who for many years led a pious life, fell into poverty and debts which he was in no condition to rectify. Finding himself in a state of depression, one day he ran towards the Moscow river with the intent of drowning himself.

A few steps before he reached the river Anthony the Fool appeared before him and said, "You are going to drown yourself, go back! They brought the money to you with which you will pay your debts, and you will live better than you lived before."

"And who are you?" asked the merchant.

"Anthony of Valaam," came the reply.

The merchant buried his face in his hands, closed his eyes, and in a few minutes wanted to continue his questions, but the vision was gone. The merchant returned home, found the money and in a year came to Valaam to thank his deliverer, Anthony the Fool. But the latter did not receive him. The merchant found out that, at the time when the Fool appeared to him, Anthony Ivanovich had been permanently residing on Valaam.

One day the Fool-for-Christ told Schemamonk Michael (Chikhachov),[1] originally from St. Sergius Hermitage on the gulf of Finland: "Before my death you will come to me to bid farewell."

After several years Metropolitan Nicanor visited the St. Sergius Hermitage and told Fr. Michael to go to Valaam at once, saying that he was needed there. When he arrived at Valaam Monastery, it was the day of the eve of the death of Anthony the Fool. Parting with him, Fr. Michael heard from Anthony these words: "Ah, you came to say goodbye to me just as I told you."

The next day the Blessed Fool fell asleep in the Lord.

While Fathers Theodore, Cleopas and Leonid lived on Valaam, Blessed Anthony knew them well and after their departure used to say in his cryptic way: "They traded

---

1. A friend of (Saint) Bishop Ignatius Brianchaninov.

well." Considering what deep influence they left on the monastic life at Valaam among the spiritually minded monks, it was quite appropriate that Blessed Anthony commented: "As the Gospel teaches, they made spiritual profit unto the Lord."

Fr. Anthony Bochkov, the monk who initially began compiling the Life of Elder Leonid, wrote a poem about Blessed Anthony.

Source: *Russian Monk,* no. 24,
December, 1910, pp. 56-57.

The earliest portrait of Elder Leonid, from the Optina Archives

APPENDIX III

The "Pancake" Commemoration of Elder Leonid

Every monastery is traditionally endowed with the right to venerate their own righteous ascetics. This is first expressed by panikhidas, later by solemn commemorations over their graves and, finally, even by local canonizations.

In Optina, the beginning of such a glorification of the founding father, Elder Leonid, was laid down for posterity by Archimandrite Moses, the founder of the very Skete where St. Leonid (in Schema Leo) labored, suffered, met his righteous death and was venerated as a saint.

The following account[1] shows the esteem in which Elder Leonid was held after his repose by the Optina community. It was written by Sergei Nilus, as an entry to his spiritual diary, on July 25th, 1909.

———

A rumor went around that one of the Optina fathers had advised Fr. Archimandrite (i.e., the Abbot of Optina at

---

1. Taken from the book *On the Banks of God's River*, pp. 244-246, containing the diary of Sergei Nilus during a portion of his five-year stay at Optina Monastery.

that time) to cut down the age-old pine trees which grow between the Skete and the Monastery, in order to mill them [for money]. The rationale was that it would be all the same anyhow since they were rotting at the roots from old age.

Today our friend from the Skete, Fr. Nectarius,[2] visited us. "Did you hear?" I asked.

"About what?"

I told of the rumor.

"This," Fr. Nectarius cried out in animation, "will never take place, for a commandment was set down by our great Elders never to disturb the forest between the Skete and the Monastery. Not even a bush is allowed to be cut, let alone an ancient tree."

And then he told me the following:

"When the Elder Fr. Leo was dying, he gave a testament to the Skete, saying that the day of his repose should be commemorated by a "consolation" for the brothers and that pancakes should be cooked for them on this day. After his death it was instituted by our Elders, Fathers Moses and Macarius, that a panikhida be served on that day and attended by all. Thus was this testament observed for a long time, until the days of Abbot Isaac and the Skete Superior Hilarion. During their time the following 'temptation' occurred. On the eve of the memorial of Fr. Leonid, the sexton Theodosius came to the Abbot and said: 'It's not in accordance with accepted practice to serve, on tomorrow's date, a panikhida that everyone is obliged to attend.'

"The Abbot insisted, 'But this is my wish!'

"And what do you think happened after this? Theodosius saw in a dream: Father Leo grabbed him by the scruff of the neck, took him by the hair to the cross on top of the belfry, and threatened him three times, 'Do you want me to drop you now?' And at this moment he showed

---

2. Later, Elder Nectarius of Optina (†1928).

him a terrible abyss beneath the bell tower. When Theodosius woke up, he felt a pain between his shoulders. Then a carbuncle formed. He suffered for more than a month and even despaired of his life. From that time on, those who had wanted to stop the common memorial became quite shaken up.

"And in the Skete, on that very same day, the cell-attendant of Fr. Hilarion, Nilus, began to persuade the Skete Superior Fr. Hilarion to do away with the serving of pancakes. 'Batiushka,' he said, 'how much coarse flour will be wasted on them! The pancakes will have to be cooked in the workers' kitchen; it will take the workers away from their work, and we will also have to treat the workers. Where are we going to find that much flour?'

"And so Nilus managed after all to bend the will of the Skete Superior — they abolished the pancakes. Then something more serious than Theodosius' carbuncle occurred. From that day on Fr. Hilarion fell ill and until the end of his life could no longer celebrate the Divine Service. Nilus in turn was stricken by leprosy from which he died, having lost his strength during his lifetime to such an extent that a worker had to wheel him in a wheelchair to the temple of God. As if that were not enough, that very night, when that ill-fated cancellation of the 'consolation' occurred, in the workers' kitchen in the Skete a worker died from smoke inhalation. How much trouble there was with the police! And then the God-loving benefactors stopped donating the flour itself to the Skete. . . .

"Do you see what obedience to the commandments of the Elders means for us?" Fr. Nectarius added to his story. He concluded with these words:

"As long as eldership is upheld in Optina, the testaments of the Elders will be carried out. Then when the cabins of the Elders are sealed, when locks will be hung on the doors of their cells, alas then! . . . everything can then be expected, but as for now, 'the time has not yet come.'"

Batiushka fell silent for awhile, then smiled with his radiant kindhearted smile and said, "In the meantime let our beautiful pines beautify this place right where they stand!"[3]

Truly they are beautiful.

3. From the words of Bishop Nektary of Seattle (†1983) it is known that when the Soviet government liquidated the Monastery, one of the first things it did was to cut these very pine trees between the Monastery and the Skete. After the passage of 80 years, part of the forest has grown back, but not all. Now the young monks who have settled again at Optina wish to restore once more all the traditions to the minutest detail—which is not a simple matter, since the century-old chain of eldership has been severed.

A HOUSE ETERNAL IN THE HEAVENS

Seven years after the death of Elder Leonid, in 1848, Elder Macarius wrote the following letter in which the passage of Elder Leonid "from death to life" and his intercession before the throne of God for his spiritual children is portrayed. The vision described is fully in harmony with the rich treasury of Orthodox ascetic literature and shows how the saints make known to those pained in heart the favor they have found with God. Coming from the pen of Elder Macarius in so matter-of-fact a style, it can be considered as one of the earliest steps toward the recent canonization of Elder Leonid of Optina.

Letter 46

… Abbess Magdalena of Sevsk reposed on the 25th of August at twelve o'clock. The convent became orphaned…. Several days before her death, the Abbot of Ploshchansk saw a vision: it was as if the heavens had suddenly opened up and Fr. Leonid (Leo) from thence said to the Abbess, "Magdalena! Will you come to me soon? I have long awaited you and have built a cell for you." And she in turn replied, "Soon, very soon, Batiushka, I will come." While reading the moving account of her repose no one can refrain from tears, especially when thinking of her spiritual children smitten with sorrow….

Hieromonk Macarius
September 1, 1848

SOURCE: *Collected Letters [to Monastics] of Elder Hiero-schemamonk Macarius of Blessed Memory,* Optina Monastery, Moscow, 1862, p. 65.

GLOSSARY

akathist: a special group of hymns of praise to our Lord Jesus Christ, the Mother of God or a saint, during which everyone should stand. (The word is derived from the Greek "not sitting.")

archimandrite: an abbot in priestly rank.

canon: a set of hymns and verses sung to a particular saint or in honor of a feast.

catholicon: the main church of a monastery.

cliros: the place in church where the services are read and sung.

coenobitic monasticism: the type of monasticism in which a group of monks or nuns live a communal life under an abbot or an abbess.

confessor: a priest who administers the Sacrament of Confession.

epitimia: a penance.

epitrachelion: a vestment which hangs from the neck of the priest and is the one indispensable vestment for all priestly ministrations.

hesychasm: an ascetic practice associated with the anchoretic way of life and involving mental stillness, inner spiritual concentration and unceasing prayer of the heart.

hieromonk: a monk in priestly rank.

Holy Mysteries: the Sacrament of Holy Communion.

Holy Synod: a council of bishops.

Jesus Prayer: "Lord Jesus Christ, Son of God, have mercy on me, a sinner." This prayer expresses the true relationship of man to God. It is said by many Orthodox Christians, and especially monastics, who repeat the prayer from the depth of their souls, aflame with love for God.

kamilavka (pl. *kamilavki*): head covering worn by monastics.

lavra: a large coenobitic monastery.

Lity: a procession and solemn intercession at Vespers for special feasts, taking place in the narthex of the church. Also, the shortened Office of the Dead which can be sung at the end of Divine Liturgy.

mantia: a mantle; the pleated outer robe worn by tonsured monastics.

mental prayer: inner or "noetic" prayer. To practice inner prayer it is essential to keep one's attention in the heart before the Lord.

metropolitan: the chief hierarch of a city.

Moleben: a prayer service in which the faithful ask for heavenly help or give thanks to God.

monastic rule: an additional set of prayers, outside the daily cycle of services, which are to be said daily by each monk or nun.

Old-Believers: schismatic Orthodox believers who refused to accept the reforms of Patriarch Nikon in the 17th century in Russia.

Panikhida: a service of prayer for those who have reposed.

paraman: a square piece of cloth with a cross embroidered on it, worn by tonsured monks and nuns.

Patericon: a collection of sayings by and about the Holy Fathers.

polyeleos: a term meaning "all-merciful," referring to Psalms 134 and 135 and a selection of verses from other Psalms chanted antiphonally in Matins on feast days.

ryassa: the outer robe worn by monastics and priests.

schemamonk: one who has taken on the highest and strictest monastic discipline, leading a life of seclusion and prayer. He wears the schema, a special cowl and stole.

skete: a small monastery; usually a close-knit "family" of up to 12 monastics with the abbot or abbess as their head.

sobriety: spiritual vigilance, alertness, watchfulness; an attitude of guarding the heart and intellect from evil thoughts and desires; seeing reality as it is.

stylite: a saint who takes on the ascetic feat of standing on a pillar for years and praying for the world.

tonsure: the rite whereby a novice is clothed into the monastic habit and becomes a monk or nun.

Trisagion: a series of prayers in the Orthodox Church beginning with "Holy God" and ending with "Our Father. . . ."

ukase: a declaration made by a ruling bishop or a council of bishops.

Unction: the Sacrament of anointing, usually for the sick or dying.

vigil: a service sung on the eve of a special feast; it is comprised of Vespers and Matins.

INDEX

St. Herman Press

ST. HERMAN OF ALASKA BROTHERHOOD